TROUNCING THE DOW

A Value-Based Method for Making Huge Profits

Kenneth Lee

McGraw-Hill

New York   San Francisco   Washington, DC   Aukland   Bogotá
Caracas   Lisbon   London   Madrid   Mexico City   Milan
Montreal   New Delhi   San Juan   Singapore
Sydney   Tokyo   Toronto

Library of Congress Cataloging-in-Publication Data

Lee, Kenneth
    Trouncing the Dow : a value-based method for making huge profits /
by Kenneth Lee
       p.   cm.
    ISBN 0-07-038301-4
    1. Investments—United States.   2. Stocks—United States.
I. Title.
HG4910.L445   1998
332.63 ' 22—dc21   98–8619
                                                                        CIP

McGraw-Hill

A Division of The **McGraw·Hill** Companies

1 2 3 4 5 6 7 8 9 0 DOC/DOC 9 0 3 2 1 0 9 8

ISBN 0-07-038301-4

The sponsoring editor for this book was Stephen Isaacs, the editing supervisor was
John M. Morriss, and the production supervisor was Suzanne W. B. Rapcavage. It
was set in Palatino by Carol Barnstable of Carol Graphics.

Printed and bound by R.R. Donnelley & Sons Company.

McGraw-Hill books are available at special quantity discounts to use as
premiums and sales promotions, or for use in corporate training programs.
for more information, please write to the Director of Special Sales, McGraw-Hill, 11
West 19th Street, New York, NY 10011. Or contact your local bookstore.

 This book is printed on recycled, acid-free paper containing a minimum of
50% recycled de-inked fiber.

To my wife, Karen,
and to my children, Jonathan,
Matthew, Michelle, and Joseph

I love you all very much.

CONTENTS

Chapter 12

Benchmark's Self-Test

APPENDIX

DISCLAIMER

Because of the extreme risk inherent in any stock investment, there is no guarantee that the benchmark investing method will be profitable in specific applications. Although the method of stock investment described in this book is believed to be effective, there can be no assurance that the method will be profitable in its real-time application. *Indeed, there are several instances described in the book where benchmark investing would have lost or did lose money.*

Thus, neither the publisher nor the author assumes liability for any losses that may be sustained by use of the method described in this book, and any such liability is hereby expressly disclaimed. Nor is the benchmarking method a recommendation to purchase or sell the securities of any of the companies herein discussed.

In addition, the views expressed in this book are those of the author and do not represent the views of the broker-dealer for which he is employed, its officers, or its other employees.

Unless otherwise specified, annual returns for the *Trouncing the Dow* portfolios and the Dow Jones Industrial Average were calculated by taking period-end prices, subtracting them from the prices at the end of the following period, and adding dividends received for the period. Of course, adjustments were made for any stock splits that occurred during the year.

All total returns are figured before taxes, commissions, and/or fees.

Historical returns are compounded annually. Compound annual return simply expresses geometric progression as a yearly figure, in contrast to average annual return. Compound annual return is also known as the geometric average, whereas average annual return is known as the arithmetic average. The distinction can be very deceiving.

For our purposes, we will use compound annual return exclusively when discussing performance.

INTRODUCTION

The real tragedy of life is when men are afraid of the light.

Plato
The Republic

Over the years, countless methods have been devised to make money in the stock market. They inevitably are back-tests constructed from historical data, and are designed to have worked profitably if they had been used during the most recent period of time. Nevertheless, few have fulfilled their great expectations long into the future.

That's not to say that all innovative investment systems should be shunned. The new method advocated and taught in this book differs in one critical sense: it has been used quite successfully over the years in real-time investing. The following pages detail how anyone can duplicate these impressive results to beat the stock market and, in particular, the Dow Jones Industrial Average.

So, how can those wholly unfamiliar with the stock market attain a working knowledge of stocks so that they can *trounce* the Dow and cast off their dependence upon Wall Street advisers to become successful investors on their own? The answer can be found in this book, which provides novices and market veterans alike who wish to generate superior returns with a practical new approach called *benchmark* investing.

Successful investing doesn't require advanced degrees, superior intellect, wealthy relatives, insider information, or arcane business skills. To quote Omaha billionaire Warren Buffett, what's needed is "a sound intellectual framework for making decisions and the ability to keep emotions from corroding that framework."[1]

Who would disagree with Buffett—the greatest investor of all time—when the topic is investing? In fact, this book provides

---

1 Warren Buffett, preface to Benjamin Graham, *The Intelligent Investor* (New York, Harper & Row, 1976), p. vii. (Graham's work was originally published in 1949.)

investors with the intellectual framework by showing them how to buy a stock for far less than its intrinsic value. Rather than trusting in Wall Street hype that has little hope of ever paying off, investors can now rely upon themselves to make their own important investment decisions.

Nowadays, people often delegate and are eager to abdicate responsibility to advisers for financial decisions that they should make for themselves. One reason is the widespread belief that advisers with impressive credentials know more about the future than anyone else. If we're too busy to understand how something works, we turn to experts. We are so convinced we can't beat the market that we don't bother to try. We assume that anyone with an MBA or Ph.D. possesses all-knowing wisdom. When it comes to Wall Street, with its promise of quick, easy money, we are especially vulnerable. It is here that even U.S. presidents have lost entire personal fortunes to advisers—Ulysses S. Grant was swindled out of $2.6 million in 1884 by Wall Street operator Ferdinand Ward. That's just one of many reasons that investors should think for themselves rather than outsource the job to high-priced professionals.

This book is a guide for those who are willing to accept responsibility for their investments and who want to be successful. Benchmark investing shatters the myth that only certain enlightened experts know the secrets of Wall Street. Investing in stocks is simpler than most people think. Rather than focusing on credentials, investors will discover that there is no substitute for rational, independent thinking.

Another myth is that novice investors can't outperform institutional investors. Nothing could be further from the truth. Institutional money managers have a very difficult time beating the indexes because they are the market. The pros are competing with themselves, whereas independent investors can take advantage of the bargains created by Wall Street managers. According to Michael O'Higgins, institutional investors have "created more opportunities than disadvantages for personal investors."[2]

Independent investors need only know how to value stocks before making serious investment decisions. The biggest and most consistent winners are the investors willing and able to act differ-

---

2   Michael O'Higgins, *Beating the Dow* (Harper Collins Publishers, 1992), p. 4.

ently from the institutional managers, who are typically involved in self-destructive, shorter-term investing that encourages portfolio turnover and below-par results.

According to Jay Palmer, the problem with most money managers is that they're flesh and blood. "If managers could just strip away those attributes, and adopt a cold, robotic investment strategy, they would do much better in the stock market."[3]

This is not meant to be a condemnation of contemporary institutional investors. On the contrary, they are a skilled and dedicated group. They're also highly educated, hardworking, and exceedingly motivated. As Michael DiCarlo, head of John Hancock's Special Equities Fund and one of the most successful fund managers in America, noted: "Look, in this business, everybody is a workaholic and everyone is incredibly bright."[4]

Although the collective purpose of the professionals is to beat the market, the truth is that they are not beating the market. The stark reality is that the market is beating them. "The evidence is consistent and overpowering that 'beating' the stock market is an extremely difficult challenge for any equity portfolio manager," noted Vanguard mutual fund chairman John Bogle.[5]

"Too many clever and experienced people are engaged simultaneously in trying to outwit one another in the market," wrote Benjamin Graham, the father of value investing. "The result, we believe, is that all their skill and efforts tend to be self-neutralizing or to cancel out, so that each experience and highly informed conclusion ends up by being no more dependable than the toss of a coin."[6] As a result, benchmark investors enjoy significant advantages over professional investors.

Benchmark investing is based solely on the belief that the price of a company tells absolutely nothing about its true value. At the same time, it asks the question that should be on every investor's mind: "Can the stock be purchased at a discount to its true value?"

---

3   Jay Palmer, "Growth vs. Value," *Barron's*, 1997.

4   Diane K. Shah, "Holding on to The Bull," *The New York Times Magazine*, December 1, 1996, p. 105.

5   John C. Bogle, Ferris Lecture at Trinity College, Cambridge, November 18, 1990.

6   Adam Smith quoting Benjamin Graham, *Supermoney* (New York: Random House, 1972), pp. 183–84.

The goal of the benchmark investor is the same as Buffett's—that is, to have the purchase price so attractive that even a mediocre sale provides good results. Too many people are trying to find the next Intel. Too few are trying to find the next Sears or Caterpillar when it is temporarily out of favor.

When investors find a significant difference between the price and the value of a stock, they should buy or sell, as appropriate, to capture the difference between that price and value. Indeed, there are few things as fascinating, or rewarding, as buying a company's stock when it's selling for pennies on the dollar.

This strategy of learning how to figure out a company's true value gives the investor the ability to (1) find an entry price that will minimize downside risk, (2) participate in the market at a significant discount, and (3) consistently outperform the market over long periods of time while mitigating risk. Just as important, benchmark investing instills confidence. The common denominator of all successful investors, regardless of investment style, is their ability to curb their destructive emotions and display patience and fortitude at all times. The important test of any investment strategy is the investor's ability to adhere to it over the long term, even when short-term results are disappointing. This kind of confidence can lead to mastery and noteworthy results.

Benchmark investing works because stocks are subject to irrational and excessive price fluctuations in both directions as a result of investors' tendency to speculate or gamble out of hope, fear, and greed.

Because of investors' illogical emotions, the chief roadblock to attaining desired investment results is likely to be investors themselves. Most people lose money in the market because they are unable to control their own greed and fear. They lack a discipline that protects them from their emotions. In fact, it baffles Buffett to see investors recklessly chasing after one Wall Street fad after another when the secret to above-average gains is right under their noses.

Therefore, the second aim of this book is to clad its readers in the full protective armor of practical knowledge. The more you know about yourself as an investor and the more you understand the stock market, the more you will know how to invest with discipline and confidence. Benchmark investing takes emotion, opinion, and guesswork out of all the most important investment decisions and gives investors an objective, historical approach to building their stock portfolios.

The lessons taught in this book can shield investors from the greed, hope, and fear that lead to perilous stock choices. Whenever euphoria or paranoia replaces common sense in the market, benchmark investors will be able to keep their wits about them. Concrete examples are provided to give you a better understanding of how to use benchmarks to make informed decisions. A set of 30 exercises is also included at the end of the book to help you decide whether you're ready to begin using the benchmark strategy with real money. This self-test should reinforce the ideas taught in these pages.

As a result, you will learn how to become a disciplined, rational investor who neither follows the crowd on Wall Street nor plays short-term market gyrations for a quick buck. Benchmark investors can profit from the folly of others rather than participate in it.

It must be stressed, however, that investment success is not synonymous with infallibility. Even Buffett has made investment mistakes over the years. Peter Lynch, once legendary as Fidelity Magellan manager, admitted that whenever the stock market did poorly, Magellan did worse. Benchmark investors must be prepared to experience significant and extended falls as well as growth in the value of their stocks. The acid test of an investor, according to Buffett, is to be able to see a stock decline 50 percent or more and not panic into selling so long as the intrinsic value remains.

Benchmark investors will learn how to mitigate these inevitable setbacks. It's important to remember that just because money is lost on a stock does not mean that the decision was a bad one. After all, the word "speculation" implies and accepts added risk and a certain number of missed calls. In the long run, it is these same risks that bring worthwhile rewards to benchmark investors.

How is it that the stock market allows a company's shares to get undervalued, then invariably wakes up and drives the price into the correct or even overvalued range? There lies one of the great mysteries of Wall Street. Experience has shown, however, that eventually the market catches up with a company's true value. One way or another, it happens. And as you will discover, buying good values at depressed prices achieves superior returns over time with relatively low risk.

This book also hopes to dispel the efficient market theory. Its followers believe that all the information available about a company is already known in the investment community so that no analyst or investor can have an advantage over any other. These "random walkers" believe that an investor can do as well by randomly picking shares as he or she can by poring over corporate reports. Most value investors, especially those who outperform the market every year, consider the efficient market theory as utter nonsense.

"I'd be a bum on the street with a tin cup if the markets were efficient," says Buffett.[7]

It's my observation that markets are not efficient, but they are constantly in the process of moving toward efficiency. There's too much evidence of great investors who consistently take advantage of market inefficiencies to support any other belief. Throughout my career as a professional investment consultant and adviser, I have stressed to my clients that historical performance is unsuited as a criteria for evaluating money managers. In fact, research clearly shows the absence of any predictive value in historical performance rankings of money managers.

But if historical performance has no discriminating value for investors, why should anyone consider benchmark investing's superior results from 1973 to 1996? The answer is compelling, because benchmark investing provides investors with several qualities that every great money manager exhibits:

- *Independent thinking.* A professional investor must adopt a nonconsensus view in order to achieve superior results. Buffett is the ideal independent thinker, and benchmark investing allows anyone to mimic this great mentor by taking advantage of superior Dow companies that are temporarily out of favor with the consensus on Wall Street.
- *Unencumbered decision making.* If the process of following through with original ideas is difficult, only easy and generally less rewarding decisions will be made. Complex, time-consuming information makes decision more difficult. Benchmark investing is a straightforward process that allows for objective, scientific, and unobstructed decision making.
- *Personal discipline.* Successful money managers tend to be highly focused, intense, and enthusiastic in their pursuits. Benchmark investing's focus on 30 of the best companies in the world offers superior discipline for investors.

---

7   Janet Lowe, *Value Investing* (New York: McGraw-Hill, 1996), p. 16.

♦ *Flexibility.* Portfolio management requires a great commitment to change. All investments must be reviewed continually to ensure that they reflect the newest and best available information. The successful manager must always be willing to reverse an earlier decision, regardless of whether it was good or bad, without the slightest hesitation. Benchmark investing provides the flexibility for investors to take a long-term approach, which they can appraise on a quarterly basis.

Benchmark investing supplies investors with all the qualities necessary to beat the Dow, and it does so in a consistent, straightforward manner. In addition, it stresses a low-turnover approach that is highly advantageous for taxable investors.

The rational foundation to support benchmark investing rests in its real-time record, which has outperformed the market since the technique's inception (see Figure I.1). Of course, it is the nature of things that only the reader can determine how useful my new strategy is. I do not claim to present all the answers about investing here or to offer the ultimate truth about investing. To some, my technique may seem too simple to be convincing. It's not sexy or sensational or exotic like futures trading, risk arbitrage, or mergers and acquisitions. In fact, its sole reliance is on a single criterion of price attractiveness. Nevertheless, Sir William of Occam essentially said that the simpler the explanation, the more likely it is to be correct (Occam's Razor). Ideas don't need to be complicated to work. And my ideas are intended to be understandable to anyone with a general knowledge of finance.

Benchmark investing simply translates into a highly reliable method that works in all types of market conditions. Because people shy away from reading large, comprehensive works, intimidated by their size, I've endeavored to "let my light shine" as simply as possible in these few pages. This book is intended to serve as an avenue for those who are seeking a high-quality, low-cost method of investing without the confusion or noise from Wall Street. You'll never have to rely on hype, hope, or guesswork again. I earnestly hope that this book will encourage, educate and enlighten amateur investors so that they enjoy many years of successful, disciplined investing all on their very own.

FIGURE I.1

Benchmark Investing versus DJIA: Three-year Rolling Average Total Returns

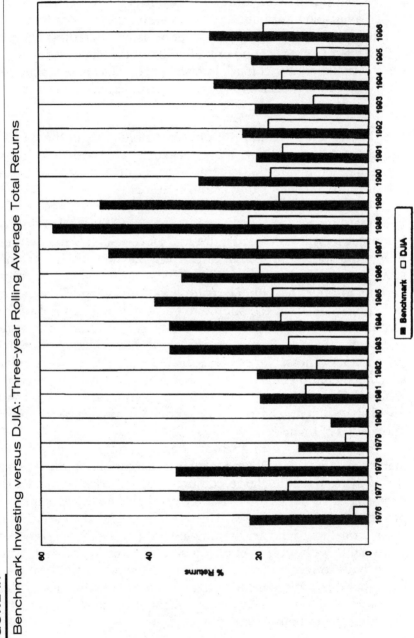

One last word of encouragement. This is one endeavor where even the mightiest players can be outdone by the little folks with the determination to succeed. Graham was convinced that an individual investor with sound principles could invest better over the long term than a large institution. And Lynch based his long-term success at Fidelity Magellan on trying to act like an individual investor, not an institutional investor. It is my hope that this book will show you the advantages that amateurs truly enjoy, so that you too can outperform the mighty professionals of Wall Street.

CHAPTER 1

The Wall Street Money Machine

Everyone wants to be rich, but few want to work for it.

Richard Driehaus,
Investment Gurus, foreword, p. xv.*

In the spring of 1951, the father of value investing had some advice for his best pupil. With the Dow Jones Industrial Average trading around 250, Benjamin Graham advised former Columbia graduate student Warren Buffett to postpone his investment career until the Dow dropped back below 200. Ben Graham was not your typical professor. One of the first modern Wall Street analysts, he wrote two of the all-time classics on investing: *Securities Analysis* and *The Intelligent Investor*. Graham also was an outstanding investor. From 1929 to 1956 he averaged 17 percent annual returns. But his advice to Buffett violated one of his major strictures against trying to predict the market.

Fortunately, Buffett didn't listen to his esteemed mentor. The Dow didn't go back to 200 that year or any other year since. Buffett's move foreshadowed his amazing ability to ignore the conventional wisdom of others on Wall Street. "I had about 10 thousand bucks. If I'd taken (Graham's) advice, I'd probably still have about

---

* Peter Tanous, *Investment Gurus* (New York: New York Institute of Finance, 1997).

10 thousand bucks," Buffett told *Wall Street Journal* reporter Roger Lowenstein.[1]

Today, Buffett is a billionaire who is generally considered to be the greatest investor of all time. Beyond doubt, Buffett is the most interesting, the most influential, and the most important investor of any era. By 1997, Buffett had turned his $10,000 life savings into a stock portfolio worth over $23 billion by buying into the teeth of panic. That is, he built his vast wealth by buying stocks only after they became extremely unpopular on Wall Street. One of his landmark trades came in 1964, when American Express collapsed in the Michael De Angelis salad oil scandal. Buffett bought heavily after determining that the danger of losses was limited thanks to American Express's basic strengths in the credit card and traveler's check operations. His timely investment increased fivefold in the next five years as a result of his ability to recognize a great bargain and to have the character to bet against the high priests of Wall Street.

Thirty years later, in 1994, Buffett was up to his old tricks again. This time, however, he believed that things went better with Coke. That's when he snapped up nearly 1.6 million shares of Coca-Cola for roughly $64 million. As reported in *The Wall Street Journal*, Buffett's purchases between June 23 and June 30 averaged $40.66 per share (in presplit 1994 prices) at a time when Wall Street had seemed "particularly divided" about Coke's prospects.

Although many high-paid analysts were unimpressed with Coke, anyone taking a close look at the company in 1994 could have seen that the shares were trading at historically low levels after stagnating for nearly three years. Buffett's approach highlights one of the tremendous advantages that amateur investors have over professionals. As someone with no clients to please and no policy guidelines, the independent investor has a huge advantage. Institutional managers are keenly aware of what the Street thinks about a particular company. As a result, the professionals tend to lean toward homogeneous research, making them herd followers rather than original thinkers. Of course, the reason is that professionals have to worry about keeping their jobs. And keeping their jobs isn't about maximizing performance. Perhaps that's why only 8 out of

---

1   Roger Lowenstein, "The DJIA's Past Isn't Prologue," *The Wall Street Journal*, April 4, 1996 p. C1.

Warren Buffet's Wealth Progression

Warren Buffett began his investment career in 1956 with $10,000. By 1969, he'd built his net worth to $25 million. In 1982, *Forbes* began ranking the world's richest people, listing Buffett at eighty-second, with a net worth of $250 million. Below is a record of how the Oracle of Omaha fared in succeeding years.

- 1983, thirty-first, with $520 million
- 1984, twenty-third, with $665 million
- 1985, twelfth, with $1.4 billion
- 1986, fifth, with $1.4 billion
- 1987, seventh, with $2.1 billion
- 1988, ninth, with $2.2 billion
- 1989, second, with $4.2 billion
- 1990, second, with $5.3 billion
- 1991, fourth, with $4.3 billion
- 1992, fourth, with $4.3 billion
- 1993, first, with $8.3 billion
- 1994, second, with $9.35 billion
- 1995, second, with $12 billion
- 1996, second, with $15 billion
- 1997, second, with $23 billion

3993 mutual funds tracked by *Morningstar* had outperformed the market over 1-, 3-, 5-, 10-, 15-, and 20-year periods as of September 30, 1996. Eight out of 3993 means that only 1 out of every 499 mutual funds beat the market over extended periods of time.

Professionals are loath to play the skeleton at the feast. In other words, few are willing to venture out on a limb. They dread bucking the crowd with independent opinions. What they fear most is not being wrong but being out of step with their peers. They'd all rather be wrong together than wrong alone, and they worry mainly about being second-guessed over the next three months. Moreover, an analyst who writes a negative report on XYZ Corp. has to consider that his or her firm's investment bankers will probably not be hired

> Coca-Cola is not a cheap stock. We're somewhat concerned about the price/earnings multiple.
>
> All-Star Analysts 1993 Survey, *The Wall Street Journal*, September 15, 1993, p. A2

to underwrite XYZ's next stock issue. The analyst also has to face uncooperative management the next time a quarterly report is due. Ironically, professional money managers and analysts are driven by the same compelling forces of fear and greed that supposedly afflict only novice investors.

"To keep their jobs, professional money managers typically invest in assets that are popular with other money managers, that get good press, and that are easily explained to folks who know just enough about stock picking to be dangerous," wrote *Worth* journalist Clint Willis. "In other words," Willis continued, "the pros end up buying expensive investments and shunning cheap ones.[2]

In the summer of 1994, it didn't take a rocket scientist to learn that Coke's worldwide volume had just started to rise in the first quarter. It was public knowledge, available to all. Nor did it take a Wall Street wizard to see that Coke's profits were up 15 percent that quarter.

In fact, it didn't even take a Harvard MBA to realize that the lion's share of Coke's gains was coming from outside the United States, in places where the company had done little or no business up to that point. Coca-Cola had just completed the infrastructure necessary to begin to fully support growth in Eastern Europe and other largely untapped markets, including China and India. At the same time, Coke had aggressively been buying back its stock. In 1994 alone, the company bought back approximately 25 million of its own shares, a clear signal to the investment community that management was bullish on its stock's future.

With as little as a few minutes invested in researching Coke during that summer of 1994, any amateur benchmark investor could have been just as confident as Buffett that Coke was an excellent

---

2   Clint Willis, "8 Ways to Beat the Pros," *Worth* (December–January 1997), p. 76.

bargain. Anyone could have seen that Coke's stock was primed to make a dramatic rise over the foreseeable future. And rise it did. By the end of 1997, Buffett's $64 million investment in Coke had more than tripled.

Remarkably, Buffett doesn't rely on fancy computer models to make his investment decisions. In fact, he doesn't even have a stock quote machine in his office. Buffett makes his money with common sense, patience, and fundamental analysis—traits that he sticks with even in the bleakest of times. His great wealth has been earned by simply buying great businesses at reasonable prices and having the temperament and conviction to stand pat, just as any amateur or veteran investor can learn to do.

Buffett first calculates the downside of a company before making investment decisions. He makes sure he has a "margin of safety" before investing, much like engineers who build bridges with added structural support to compensate for expected traffic loads. His favorite time to invest in a stock is after it's been dumped by panic-stricken Wall Streeters and left for dead. Buffett's belief is that even some of the best businesses run into problems. But before he invests, he does his homework and waits patiently for the right, undervalued price.

He doesn't worry about day-to-day fluctuations in the price of his stocks after he invests. *Nor does he worry about the economy or the stock market.* In short, Buffett waits patiently for the market to realize the true value of his convictions. And all the while, he ignores Wall Street pundits, who have never been able to top Buffett even with all their credentials, honors, and enormous salaries. Indeed, to paraphrase Ralph Waldo Emerson, Buffett is a great investor who keeps his own independence in the midst of the crowd.

What investors fail to realize is that these Buffett-like investments are available at all times to those patient enough to invest in research and brave enough to stand by their convictions. For those willing and able to do so, above-average gains will be the reward. The problem is that most investors have been conditioned to fear the risk of losing everything if they invest in the stock market on their own. For most people, the thought of picking individual stocks is terrifying. A trip to the dentist is less feared.

Certainly, the stock market is a chameleon with the ability to change its stripes instantly for any reason. It's also a dangerously unpredictable animal that moves unexpectedly and chaotically.

Wall Street has the uncanny ability to focus on a vision of the future, reach virtual unanimity, and just as quickly turn around and dismiss its conclusions completely when the first earnings report doesn't pan out. The truth is that the stock market is really nothing more than checking the investor's mercurial temperature, which, in trying to find its equilibrium, changes from minute to minute. That's why most people do so poorly with their stock investing. It seems that investors instinctively tend to be shortsighted, impatient, and herdlike.

Consider that during one particularly hair-raising seven-day period in July 1996 the amount of money moved in and out of mutual funds by participants in some large 401(k) plans spiked as much as sixfold. As reported in *The Wall Street Journal*, the participants nervously dumped shares of stock funds on days that the market was down. Then, just as illogically, they scooped the shares back up again after the stock prices inched higher.

It's not surprising to learn that most of the participants sold low and bought back at a higher price. *Shortsighted, impatient, and herdlike* behavior occurs all too frequently because investors listen to the investment media in an effort to decipher the health of the market. Unfortunately, the vast majority of investors are most enamored of investment media at times when markets are overvalued. Their love affair does nothing more than add to the confusion already caused by the quickly changing reports flowing from Wall Street. The not-so-obvious problem is that the market's daily rises and falls mirror only feelings of the moment. They fail to give investors much of a clue as to the market's future direction.

As a result, most investors find it easier to seek out the recommendations of market gurus or turn their money over to the hottest fund manager and hope for the best. After all, if they can't trust an analyst who boasts a $5 million salary or a fund manager who earned the highest returns during the last year, whom can they trust? Sadly, these same investors underperform the market when all the while they could be taking advantage of the market's unpredictability and reaping superior, long-term gains.

There are those who will remain convinced that special skills are required to invest successfully in the stock market. And many investors will continue to believe that they need a professional to tell them which stocks to buy and sell. Wall Street gurus often shroud their predictions in so much fog and mist that they later can claim they were right regardless of what happens in the market. As a result, too many sheeplike investors are disappointed when their gurus fail to live up to their inflated expectations. And those who place their financial faith in yesterday's hot fund managers also find out too late how disastrous that strategy can be.

What most people fail to realize is that they can invest in high-quality, undervalued companies all on their own, without the expense and frustration of outside assistance. And doing so can absolutely improve their financial results. Another common misconception is that investors have to be rich to make money in the stock market. Nothing could be further from the truth. As *Forbes* columnist Kenneth L. Fisher noted, "rich Americans have, in general, been terrible investors."[3] According to Fisher, only a "precious few" of the original 1981 *Forbes* list of the 400 wealthiest people in America had made the list again 15 years later, in 1996. He found that not one of the original 10 richest remained in the top 10 in 1996. And of 1986's top 10, only two remained: Warren Buffett and John Kluge.

Remember that Buffett began with "10 thousand bucks" in 1956. Today, he's one of the wealthiest people in the world. How did he do it? By averaging 26.9 percent returns between 1956 and the end of 1997, that's how. A $10,000 investment with Buffett when he began his career would have been worth $80 million at the end of 1984, and more than $194 million at the end of 1997.

An investor who starts with $10,000 and earns "just" 20 percent returns for the next 10 years will end up with $61,977 before taxes. In 20 years, that figure grows to $383,376. And in 30 years, the sum will be $2,373,763. However, an investor fortunate enough to experience the same average returns as Buffett, or 26.9 percent, would see those totals swell to $108,296 in 10 years, $1,172,822 in 20 years, and $12,701,314 in 30 years (see Figure 1.1 and Table 1.1).

Although it may seem incredible that the average investor can generate those kinds of returns, it should be noted that the benchmark investing approach enjoyed even better results than Buffett's between 1991 and 1996. This is not to imply that amateur investors using benchmark investing will outperform Warren Buffett, *who deserves nothing but the greatest respect*. However, by investing in only the most undervalued stocks in the Dow Jones Industrial Average,

---

3   Kenneth L. Fisher, "Why the Rich Get (Relatively) Poorer," *Forbes*, October 14, 1996, p. 359.

FIGURE 1.1

Growth of $10,000

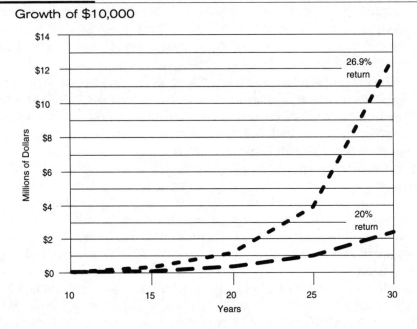

TABLE 1.1

Growth of $10,000 at Varying Rates and Intervals

Time Frame	20% Return	26.9% Return
10 years	$61,977	$108,296
20 years	$383,376	$1,172,822
30 years	$2,373,763	$12,701,314

benchmark investors averaged a 28.21 percent total return between 1991 and 1996 versus Buffett's 27.13 percent gain and the Dow's 19.14 percent average annual gain.

Rather than investing in small, unknown companies, benchmark investors can build their wealth with household names. Companies such as American Express, Walt Disney, and General Electric have all been outstanding investments in recent years after some macro- or microevent caused the bears on Wall Street to fall ravenously upon their shares. Investing in distinguished companies such as these when they're trading below their intrinsic value—below their benchmarks—is a wonderful way to create wealth. As Buffett points out, Wall Street may ignore a company's financial results, but it will, over time, confirm a company's success or failure at providing increased economic value.

Even an investment in every one of the Dow stocks over the past 22 years would have provided investors with superior results. A $100 investment in each of the 30 Dow stocks, totaling $3000, would have grown to over $1million. During that period, the United States experienced inflation, oil crises, two severe recessions, budget deficits, and much more. Even so, the Dow stocks made investors wealthy by defying the general public's accepted notion that stocks are risky business.

The stock market is really nothing more than a fashion business. It stands to reason that any style-conscious consumer would like to buy the finest, latest fashions at half price or less. Similarly, in benchmark investing, buy only when the best companies in the world (the Dow stocks) are trading at distressed prices. Then, when the price rises to a predetermined target value, it's time to sell and take profits, which then are reinvested in new undervalued companies.

Unfortunately, what was in style yesterday can quickly fall out of fashion with shortsighted speculators. As a result, stocks are chronically mispriced in relation to their true values. It's these distorted prices that allow benchmark investors to appraise a company's worth and objectively determine whether to buy, sell, or avoid. The genuine worth of any stock is thus revealed by the numbers that benchmark investors are able to calculate and evaluate.

All this can be accomplished without constant trading or market timing: benchmark investing's strategy of buying undervalued stocks from the Dow averaged just three new purchases per year between 1991 and 1997. Nor will long-term, serious benchmark investors experience sleepless nights worrying about their portfolios, because they'll know the best price to get in and have a predetermined price to get out.

Of course, no one knows for sure what the future holds. "Every age has its peculiar folly; some scheme, project, or phantasy into which it plunges, spurred on by the love of gain, the necessity of excitement, or the mere force of imitation." Charles Mackay's words are as true today as they were in 1841, when he wrote them.[4]

What's striking is that there is nothing really new in the market, just the same old errors repeated time and again. History teaches that all excesses on the upside and downside are eventually corrected, and that every extreme has been thoroughly justified and rationalized at the time it was created on Wall Street.

Thus, it seems likely that the United States will continue to experience similar events as in the past. We'll see bear markets, recessions, depressions, inflation. We'll struggle with deflation, global conflicts, catastrophes, and scandals. Yet even in the face of these serious difficulties, the stock market will continue its long secular climb toward higher highs.

That's not to say there won't be some frightening and extended downdrafts that will scare most investors away from the stock market. Economic progress is impossible without taking risks. The fact remains that large company stocks still averaged 10.7 percent a year between 1925 and 1996, a period that included horrible years such as 1931, 1973, and 1974. Therefore, it seems likely that colossal bargains should continue to be available to watchful, disciplined investors willing to wait for the right time and the right entry price.

Investors are really on their own when it comes to research and investing. That's not entirely bad news for those willing to do their own research. But by and large, patient investing eliminates most of the buying public, which neither knows how dire the situation is nor is willing to do something about it.

Consider the case of Brian McGuire, an anesthesiologist from Billings, Montana, who placed $100,000 into a fund that he thought was conservative. After all, the fund was audited by a well-known American accounting firm and had ties to a Swiss bank. Promoted as one of the world's most reputable offshore currency trading funds, it lost nearly all (95 percent) of Dr. McGuire's investment. In fact, he and 81 other investors lost $27 million in the "conservative" fund.[5]

---

4   Charles Mackay, *Extraordinary Popular Delusions and the Madness of Crowds* (New York: Harmony Books, 1841).

5   Michael R. Sesit, "Offshore Hazard," *The Wall Street Journal*, September 17, 1996, p. 1.

Less than a year later, gold fever struck investors hard when they couldn't get enough shares of a tiny Canadian gold mining outfit called Bre-X. According to *The Wall Street Journal,* what was striking about the company was that "no one suspected that the Bre-X glitter wasn't real. That it was filled with fool's gold. Even as the string of red flags grew, so did the list of Bre-X believers. Brokerage analysts toured the site and returned glowing."[6]

All of this comes as no surprise to Wall Street veteran Joe Rosenberg, chief investment strategist for Loews Corp. Bre-X investors lost billions of dollars of wealth when independent tests revealed that there wasn't any gold in any of the 268 holes drilled over a three-year testing period in Borneo. Rosenberg reported to *Barron's:* "One of the most consistent trends I've observed in over 35 years in Wall Street is the declining quality of research."[7]

Rosenberg went on to say, "Today, analysts who should know better—and very often *do* know better—simply don't publish what they know, for fear of retribution from corporations; that they'll be cut off from the information pipeline; that they'll be cut off from the investment-banking business. How do I know this? Because many of these analysts have told me so, though not on record. And the best evidence of that is that there used to be something called a 'Sell' recommendation in Wall Street."[8]

The role of Wall Street analysts has changed in recent years. Today they often juggle many different roles in addition to evaluating the merits of a company or industry. Of course, their responsibility, and one we assume they fulfill well, is to track the companies they follow. But increasingly, analysts are involved in lucrative investment banking activities that generate huge fees for their employers and big year-end bonuses for themselves. In part, because of these extra duties, they are taken away from doing the fundamental research that small investors assume they are doing on individual companies. "Professional investors have become so skeptical of the

---

6 Suzanne McGee and Mark Heninzel, "How Bre-X Holders Passed Warnings, Got Lost in Glitter," *The Wall Street Journal,* May 16, 1997, p. C1.

7 Joe Rosenberg, *Barron's,* April 14, 1997, p. 26.

8 Ibid.

analysts that many largely ignore the chorus of recommendations," wrote Reed Abelson.[9]

Of course, everybody makes mistakes at work now and then, but when a highly paid Wall Street analyst does, investors can lose millions. Consider these unfortunate blunders:

Analysts would have served their clients best by issuing a sell recommendation on high-flying Centennial Technologies before the shares plummeted from a high of $58.25 in December 1996 to a low of $1.63 just two months later. Centennial, it will be remembered, soared 451 percent to top the New York Stock Exchange in 1996. At its peak, the maker of memory cards for computers had a market value in excess of $1 billion.

Centennial was kicked off the Big Board on April 11, 1997, after evidence appeared that its president, Emanuel Pinez, had committed securities fraud. Pinez allegedly booked sales of a product that never even existed, then paid for orders with his own money to make them look real. The alleged scam went undetected for three years by its own board, by the four brokerage houses that helped Centennial raise $30 million, and by Coopers & Lybrand, the company's auditors.

"In a less-hectic stock market, lawyers and investments bankers say, underwriters might have done a thorough background search that could have raised red flags and prevented the Centennial debacle," wrote Jon Auerbach in *The Wall Street Journal*.[10] Such errors by these well-respected professionals are particularly noteworthy, since they occurred during a raging bull market. That's why it's a bad idea to blindly follow the advice of professionals.

Centennial stockholders weren't the only big losers. While the Dow Industrials roared to new highs from June 1996 to March 1997—rising 21.6 percent from 5654 to 6877—investors who had the great misfortune to rely upon some of the biggest names in small company growth funds lost as much as 47 percent. The casualty list reads like a who's who of mutual fund managers.

9   Reed Abelson, "A Guide to the Goofs of Wall Street's Wizard," *The New York Times*, December 1, 1996, Section 3, p. 1.

10 Jon G. Auerbach, "How a Salesman Built Hottest Stock of 1996 Before the Roof Fell In," *The Wall Street Journal*, April 11, 1997, p. A1.

Investors who had money in the emerging growth sector saw their funds massacred for almost a year, while the large capitalization stocks in the Dow Industrials shared a much more profitable fate. But shareholders of big, popular large cap funds also experienced poor performance compared with the Dow in 1996.

Fidelity Magellan, the largest mutual fund in America with over $53 billion in assets, returned just 9.4 percent in 1996 compared with the Dow's 26.01 percent performance. Investors have more money in Magellan than there is gold in Fort Knox and the New York Fed combined, but that didn't prevent the fund from lagging the Dow by a whopping 63 percent in 1996.

This followed a year of turmoil during which Fidelity, also the nation's biggest mutual fund company with 250 funds and $500 billion in assets under management, was stung by the defections of more than a dozen high-profile fund managers and 15 marketing and business executives. Overall, more than half of the $225 billion invested in Fidelity's stock funds had been put under new managers in 1996.[11]

Remarkably, Fidelity wasn't alone in underperforming the Dow.

The following is just a random sampling of well-known mutual funds with billions in assets that widely underperformed the Dow in 1996. Growth Fund of America, with over $9 billion in investor assets, returned 14.9 percent in 1996, barely half of the Dow's gains and well below the average stock fund gain of 19.63 percent for the year. AIM Value Fund gained just 14.3 percent. Merrill Lynch's Capital Fund, with over $3 billion in assets, gained a meager 12.1 percent. All these funds invest in large capitalization stocks like those in the Dow Industrials, underscoring how poor their 1996 performance actually was.

Investors in the above-named funds looked like huge winners compared with those unfortunate enough to have invested billions in highly aggressive growth funds in 1996. Though the average small company growth mutual fund gained 17.74 percent, according to Lipper Analytical Services, there was plenty of wreckage among the biggest and most popular.

---

11 Edward Wyatt, "Fidelity's Exit Door Swings Once More" *The New York Times*, December 8, 1996, p. F8.

As if that weren't enough, one new fund actually posted high returns in 1996, but managed big losses for its investors just the same. Incredibly, the Dreyfus Aggressive Growth Fund managed to lose $10.7 million of investors' money according to its annual report in a year when the fund recorded a total return of 81.7 percent. How? This seemingly impossible achievement happened when the fund's early gains were more than wiped out by declines after the fund had attracted close to $2 billion in new money. It's a cautionary tale that should teach investors that top performance, especially over the shorter term, is a poor indicator of future performance.

"Because past performance has been a useful indicator of future performance in various facets of people's lives, many investors naturally believe that the same decision criterion applies to investment selection," wrote Frank Campanale.[12]

So now the inevitable question: Should you to try to find a market guru or superhot fund manager who actually outperforms the market? Or would you rather become a rational, disciplined investor who takes advantage of the market's fickleness to outperform the market on your own?

If you are among those investors who choose the second alternative, you are about to discover a method of investing that will allow you literally to buy low and sell high. You're about to embark on a search for the Holy Grail of the true stock picker: a few good stocks known as real bargains.

---

12 Frank Campanale and Brett Skakun, "Why Top Performance Is a Poor Indicator of Future Performance," in Investment Management Institute's Investor Series, Vol. I, May 1997 (Smith Barney Consulting Group).

CHAPTER 2

An Investor's Best Friend

Men that hazard all do it in hope of fair advantage.

William Shakespeare,
The Merchant of Venice

Benchmark investing is an approach that can be applied at various levels of sophistication on the part of institutional and individual investors alike. Investor reaction to this new strategy, however, might well be one of skepticism, especially since people tend to seek out the dark side of anything new and unfamiliar. There's absolutely nothing wrong with having a healthy suspicion when it comes to investing. You should learn to challenge all market claims and try to understand what lies behind the numbers. Skepticism is especially beneficial in looking at claims such as the ones presented in this book. Whenever you see such a claim, it is usually a good idea to keep your wallet closed. In fact, such independence is one of the most highly valued traits of a benchmark investor. It's absolutely critical to question consensus thought and always to look behind the numbers. Those who do so will have a huge advantage over typical investors.

However, there are skeptics who insist that the market can't be beaten with any kind of market strategy, much less benchmark investing. Others question the validity of investing serious capital in the stock market at any time, not to mention when the Dow Industrials are trading at all-time highs. These are the fearful souls who resist getting caught in the next huge downturn in the stock market. Rather than invest in stocks, which historically have provided the largest returns over time, they keep their assets in sedate Treasury bills or money market funds while promising themselves that they'll invest in the market after the next correction. Of course, the law of inertia is an insuperable force. As a result, fearful investors remain prisoners of inaction and keep their money "safely" tucked away only to watch inflation and taxes destroy their future buying power. This strange affliction of inertia can be an investor's worst nightmare. It can lead investors to let large sums molder in miserly checking accounts or to stick with investments in bonds despite hearing that stocks do better in the long run. In the end, they'll completely avoid investing in the stock market.

Investing too little money in stocks, or avoiding the stock market altogether, explains why most Americans reach the age of 65 with very little savings. Paradoxically, most Americans look to their retirement years with anticipation. They look forward to having the time and money to make their dreams come true. But the brutal reality is that most people won't retire comfortably because they save too little and steer clear of stocks.

Once upon a time, retirement was simple. When a retiree—typically, the male breadwinner—turned 65, the boss held a big banquet, his colleagues gave him a gold watch, and they all bid him a fond farewell. Then, he sailed into the good life, floating comfortably on a financial cushion of a pension, Social Security, and perhaps some modest savings or inheritance. At least that was the experience of an earlier generation. But today it's pretty certain that most of the old retirement rules no longer apply, unless you're an heir to the family fortune or hit the lottery. Nowadays, reality is often a different story for those who retire.

A recent Department of Labor survey revealed some startling figures. About 45 percent of those who retire at age 65 are dependent on their relatives. Almost as astonishing, 28 percent rely entirely on welfare, charity, or Social Security. Meanwhile, 22 percent continue to work to make ends meet. Only 5 percent of retirees have enough money to meet their needs, and only 1 percent have enough money to be considered secure.

Although these statistics are alarming, there is an answer if you are determined to retire with more than the average American. The quality of your retirement years can be influenced by taking charge of your planning now. However, you must begin today, because achieving a comfortable financial future will involve both effort and time.

What's more, retirement is no longer simply a time for rest. Nowadays, retirement marks the beginning of an exciting, active phase of life that often requires higher budgets for travel and entertainment than was true in previous working years. In addition, people are living longer, thanks to medical advances, better nutrition, and an increased awareness of health. Further, workers are retiring earlier in their careers than in years past. The combination of these factors means that many may easily spend 20 years or more in retirement. It also means that workers must earn and save enough to last for many years. Otherwise, they run the very real risk of outliving their retirement savings.

Social Security, as we know it, can be a significant source of income for today's retirees. However, it was not designed to be the sole source. For example, someone retiring today from a job paying $40,000 a year would receive only about 30 percent of his or her preretirement income from Social Security—certainly not enough to live on, much less to travel extensively. And who's to say that Social Security will continue to exist in its present form? It seems certain, at the very least, that Social Security faces drastic reductions for future generations of retirees. A radical reshaping of Social Security will probably take place before the year 2000.

Former Social Security commissioner Robert Ball is backing a plan for the government to invest some Social Security funds in stocks in order to head off a taxpayer revolt. Meanwhile, a bipartisan panel agrees that some of the $400 billion of Social Security taxes collected each year should be invested in stocks.

As for pension plans, most are generally designed to replace only 25 to 45 percent of a retiree's income. Clearly, combining a pension plan along with Social Security will not allow most people to meet their retirement needs (see Table 2.1). They must make up the difference themselves or face the possibility of having to depend on relatives or charity throughout their golden years.

The future may not be secure unless workers take responsibility for saving and investing wisely before they retire. In fact, a large portion of their retirement income may need to come from their savings alone. Investing in stocks, on the other hand, can help investors plan for a secure future. Stocks are an investor's best friend.

TABLE 2.1

Social Security Income

Current Gross Annual Income	Percentage Replaced by Social Security	Approximate Annual Social Security Income
$20,000	39%	$ 7,800
$25,000	37%	$ 9,250
$30,000	35%	$10,500
$35,000	33%	$11,550
$40,000	30%	$12,000
$45,000	28%	$12,600
$50,000	27%	$13,500
$55,000	25%	$13,750
$60,000	24%	$14,400
$65,000	23%	$14,950
$70,000	21%	$14,700
$80,000	18%	$14,400

Note: These numbers may change as a result of periodic cost-of-living increases and other factors. The actual benefit may vary depending on number of years in the workplace, year of birth, earnings history, and retirement age. Assumes 4 percent annual inflation, 4 percent annual wage increase, and retirement at age 65. Retiring before 65 may reduce benefits. For more information about Social Security, call 1-800-772-1213.

Over the long term, the potential rewards of stock investing have historically outweighed the risks of the market's short-term ups and downs. In fact, stocks have significantly outperformed U.S. Treasury bonds and bills since 1925.

Figure 2.1 is updated from Jeremy Siegel's book *Stocks for the Long Run*. As the chart clearly highlights, the best way to make money grow over a long period of time is to invest in stocks of good companies. A $1 investment in stocks over the life of the study (1802 to 1996) became $358,000 after inflation. In comparison, $1 invested in Treasury bills over the same years rose to only $261 after inflation, or less than 0.0007 percent of the return on stocks. A $1 investment in Treasury bonds over the same period grew to only $752, according to Siegel.

Table 2.2 shows how much you can draw upon your retirement funds each year. Find the appropriate withdrawal rate according to the asset mix your portfolio holds and how long you expect your retirement to last. The percentage shown represents the amount you

FIGURE 2.1

Total Nominal Return Indices: 18-2–1996*

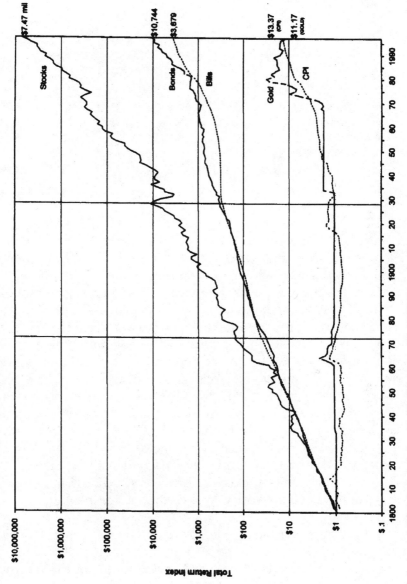

* Updated figure from Dr. Jeremy J. Siegel, *Stocks for the Long Run* (Net York: McGraw-Hill, 1994), p. 6.

TABLE 2.2

How Much You Can Pull Out of Your Retirement Funds
Each Year

	Years in Retirement				
Portfolio	**10**	**15**	**20**	**25**	**30**
70% stocks/30% bonds	12.7%	9.6%	8.1%	7.3%	6.7%
60% stocks/40% bonds	12.4%	9.3%	7.8%	6.9%	6.3%
50% stocks/50% bonds	12.2%	9.0%	7.4%	6.5%	6.0%
40% stocks/60% bonds	11.9%	8.7%	7.1%	6.2%	5.6%
30% stocks/70% bonds	11.6%	8.4%	6.8%	5.8%	5.2%
20% stocks/80% bonds	11.3%	8.1%	6.4%	5.5%	4.9%

Source: T. Rowe Price Associates.

should withdraw in the first year of your retirement. Thereafter, you should increase the amount withdrawn by the rate of inflation.

A recent phenomenon known as 401(k) millionaires proves the value of buying and holding stocks for the long term. That's because retirement savings, accumulated slowly over years in stock funds, have turned more and more ordinary people into millionaires. At Baltimore-based T. Rowe Price, records showed 120 millionaires at the end of 1995 among the firm's retirement accounts. By the middle of 1997, the number of millionaire retirement accounts had more than doubled, rising to 308. Again, nothing is more important than an investor's time horizon: the longer, the better. Of course, the public has been conditioned by the media to fear the stock market. Most Americans associate investing in stocks with the Crash of 1929. They envision panic-stricken Wall Streeters hurling themselves from the windows of New York City skyscrapers. For them, stocks are far too risky an option.

As it happens, Jeremy Siegel's research proves that stocks actually are far less risky than bonds and Treasury bills if they are held for extended periods of time: "Over the long run the returns on stocks are so stable that stocks are actually *safer* than either government bonds or Treasury bills."[1] Siegel came to his unconventional

---

1   Dr. Jeremy J. Siegel, *Stocks for the Long Run* (New York: McGraw-Hill, 1994), p. iv.

TABLE 2.3

Inflation's Long-Term Effect on Prices

	January 1, 1971	January 1, 1996
Consumer Price Index (CPI)	$100	$386
Cadillac Sedan de Ville	$5,721	$36,635
Super Bowl Ticket	$12	$250

TABLE 2.4

The Money Needed in the Future to Equal $100 Today

Years	4% Inflation
5	$122
10	$148
15	$180
20	$219
25	$267

conclusions only after conducting exhaustive market research on U.S. stocks spanning the years 1802 to 1996. He concluded that the safest long-term investment has clearly been stocks, not bonds.

Inflation makes investing in stocks a necessity. Although stock prices have historically appreciated, the purchasing power of the dollar has dramatically declined. In the past 50 years the purchasing power of $100 has fallen 83 percent, to $17.45.[2] Tables 2.3 and 2.4 underscore inflation's effects.

Remember the penny postcard? It hasn't cost a penny to mail since 1951. Thanks to inflation, it now costs 20 cents. The inflation that made the penny postcard a relic of the past could also derail your financial plans. Wealthy investors in the top tax bracket who put $1 million into bonds after World War II had only $218,000 of

2   Source: Towers Data System HYPO.

their original purchasing power left by 1996. Inflation and taxes ate up nearly 80 percent of the investment. That's why it's riskier not to invest more in stocks.

WHEN TO BUY STOCKS

One of the most agonizing tasks that an investor faces is deciding when to invest in the stock market. Many investors consider the task as difficult as hitting a moving target. Since stock prices bob up and down, their aim is to buy immediately before stock prices begin to rise. But upswings in the market, when they come, start as a series of sudden, amazing spurts in price that are concentrated in just a few days or weeks.

Investors who have been lucky enough to sell at or near a market top will have to rebuy in time for the next leg up, which is incredibly hard to do. That's because the average investor is afraid that the market's dips today might keep stocks zigzagging down. The anxiety can be particularly acute when the stock market is in the midst of a streak of hitting new record highs. Many investors—even professionals—cringe at the prospect of making an investment at the top, fearing that a major drop in stock prices will soon follow.

"I admit it. I'm nervous," revealed *Wall Street Journal* feature writer Jonathan Clements.[3] At the time of his market anxiety the Dow stood at 6255. Clements went on to explain that he was also nervous when the Dow Jones Industrial Average broke above 3000 and 4000 and 5000. So why should 6000, 7000, or 8000 be any different?

Why indeed?

Although such fears are common among investors, they're overstated when viewed in the context of the stock market's historical performance. Sure you can get killed in stocks. Just consider 1921, 1929, 1962, 1974, or 1987. *But the pain has always been temporary.* Stocks show remarkable power to recuperate from major disasters. Investors who bought stocks in 1929 and held them for the next 20 years would have been 10 times ahead of those who bought bonds, according to Siegel's extensive research.

An interesting study conducted by Smith Barney calculated just how much an investor's portfolio would have been worth over vari-

---

3 Jonathan Clements, "Nervous About Booming Stock Prices?" *The Wall Street Journal,*
   November 12, 1996, p. C1.

TABLE 2.5

Portfolio Performance and Return Comparison

Period	Market High	Market Low	T-Bills	CPI
1940–1995	7.5%	8.0%	4.3%	4.4%
1950–1995	7.2%	7.9%	5.1%	4.2%
1960–1995	7.3%	8.3%	6.0%	4.7%
1970–1995	8.8%	10.2%	6.9%	5.5%
1980–1995	10.0%	12.6%	7.2%	4.4%
1990–1995	8.7%	14.2%	4.8%	3.3%

Note: Dividends are not included in this study.
Source: Smith Barney.

ous periods if he or she had invested at the *worst* possible time—specifically, at the market's *high*—each year. Table 2.5 compares the "bad luck" investor's portfolio with a portfolio invested in 90-day Treasury bills and the return of the consumer price index over the same periods. As the table shows, even an investor with perfectly lousy investment timing would have earned returns significantly greater than those of T-bills and the rate of inflation. Further, the portfolios' returns don't include dividends, which would have increased the returns from 3.0 to 4.6 percent annually, depending on the period.

As an additional point of contrast, the hard-luck portfolio was compared with portfolios that invested at the market's *low* point each year. The conclusion of the study was that investors have been able to earn handsome returns even when their timing was very poor, and that diligently sticking to a stock investment program over long periods helps overcome short-term market declines and poorly timed investments.

Consider those luckless investors who bought at the market peak in August 1987. By 1996, they already had a return more than two times greater than that of T-bills. The worst possible day to have made a stock investment in the last 25 years was January 11, 1973, the day before the market began a two-year, 40 percent decline. If our hapless speculators had invested on that very day, it would have taken them five years to break even. However, had they remained invested until 1996, their gain would have been well over 1000 percent, compared with just 380 percent for Treasury bills.

The point is that long-term investing is the key to good fortune in the stock market, and investing long-term in undervalued companies will enhance your prospects for success. Indeed, for long-term investors, the biggest worry shouldn't be short-term market fluctuations. Instead, it should be the damage inflicted by inflation and taxes.

It should be noted that Warren Buffett made his fortune in long-term investments, not short-term. His favorite holding period, he says, is permanent. Coca-Cola went public in 1919 at $40 per share. Had your great-grandmother bought just one share, reinvested all her dividends, and held on through all the splits until the end of 1997, her single share would have grown to 95,808 shares worth over $6.3 million.

Over shorter periods, stocks are more volatile than bonds and T-bills. This may explain why most amateur investors do so poorly in the stock market. First of all, the market is a tug of war between fear and greed. Most investors move from love for their stocks to hate to neglect. *The problem is that stocks are loved when they are overpriced.* The average investor hurls his or her life savings into the market at such times on the reasonable assumption that when people exude extreme, euphoric optimism, the market is climbing higher. The truth is that most investors place their bets when they should be selling. And just as night follows day, most investors sell when they should be buying. Euphoria and rampant greed cause investors to buy at selling time, while fear and loathing compel most of them to sell at buying time.

It should now be clear why most investors will benefit from a discipline like benchmark investing, which eliminates emotions and seeks out objective answers. Benchmark investing allows investors to step back from the intensity and emotionalism of the stock market. Investing in undervalued stocks and adding to them regularly over a few decades should make most investors more than just well off. They should forget about trying to time the market and instead let compounding go to work for them. The trouble, of course, is that we are all creatures with a short-term orientation. We are afraid of looking stupid holding stocks when the market takes its inevitable dive.

Table 2.6 shows what $1000 would be worth in 10, 20, 30, and 40 years if you allowed it to compound tax-free at varying rates of return. The difference that a few percentage points can make is astonishing. At 10 percent for 10 years, your $1000 would grow to $2593 when allowed to compound tax-free. But look at the incredible

TABLE 2.6

The Power of Compounding

Period	10%	15%	20%	25%
10 years	$2,593	$4,045	$6,191	$9,313
20 years	$6,725	$16,367	$38,338	$86,736
30 years	$17,449	$66,211	$237,376	$807,793
40 years	$45,259	$267,863	$1,468,771	$7,523,163

difference you would enjoy with a 15 percent annual gain. Then add 5 percent and 10 years, and your $1000 initial investment would grow to $38,338. If you're young enough, go to 25 percent for 40 years, and you'll see the original $1000 climb astronomically to $7.5 million!

If you want to do well in the stock market, you need to consider benchmark investing's strategy of buying high-quality companies at bargain prices. However, you should remain skeptical about benchmark investing until you see how it actually works. What you will find is a simple strategy that has delivered exceedingly well during the last few years.

From the beginning of 1991 to the end of 1996, benchmark investing enjoyed a cumulative (geometric) total return of 344.12 percent while annually compounding at an average of 28.21 percent. Extrapolating those kinds of returns over varying periods, you can see that your portfolio would grow very quickly. Meanwhile, during the same period the Dow Jones Industrial Average had a cumulative increase of 185.94 percent while averaging 19.14 percent in annual compound returns—less than its "average" return of 19.67 percent (see Chapter 3). What's interesting is that benchmark investing picked the best-performing Dow stock only once during those six years, yet it still managed to beat the mighty Dow index.

Perhaps a large dose of humility is in order at this point. You should never expect to be right all the time with any strategy, including benchmark investing. In the future, for one reason or another, benchmark investing will be wrong in many cases. Eight of the 23 benchmark picks either lost money or underperformed the Dow between 1991 and 1996. Future selections will, without a doubt, disappoint investors. Benchmark investing stresses downside protection versus upside potential, a point worth remembering when a different segment of the market heats up while your benchmark picks languish.

In any event, benchmark stocks will have periods of mediocre or substandard performance compared with other categories of stocks. It is at these times that the benchmark investor must practice the patience and fortitude of a saint. If you have any doubts that this will ever occur, please be assured that Wall Street is littered with banana peels. It can only be hoped that benchmark investing will continue to outperform the Dow in years to come. A more realistic possibility is that there will be disappointing years.

That's the bad news. The good news is that financial manias will provide a rich depository of mistakes over and over again from which to profit. Benjamin Graham taught that the average investor will make the wrong decisions most of the time and that the path to success is best found by doing the opposite of what everyone else is doing. Benchmark investing allows investors to do what Graham taught.

As a valuation tool, benchmark investing provides investors with a discipline that aims at removing emotionalism from the marketplace. It consistently identifies when stocks are cheap and when they are dear. Remember, value usually differs from a stock's current price, making for either incredible bargains or extremely overpriced securities. And as the Dow's creator, Charles H. Dow, insisted, every investor should "first of all know value." What matters is that the patient, disciplined benchmark investor will buy in a period of disenchantment, then watch as stock prices appreciate when other investors recognize the true value in benchmark stocks.

A benchmark investor will achieve what most professional managers have failed to accomplish over the years if he or she can just match market gains. A vital reason benchmark investing has enjoyed a superior record over the Dow is that it is a disciplined approach. Any discipline works better than no discipline. Those with a consistent approach are bound to produce better results than managers who stick a finger in the air and try to go with the flow of the moment. If a benchmark investor can match or exceed the market's average gains, the returns will be both rewarding and compelling. You may not make it to the *Forbes* list of the 400 wealthiest people in America, but you will be more than well off.

CHAPTER 3

Trouncing the Dow

Price is what you pay. Value is what you get.
Warren Buffett,
Letter to Partners, Jan. 20, 1966

It was not the end of the world, but a day that bedlam reigned on the floor of the New York Stock Exchange. The day that indescribable atrocity loosed itself like a firestorm upon the canyons of Wall Street. Investors around the world, from Tokyo to Toledo, were shocked by the gruesome slaughter that occurred that Monday. There was blood in the Street as a surging, screaming mass of traders fought to sell off shares that nobody wanted. The free fall was accentuated in Chicago by index futures and options trading as successive waves of selling inspired by portfolio insurance fed on themselves.

In stark contrast, all this havoc on Wall Street followed a sublime 700 point, 40 percent increase in the Dow in the preceding seven months that left investors—both amateur and professional alike—profoundly complacent as to the incredible damage a bear market could inflict. As usual, few investors suspected what was going to happen. But soon enough, they would learn that Benjamin Graham was right to insist that the only thing investors had to fear was the absence of fear.

Then, tragedy came out of nowhere as $560 billion simply vanished. In a matter of a single trading session, the stock market experienced a full-scale selling panic that sent the Dow crashing 508 points—a modern-day meltdown of epic proportions. More important, it was an agonizing 22.6 percent disintegration that seriously called into question whether capitalism American-style would survive.

It was also the day that benchmark investing was born: Monday, October 19, 1987.

Prior to the crash, I had studied a multitude of investment strategies in an effort to find a safer way to invest in stocks. As a financial professional as well as a serious and dedicated student of the stock market, I followed scores of investment newsletters, magazines, and journals to keep up with indicators such as money supply growth, put-call ratios, insider buying and selling, and advisory sentiment. I also paid close attention to advance-decline lines, initial public offering prices, chart patterns, moving averages, sector analysis, interest rate directions, foreign trade deficits, and price-earnings models, along with several other indicators. But in spite of my efforts, I was as completely surprised by Black Monday's crash as anyone in America.

All the indicators failed to give me a clear warning of impending financial disaster. Still, there had to be a way to know when the market was too high. And if such a way existed, I was determined to discover its secret. Thus began an intense search to uncover an investment strategy that worked: a search to find the way to know when to buy a stock at undervalued levels and when to sell at dizzying heights. It had to be uncomplicated so that anyone could understand it and use it to make stock decisions. What I discovered—through exhaustive trial and error—was *so* simple that I almost removed it from consideration until it began beating the stock market month after month. Just as surprising, this new strategy I began calling *benchmark investing* would have sent a strong warning signal that the stock market was too high in the summer of 1987 (see Table 3.1).

In its first 12 months, benchmark investing outperformed the stock market with a 37.63 percent total return. Just as amazing to me, benchmark investing continued to outperform the Dow Industrials month after month and year after year. Most important, this simple strategy avoided most, but not all, of the losers in the Dow Jones Industrial Average over the years.

Today, the great news is that investors don't have to follow 1500 stocks like I did when I first began using benchmark investing. That's because the technique works just as well, if not better, with the 30 Dow Industrial stocks as it does with a much larger universe. And,

TABLE 3.1

Benchmark's 1987 Dow Jones Industrial
Average Monitor

DJIA Stocks	12/31/86 Price	Historical Market/ Book Low	High	ROE Ratio	1987 Book Value	Downside Target	Upside Target
AlliedSignal	$40.13	0.81	1.25	1.16	$20.87	$19.61	$30.26
Alcoa	$33.88	0.70	1.03	0.94	$43.62	$28.70	$42.23
American Can	$84.13	0.70	0.88	1.37	$53.25	$51.07	$64.20
American Express	$57.50	1.38	2.15	0.51	$20.22	$14.23	$22.17
AT&T	$25.00	1.37	1.80	1.30	$13.46	$23.97	$31.50
Bethlehem Steel	$6.25	0.33	0.48	0.51	$14.74	$2.48	$3.61
Chevron	$45.38	0.74	1.13	0.34	$46.13	$11.61	$17.72
DuPont	$84.00	0.89	1.30	0.99	$58.65	$51.68	$75.48
Eastman Kodak	$68.59	1.40	2.05	1.45	$27.83	$56.49	$82.72
Exxon	$70.13	0.95	1.30	0.81	$48.76	$37.52	$51.34
General Electric	$86.00	1.62	1.90	0.99	$36.50	$58.54	$68.66
General Motors	$66.00	0.77	1.07	0.88	$89.09	$60.37	$83.89
Goodyear Tire	$41.88	0.63	0.94	2.15	$32.19	$43.60	$65.06
IBM	$120.00	2.12	2.98	0.66	$64.06	$89.63	$125.99
Inco	$11.75	0.82	1.41	0.55	$9.40	$4.24	$7.29
International Paper	$75.13	0.64	0.91	1.00	$72.62	$46.48	$66.08
McDonald's	$60.75	1.88	2.81	0.96	$15.44	$27.87	$41.65
Merck	$124.00	2.60	3.83	2.03	$16.11	$85.03	$125.25
MMM	$116.63	2.11	2.82	0.94	$44.48	$88.22	$117.91
Navistar	$4.75	0.45	0.67	NMF	($0.50)	$0.00	$0.00
Owens-Illinois	$53.00	0.45	0.63	1.21	$55.65	$30.30	$42.42
Philip Morris	$72.00	1.68	2.44	1.22	$28.83	$59.09	$85.82
Procter & Gamble	$76.38	1.67	2.22	0.78	$35.44	$46.16	$61.37
Sears	$39.75	0.85	1.24	1.11	$35.89	$33.86	$49.40
Texaco	$35.88	0.54	0.80	0.41	$37.36	$8.27	$12.25
Union Carbide	$22.50	0.65	1.02	2.47	$9.43	$15.14	$23.76
United Technologies	$46.00	0.96	1.44	1.04	$32.90	$32.85	$49.27
USX	$21.50	0.50	0.75	0.70	$23.00	$8.05	$12.08
Westinghouse	$55.75	1.00	1.58	1.29	$24.92	$32.15	$50.79
Woolworth	$38.63	0.69	1.09	1.26	$26.54	$23.07	$36.45
DJIA	1895.95	1.06	1.52	1.07	35.75	1370.30	1964.95

obviously, it's far less time-consuming to follow the 30 stocks in the
Dow than the 1500 or so covered in *Value Line.*

The overview in Table 3.2 provides a better understanding of
how benchmark investing has worked in real-time investing during
the volatile 1990s. It must be noted that only those companies recommended at the *beginning* of each year have been included in the
yearly returns so as to fairly compare the results of the Dow with
those of benchmark investing. Actually, there were many additional
recommendations each year that would have improved benchmark
investing's annual results. Still, the table provides an understanding
of how the strategy operates.

1991

Could there have been a worst time to invest? The United States had
gone to war with Saddam Hussein and Iraq at the outset of 1991, and
along with its stunning military success came an end to months of
suspense over the prospects of the stock market. Wall Street fired off
its own equivalent to a 21-gun salute in late January, when the Dow
soared more than 114 points in one day, its second-biggest gain in history up to that point in time. In the process, the Dow turned around
a year that had started on a distinctly sour note (see Figure 3.1).

As if war in the volatile Mideast wasn't enough to worry about,
Wall Street was also troubled over the debt binge created by Drexel (remember that?), plunging real estate prices, higher oil prices, and inflation. Again, the market defied expectations for a bad year by posting a healthy 23.93 percent total return (including dividends) in 1991.

Meanwhile, benchmark investing's recommendations (see Table 3.3) beat the Dow's 1991 showing, even though none of the top six
Dow performers were recommended. The four benchmark investing
stocks selected gained 25.69 percent. The list was led by Sears, which
had the seventh-highest total return that year among the Dow Industrials (see Tables 3.4 and 3.5).

1991 Benchmark Recommendations	12-31-90 Price	12-31-91 Price	1991 Dividend	1991 Total Return
American Express	$20.63	$20.50	$0.94	3.93%
AT&T	$30.13	$39.13	$1.32	34.25%
Boeing	$45.38	$47.75	$1.00	7.43%
Sears	$25.23	$37.88	$2.00	57.13%
Benchmark picks				25.69%
DJIA's total return				23.93%

TABLE 3.2

Benchmark Investing Results: 1973–1997

Stocks Selected	Year	Benchmark Results	DJIA Results
14	1973	−3.22%	−13.12%
14	1974	−5.13%	−23.14%
5	1975	73.28%	44.40%
19	1976	35.01%	22.72%
14	1977	−3.16%	−12.71%
16	1978	6.24%	2.69%
20	1979	17.43%	10.52%
15	1980	35.44%	21.41%
9	1981	7.84%	−3.40%
5	1982	65.20%	25.79%
7	1983	35.67%	25.65%
3	1984	16.16%	1.08%
1	1985	50.33%	32.78%
1	1986	68.27%	26.92%
1	1987	47.09%	6.02%
6	1988	23.05%	15.95%
5	1989	21.03%	31.71%
2	1990	15.63%	−0.57%
4	1991	25.69%	23.93%
3	1992	14.92%	7.34%
4	1993	38.04%	16.72%
2	1994	11.36%	4.95%
8	1995	37.81%	36.48%
2	1996	45.14%	28.57%
2	1997	31.88%	24.91%
	Cumulative Gain	36932.76%	2128.66%
	Annual Compound Rate	26.68%	13.01%
	Average Annual Percent	28.44%	14.30%

Note: All dividends are included for both the benchmark investing strategy and the DJIA, and do not reflect sales charges, commissions, expenses, or taxes. Past performance is no guarantee of future results.

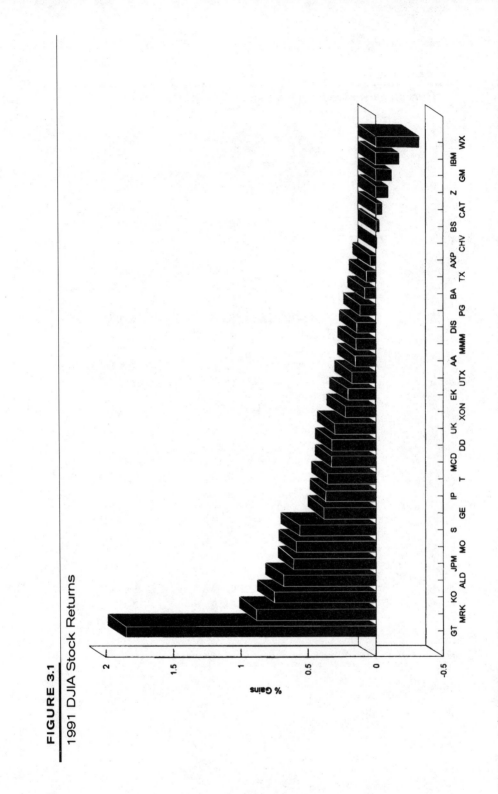

FIGURE 3.1

1991 DJIA Stock Returns

32

TABLE 3.3

Benchmark's 1991 Dow Jones Industrial Average Monitor

DJIA Stocks	12/31/90 Price	Historical Market/ Book Low	High	ROE Ratio	1991 Book Value	Downside Target	Upside Target
AlliedSignal	$27.00	0.97	1.47	1.08	$26.05	$27.29	$41.36
Alcoa	$57.63	0.86	1.33	1.10	$66.35	$62.77	$97.07
American Express	$20.63	1.65	2.67	1.07	$15.15	$26.75	$43.28
AT&T	$30.13	1.79	2.62	1.26	$14.80	$33.38	$48.86
Bethlehem Steel	$14.75	0.47	0.89	0.42	$23.00	$4.54	$8.60
Boeing	$45.38	1.23	2.00	1.56	$25.00	$47.97	$78.00
Caterpillar	$47.00	0.55	0.83	NMF	$40.08	NMF	NMF
Chevron	$72.63	0.86	1.27	1.22	$44.20	$46.37	$68.48
Coca-Cola	$46.50	3.30	5.19	1.38	$6.68	$30.42	$47.84
Disney	$101.50	2.43	4.21	1.05	$29.50	$75.27	$130.40
DuPont	$36.75	1.05	1.53	1.20	$26.20	$33.01	$48.10
Eastman Kodak	$41.63	1.65	2.33	1.44	$21.65	$51.44	$72.64
Exxon	$51.75	1.25	1.67	0.93	$28.00	$32.55	$43.49
General Electric	$57.38	1.86	2.66	1.11	$27.20	$56.16	$80.31
General Motors	$34.38	0.63	0.94	0.47	$62.95	$18.64	$27.81
Goodyear Tire	$18.88	0.84	1.40	0.27	$34.10	$7.73	$12.89
IBM	$113.00	1.75	2.46	0.81	$76.35	$108.23	$152.14
International Paper	$53.50	0.74	1.19	1.05	$56.55	$43.94	$70.66
McDonald's	$29.13	2.12	3.25	1.00	$12.90	$27.35	$41.93
Merck	$89.96	4.62	6.76	1.38	$13.25	$84.48	$123.61
Minnesota Mining	$85.75	2.19	2.98	1.11	$30.30	$73.66	$100.23
Philip Morris	$51.75	2.25	3.42	1.25	$14.90	$41.91	$63.70
J. P. Morgan	$44.38	1.00	1.56	1.49	$29.41	$43.82	$68.36
Procter & Gamble	$86.63	1.98	2.85	1.32	$22.05	$57.63	$82.95
Sears	$25.38	0.83	1.31	0.80	$42.15	$27.99	$44.17
Texaco	$60.50	0.72	1.03	1.46	$33.60	$35.32	$50.53
Union Carbide	$16.38	0.86	1.45	0.55	$18.50	$8.75	$14.75
United Technologies	$47.88	1.00	1.52	1.03	$41.55	$42.80	$65.05
Westinghouse	$28.50	1.36	2.12	1.17	$18.35	$29.20	$45.52
Woolworth	$30.25	1.06	1.76	1.20	$19.95	$25.38	$42.13
DJIA	2633.66	1.49	2.27	1.08	$30.37	2674.54	4074.64

TABLE 3.4

1991 Dow Jones Industrial Average Total Returns:
Alphabetical List

DJIA Stocks	12/31/90 Price	12/31/91 Price	1991 Dividend	1991 Total Return
AlliedSignal	$27.00	$43.88	$1.60	68.44%
Alcoa	$57.63	$64.38	$1.78	14.80%
American Express	$20.63	$20.50	$0.94	3.93%
AT&T	$30.13	$39.13	$1.32	34.25%
Bethlehem Steel	$14.75	$14.00	$0.40	−2.37%
Boeing	$45.38	$47.75	$1.00	7.43%
Caterpillar	$47.00	$43.88	$1.05	−4.40%
Chevron	$72.63	$69.00	$3.25	−0.52%
Coca-Cola	$46.50	$80.25	$0.96	74.65%
Disney	$101.50	$114.50	$0.67	13.47%
DuPont	$36.75	$46.63	$1.68	31.46%
Eastman Kodak	$41.63	$48.25	$2.00	20.71%
Exxon	$51.75	$60.88	$2.68	22.82%
General Electric	$57.38	$76.50	$2.04	36.88%
General Motors	$34.38	$28.88	$1.60	−11.34%
Goodyear Tire	$18.88	$53.50	$0.40	185.49%
IBM	$113.00	$89.00	$4.84	−16.96%
International Paper	$53.50	$70.75	$1.68	35.38%
McDonald's	$29.13	$38.00	$0.36	31.69%
Merck	$89.88	$166.65	$2.31	87.98%
MMM	$85.75	$95.25	$3.12	14.72%
Philip Morris	$51.75	$80.25	$1.82	58.59%
J. P. Morgan	$44.38	$68.63	$1.98	59.10%
Procter & Gamble	$86.63	$93.88	$1.95	10.62%
Sears	$25.38	$37.88	$2.00	57.13%
Texaco	$60.50	$61.25	$3.20	6.53%
Union Carbide	$16.38	$20.25	$1.00	29.73%
United Technologies	$47.88	$54.25	$1.80	17.06%
Westinghouse	$28.50	$18.00	$1.40	−31.93%
Woolworth	$30.25	$26.50	$1.07	− 8.86%
DJIA	2633.66	3168.83		23.93%

TABLE 3.5

1991 Dow Jones Industrial Average Total Returns:
Ranked by Performance

DJIA Stocks	12/31/90 Price	12/31/91 Price	1991 Dividend	1991 Total Return
1　Goodyear Tire	$18.88	$53.50	$0.40	185.49%
2　Merck	$89.88	$166.65	$2.31	87.98%
3　Coca-Cola	$46.50	$80.25	$0.96	74.65%
4　AlliedSignal	$27.00	$43.88	$1.60	68.44%
5　J. P. Morgan	$44.38	$68.63	$1.98	59.10%
6　Philip Morris	$51.75	$80.25	$1.82	58.59%
7　Sears	$25.38	$37.88	$2.00	57.13%
8　General Electric	$57.38	$76.50	$2.04	36.88%
9　International Paper	$53.50	$70.75	$1.68	35.38%
10　AT&T	$30.13	$39.13	$1.32	34.25%
11　McDonald's	$29.13	$38.00	$0.36	31.69%
12　DuPont	$36.75	$46.63	$1.68	31.46%
13　Union Carbide	$16.38	$20.25	$1.00	29.73%
14　Exxon	$51.75	$60.88	$2.68	22.82%
15　Eastman Kodak	$41.63	$48.25	$2.00	20.71%
16　United Technologies	$47.88	$54.25	$1.80	17.06%
17　Alcoa	$57.63	$64.38	$1.78	14.80%
18　MMM	$85.75	$95.25	$3.12	14.72%
19　Disney	$101.50	$114.50	$0.67	13.47%
20　Procter & Gamble	$86.63	$93.88	$1.95	10.62%
21　Boeing	$45.38	$47.75	$1.00	7.43%
22　Texaco	$60.50	$61.25	$3.20	6.53%
23　American Express	$20.63	$20.50	$0.94	3.93%
24　Chevron	$72.63	$69.00	$3.25	−0.52%
25　Bethlehem Steel	$14.75	$14.00	$0.40	−2.37%
26　Caterpillar	$47.00	$43.88	$1.05	−4.40%
27　Woolworth	$30.25	$26.50	$1.07	−8.86%
28　General Motors	$34.38	$28.88	$1.60	−11.34%
29　IBM	$113.00	$89.00	$4.84	−16.96%
30　Westinghouse	$28.50	$18.00	$1.40	−31.93%

1992

Each January *Barron's* hosts a roundtable panel with some of the brightest and best money managers from Wall Street to discuss the economy and stock market. Its 1992 panel predicted a sharp correction for the year. After all, we were in a recession. Invest in stocks? Get real. Yet the Dow managed to provide a 7.34 percent total return, far from the sharp correction many of the experts had predicted (see Figure 3.2). At the same time, benchmark investing (see Table 3.6) more than doubled the Dow's performance with a 14.92 percent gain. Third-place Dow finisher AT&T was benchmark investing's top recommendation in 1992 at 33.71 percent, followed by ninth-place Caterpillar (see Tables 3.7 and 3.8).

1992 Benchmark Recommendations	12-31-91 Price	12-31-92 Price	1992 Dividend	1992 Total Return
AT&T	$39.13	$51.00	$1.32	33.71%
Caterpillar	$43.88	$53.63	$0.60	23.59%
Eastman Kodak	$48.25	$40.50	$1.70	−12.54%
Benchmark picks				14.92%
DJIA's total return				7.34%

1993

The year began with anguished cries of stock bashing. That's because Americans were swearing in a new president who caused many to swear off the stock market. Meanwhile, the scientists of Wall Street were worried over such myriad issues as cellular phones causing brain cancer, a further collapse of the Tokyo stock market, IBM slashing its dividend by more than half and firing its chairman, American Express replacing long-time CEO James Robinson III with Harvey Golub, and Sears closing the books on its famed catalog along with 50,000 jobs. Wall Streeters were in a general funk over corporate America's relentless shedding of jobs at an alarming rate, which they reckoned couldn't be good for the stock market.

Nonetheless, the mighty Dow turned in an above-average 16.72 percent total return in 1993 (see Figure 3.3). It wasn't until late in the year that *Barron's* informed the world of its latest quarterly poll, which showed institutional money managers becoming more bullish. Meanwhile, benchmark investing's choices at the beginning of 1993 topped the Dow with a 38.04 percent total return (see Table 3.9).

FIGURE 3.2

1992 DJIA Stock Returns

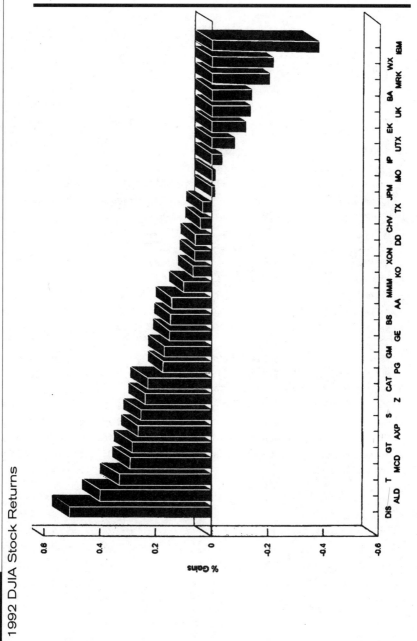

TABLE 3.6

Benchmark's 1992 Dow Jones Industrial Average Monitor

DJIA Stocks	12/31/91 Price	Historical Market/ Book Low	High	ROE Ratio	1992 Book Value	Downside Target	Upside Target
AlliedSignal	$43.88	1.02	1.55	1.17	$24.30	$29.00	$44.07
Alcoa	$64.38	0.81	1.19	0.63	$59.40	$30.31	$44.53
American Express	$20.50	1.49	2.39	0.76	$16.65	$18.85	$30.24
AT&T	$39.13	1.89	2.68	1.66	$14.95	$46.90	$66.51
Bethlehem Steel	$14.00	0.44	0.80	NMF	$3.50	$0.00	$0.00
Boeing	$47.75	1.35	2.04	1.23	$27.50	$45.66	$69.00
Caterpillar	$43.88	1.08	1.63	1.43	$40.75	$62.93	$94.98
Chevron	$69.00	0.94	1.38	0.83	$43.15	$33.67	$49.42
Coca-Cola	$80.25	3.95	6.52	1.36	$7.85	$42.17	$69.61
Disney	$114.50	2.69	4.40	1.10	$35.20	$104.16	$170.37
DuPont	$46.63	1.13	1.62	0.87	$25.50	$25.07	$35.94
Eastman Kodak	$48.25	1.64	2.31	1.48	$20.90	$50.73	$71.45
Exxon	$60.88	1.33	1.73	0.84	$28.35	$31.67	$41.20
General Electric	$76.50	1.92	2.64	1.11	$27.95	$59.57	$81.90
General Motors	$28.88	0.66	0.98	NMF	$39.40	$0.00	$0.00
Goodyear Tire	$53.50	0.78	1.33	0.86	$41.70	$27.97	$47.70
IBM	$89.00	1.69	2.42	0.57	$75.80	$73.02	$104.56
International Paper	$70.75	0.81	1.15	0.81	$55.10	$36.15	$51.33
McDonald's	$38.00	2.16	3.16	0.94	$14.70	$29.85	$43.66
Merck	$166.66	5.29	7.87	1.39	$16.50	$121.33	$180.50
Minnesota Mining	$95.25	2.36	2.94	0.94	$30.90	$68.55	$85.40
Philip Morris	$80.25	2.73	3.96	1.33	$16.15	$58.64	$85.06
J. P. Morgan	$68.63	1.10	1.72	1.21	$32.65	$43.46	$67.95
Procter & Gamble	$93.88	2.40	3.27	1.19	$20.20	$57.69	$78.60
Sears	$37.88	0.80	1.24	1.11	$40.85	$36.27	$56.23
Texaco	$61.25	0.81	1.13	1.01	$34.75	$28.43	$39.66
Union Carbide	$20.25	0.80	1.32	0.92	$18.40	$13.54	$22.34
United Technologies	$54.25	1.07	1.56	1.04	$28.60	$31.83	$46.40
Westinghouse	$18.00	1.34	2.10	0.96	$10.85	$13.96	$21.87
Woolworth	$26.50	1.09	1.76	1.23	$17.25	$23.13	$37.34
DJIA	3168.83	1.62	2.41	1.03	$28.66	2627.28	3908.49

TABLE 3.7

1992 Dow Jones Industrial Average Total Returns:
Alphabetical List

DJIA Stocks	12/31/91 Price	12/31/92 Price	1992 Dividend	1992 Total Return
AlliedSignal	$43.88	$60.50	$1.00	40.15%
Alcoa	$64.38	$71.63	$1.60	13.75%
American Express	$20.50	$24.88	$1.00	26.24%
AT&T	$39.13	$51.00	$1.32	33.71%
Bethlehem Steel	$14.00	$16.00	$0.00	14.29%
Boeing	$47.75	$40.13	$1.00	−13.86%
Caterpillar	$43.88	$53.63	$0.30	22.90%
Chevron	$69.00	$69.50	$1.65	3.12%
Coca-Cola	$40.13	$41.88	$0.56	5.76%
Disney	$28.63	$43.00	$0.20	50.89%
DuPont	$46.63	$47.13	$1.74	4.80%
Eastman Kodak	$48.25	$40.50	$2.00	−11.92%
Exxon	$60.88	$61.13	$2.83	5.06%
General Electric	$76.50	$85.50	$2.24	14.69%
General Motors	$28.88	$32.25	$1.40	16.52%
Goodyear Tire	$53.50	$68.38	$0.56	28.86%
IBM	$89.00	$50.38	$4.84	−37.96%
International Paper	$70.75	$66.63	$1.68	−3.45%
McDonald's	$38.00	$48.75	$0.40	29.34%
Merck	$55.55	$43.38	$0.92	−20.25%
MMM	$95.25	$100.63	$3.20	9.01%
Philip Morris	$80.25	$77.13	$2.23	−1.11%
J. P. Morgan	$68.63	$65.75	$2.18	−1.02%
Procter & Gamble	$46.94	$53.63	$1.08	16.55%
Sears	$37.88	$45.50	$2.00	25.40%
Texaco	$61.25	$59.75	$3.20	2.78%
Union Carbide	$20.25	$16.63	$0.88	−13.53%
United Technologies	$54.25	$48.13	$1.80	−7.96%
Westinghouse	$18.00	$13.38	$0.72	−21.67%
Woolworth	$26.50	$31.63	$1.11	23.55%
DJIA	3168.83	3301.11		4.17%

TABLE 3.8

1992 Dow Jones Industrial Average Total Returns:
Ranked by Performance

DJIA Stocks	12/31/91 Price	12/31/92 Price	1992 Dividend	1992 Total Return
1 Disney	$28.63	$43.00	$0.20	50.89%
2 AlliedSignal	$43.88	$60.50	$1.00	40.15%
3 AT&T	$39.13	$51.00	$1.32	33.71%
4 McDonald's	$38.00	$48.75	$0.40	29.34%
5 Goodyear Tire	$53.50	$68.38	$0.56	28.86%
6 American Express	$20.50	$24.88	$1.00	26.24%
7 Sears	$37.88	$45.50	$2.00	25.40%
8 Woolworth	$26.50	$31.63	$1.11	23.55%
9 Caterpillar	$43.88	$53.63	$0.30	22.90%
10 Procter & Gamble	$46.94	$53.63	$1.08	16.55%
11 General Motors	$28.88	$32.25	$1.40	16.52%
12 General Electric	$76.50	$85.50	$2.24	14.69%
13 Bethlehem Steel	$14.00	$16.00	$0.00	14.29%
14 Alcoa	$64.38	$71.63	$1.60	13.75%
15 MMM	$95.25	$100.63	$3.20	9.01%
16 Coca-Cola	$40.13	$41.88	$0.56	5.76%
17 Exxon	$60.88	$61.13	$2.83	5.06%
18 DuPont	$46.63	$47.13	$1.74	4.80%
19 Chevron	$69.00	$69.50	$1.65	3.12%
20 Texaco	$61.25	$59.75	$3.20	2.78%
21 J. P. Morgan	$68.63	$65.75	$2.18	−1.02%
22 Philip Morris	$80.25	$77.13	$2.23	−1.11%
23 International Paper	$70.75	$66.63	$1.68	−3.45%
24 United Technologies	$54.25	$48.13	$1.80	−7.96%
25 Eastman Kodak	$48.25	$40.50	$2.00	−11.92%
26 Union Carbide	$20.25	$16.63	$0.88	−13.53%
27 Boeing	$47.75	$40.13	$1.00	−13.86%
28 Merck	$55.55	$43.38	$0.92	−20.25%
29 Westinghouse	$18.00	$13.38	$0.72	−21.67%
30 IBM	$89.00	$50.38	$4.84	−37.96%

FIGURE 3.3

1993 DJIA Stock Returns

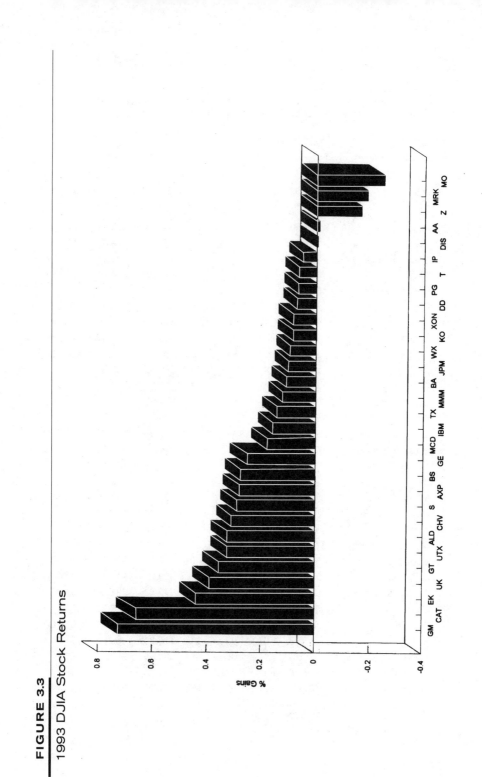

TABLE 3.9

Benchmark's 1993 Dow Jones Industrial Average Monitor

DJIA Stocks	12/31/92 Price	Historical Market/ Book Low	High	ROE Ratio	1993 Book Value	Downside Target	Upside Target
AlliedSignal	$60.50	1.17	1.76	1.18	$28.60	$39.49	$59.40
Alcoa	$71.63	0.85	1.27	0.96	$61.05	$49.82	$74.43
American Express	$24.88	1.63	2.57	0.98	$15.90	$25.40	$40.05
AT&T	$51.00	1.96	2.79	1.48	$15.25	$44.24	$62.97
Bethlehem Steel	$16.00	0.66	1.31	0.73	$4.20	$2.02	$4.02
Boeing	$40.13	1.36	2.10	1.35	$28.50	$52.33	$80.80
Caterpillar	$53.63	1.10	1.66	1.27	$41.00	$57.28	$86.44
Chevron	$69.50	0.99	1.39	1.13	$43.40	$48.55	$68.17
Coca-Cola	$41.88	5.07	7.84	1.46	$4.00	$29.61	$45.79
Disney	$43.00	2.82	4.58	1.04	$10.35	$30.35	$49.30
DuPont	$47.13	1.21	1.72	1.13	$27.50	$37.60	$53.45
Eastman Kodak	$40.50	1.74	2.42	1.67	$21.90	$63.64	$88.51
Exxon	$61.13	1.45	1.88	0.87	$29.65	$37.40	$48.50
General Electric	$85.50	2.06	2.81	1.08	$30.90	$68.75	$93.78
General Motors	$32.25	0.59	0.85	0.72	$34.60	$14.70	$21.18
Goodyear Tire	$68.38	0.97	1.57	1.15	$47.90	$53.43	$86.48
IBM	$50.38	1.65	2.34	0.63	$63.45	$65.96	$93.54
International Paper	$66.63	0.85	1.23	0.77	$55.55	$36.36	$52.61
McDonald's	$48.75	2.25	3.33	0.89	$17.75	$35.54	$52.61
Merck	$43.38	5.67	8.79	1.07	$6.95	$42.16	$65.37
Minnesota Mining	$100.63	2.40	3.16	0.94	$34.70	$78.28	$103.07
Philip Morris	$77.13	3.05	4.51	1.40	$16.80	$71.74	$106.08
J. P. Morgan	$65.75	1.12	1.73	1.13	$38.25	$48.41	$74.77
Procter & Gamble	$53.63	2.59	3.52	1.20	$12.00	$37.30	$50.69
Sears	$45.50	0.87	1.33	1.19	$37.40	$38.72	$59.19
Texaco	$59.75	0.92	1.25	1.21	$35.70	$39.74	$54.00
Union Carbide	$16.63	1.07	1.94	0.61	$15.20	$9.92	$17.99
United Technologies	$48.13	1.14	1.65	1.05	$31.15	$37.29	$53.97
Westinghouse	$13.38	1.46	2.38	0.74	$11.45	$12.37	$20.17
Woolworth	$31.63	1.27	2.01	0.95	$17.70	$21.36	$33.80
DJIA	3301.11	1.69	2.53	1.03	$27.01	3165.65	4734.45

Benchmark picked the second-best Dow performer with its recommendation of Caterpillar, followed by third-place Eastman Kodak and tenth-place American Express. Rounding out the benchmark portfolio was IBM, which trailed the Dow with only a 13.14 percent increase (see Tables 3.10 and 3.11).

1993 Benchmark Recommendations	12-31-92 Price	12-31-93 Price	1993 Dividend	1993 Total Return
American Express	$24.88	$30.88	$1.00	28.14%
Caterpillar	$53.63	$89.00	$0.60	67.07%
Eastman Kodak	$40.50	$56.25	$2.00	43.83%
IBM	$50.38	$56.50	$0.50	13.14%
Benchmark picks				38.04%
DJIA's total return				16.72%

1994

Although the consensus of the smart, witty, literate, and sensible market pros featured in *Barron's* roundtable were comfortable with the investment climate on Wall Street at the beginning of 1994, the following 12 months would prove to be dismal for stocks. Quite simply, most struggled to break even in 1994 (see Table 3.12). Many suffered sharp declines as the Dow gained just 4.95 percent (see Figure 3.4). Meanwhile, benchmark investing once again bested the Dow more than two to one with its 11.36 percent showing (see Tables 3.13 and 3.14).

Following the impressive gains of 1993, only two undervalued stocks were recommended by benchmark at the beginning of 1994: Merck and Philip Morris. Merck concluded the year as the seventh-best performer and Philip Morris finished twelfth. It should be noted that previous picks IBM, Alcoa, and Caterpillar were among the top 10 Dow performers in 1994.

1994 Benchmark Recommendations	12-31-93 Price	12-31-93 Price	1994 Dividend	1994 Total Return
Merck	$34.38	$38.13	$1.14	14.22%
Philip Morris	$55.63	$57.50	$2.86	8.50%
Benchmark picks				11.36%
DJIA's total return				4.95%

TABLE 3.10

1993 Dow Jones Industrial Average Total Returns: Alphabetical List

DJIA Stocks	12/31/92 Price	12/31/93 Price	1993 Dividend	1993 Total Return
AlliedSignal	$60.50	$79.00	$1.16	32.50%
Alcoa	$71.63	$69.38	$1.60	−0.91%
American Express	$24.88	$30.88	$1.00	28.14%
AT&T	$51.00	$52.50	$1.32	5.53%
Bethlehem Steel	$16.00	$20.38	$0.00	27.37%
Boeing	$40.13	$43.25	$1.00	10.27%
Caterpillar	$53.63	$89.00	$0.60	67.07%
Chevron	$69.50	$87.13	$3.50	30.40%
Coca-Cola	$41.88	$44.63	$0.68	8.19%
Disney	$43.00	$42.63	$0.24	−0.30%
DuPont	$47.13	$48.25	$1.76	6.11%
Eastman Kodak	$40.50	$56.25	$2.00	43.83%
Exxon	$61.13	$63.13	$2.88	7.98%
General Electric	$85.50	$104.88	$2.52	25.61%
General Motors	$32.25	$54.88	$0.80	72.65%
Goodyear Tire	$34.19	$45.75	$0.58	35.51%
IBM	$50.38	$56.50	$1.58	15.28%
International Paper	$66.63	$67.75	$1.68	4.20%
McDonald's	$48.75	$57.00	$0.42	17.78%
Merck	$43.38	$34.38	$1.03	−18.37%
MMM	$100.63	$108.75	$3.32	11.37%
Philip Morris	$77.13	$55.63	$2.60	−24.50%
J. P. Morgan	$65.75	$69.38	$2.40	9.17%
Procter & Gamble	$53.63	$55.63	$1.17	5.91%
Sears	$45.50	$57.00	$1.70	29.01%
Texaco	$59.75	$64.75	$3.20	13.72%
Union Carbide	$16.63	$22.38	$0.75	39.09%
United Technologies	$48.13	$62.00	$1.80	32.56%
Westinghouse	$13.38	$14.13	$0.40	8.59%
Woolworth	$31.63	$25.38	$1.15	−16.12%
DJIA	3301.11	3754.09		16.72%

TABLE 3.11

1993 Dow Jones Industrial Average Total Returns:
Ranked by Performance

DJIA Stocks		12/31/92 Price	12/31/93 Price	1993 Dividend	1993 Total Return
1	General Motors	$32.25	$54.88	$0.80	72.65%
2	Caterpillar	$53.63	$89.00	$0.60	67.07%
3	Eastman Kodak	$40.50	$56.25	$2.00	43.83%
4	Union Carbide	$16.63	$22.38	$0.75	39.09%
5	Goodyear Tire	$34.19	$45.75	$0.58	35.51%
6	United Technologies	$48.13	$62.00	$1.80	32.56%
7	Allied Signal	$60.50	$79.00	$1.16	32.50%
8	Chevron	$69.50	$87.13	$3.50	30.40%
9	Sears	$45.50	$57.00	$1.70	29.01%
10	American Express	$24.88	$30.88	$1.00	28.14%
11	Bethlehem Steel	$16.00	$20.38	$0.00	27.37%
12	General Electric	$85.50	$104.88	$2.52	25.61%
13	McDonald's	$48.75	$57.00	$0.42	17.78%
14	IBM	$50.38	$56.50	$1.58	15.28%
15	Texaco	$59.75	$64.75	$3.20	13.72%
16	MMM	$100.63	$108.75	$3.32	11.37%
17	Boeing	$40.13	$43.25	$1.00	10.27%
18	J. P. Morgan	$65.75	$69.38	$2.40	9.17%
19	Westinghouse	$13.38	$14.13	$0.40	8.59%
20	Coca-Cola	$41.88	$44.63	$0.68	8.19%
21	Exxon	$61.13	$63.13	$2.88	7.98%
22	DuPont	$47.13	$48.25	$1.76	6.11%
23	Procter & Gamble	$53.63	$55.63	$1.17	5.91%
24	AT&T	$51.00	$52.50	$1.32	5.53%
25	International Paper	$66.63	$67.75	$1.68	4.20%
26	Disney	$43.00	$42.63	$0.24	−0.30%
27	Alcoa	$71.63	$69.38	$1.60	−0.91%
28	Woolworth	$31.63	$25.38	$1.15	−16.12%
29	Merck	$43.38	$34.38	$1.03	−18.37%
30	Philip Morris	$77.13	$55.63	$2.60	−24.50%

TABLE 3.12

Benchmark's 1994 Dow Jones Industrial Average Monitor

DJIA Stocks	12/31/93 Price	Historical Market/ Book Low	High	ROE Ratio	1994 Book Value	Downside Target	Upside Target
AlliedSignal	$79.00	1.43	2.11	1.65	$20.80	$49.08	$72.42
Alcoa	$69.38	0.95	1.38	0.29	$38.95	$10.73	$15.59
American Express	$30.88	1.60	2.51	1.30	$13.55	$28.18	$44.21
AT&T	$52.50	2.19	3.07	1.75	$12.20	$46.76	$65.54
Bethlehem Steel	$20.38	0.82	1.57	1.24	$ 5.50	$5.59	$10.71
Boeing	$43.25	1.38	2.10	0.49	$28.00	$18.93	$28.81
Caterpillar	$89.00	1.22	1.89	2.13	$28.25	$73.41	$113.73
Chevron	$87.13	0.98	1.39	1.46	$45.25	$64.74	$91.83
Coca-Cola	$44.63	5.94	8.73	1.45	$ 4.40	$37.90	$55.70
Disney	$42.63	3.07	4.77	1.01	$11.15	$34.57	$53.72
DuPont	$48.25	1.42	1.97	1.50	$17.60	$37.49	$52.01
Eastman Kodak	$56.25	1.89	2.67	1.75	$12.10	$40.02	$56.54
Exxon	$63.13	1.57	2.02	0.82	$28.30	$36.43	$46.88
General Electric	$104.88	2.15	2.94	1.10	$32.90	$77.81	$106.40
General Motors	$54.88	0.82	1.22	2.95	$ 7.30	$17.66	$26.27
Goodyear Tire	$45.75	1.14	1.84	1.96	$18.30	$40.89	$66.00
IBM	$56.50	1.58	2.30	0.67	$33.80	$35.78	$52.09
International Paper	$67.75	0.90	1.28	0.60	$51.75	$27.95	$39.74
McDonald's	$57.00	2.37	3.44	0.85	$19.15	$38.58	$55.99
Merck	$34.38	5.20	8.09	0.72	$ 9.35	$35.01	$54.46
MMM	$108.75	2.52	3.29	1.04	$31.40	$82.29	$107.44
Philip Morris	$55.63	3.09	4.70	1.20	$15.05	$55.81	$84.88
J. P. Morgan	$69.38	1.15	1.76	1.01	$53.40	$62.02	$94.92
Procter & Gamble	$55.63	2.93	3.97	1.39	$ 9.95	$40.52	$54.91
Sears	$57.00	0.93	1.40	1.11	$31.05	$32.05	$48.25
Texaco	$64.75	1.04	1.40	1.13	$34.70	$40.78	$54.90
Union Carbide	$22.38	1.23	2.24	1.03	$ 9.20	$11.66	$21.23
United Technologies	$62.00	1.23	1.80	1.16	$26.35	$37.60	$55.02
Westinghouse	$14.13	1.71	2.77	1.01	$ 0.95	$1.64	$2.66
Woolworth	$25.38	1.31	2.09	0.76	$10.05	$10.01	$15.96
DJIA	3754.09	1.86	2.76	1.22	$22.02	3500.65	5192.58

FIGURE 3.4

1994 DJIA Stock Returns

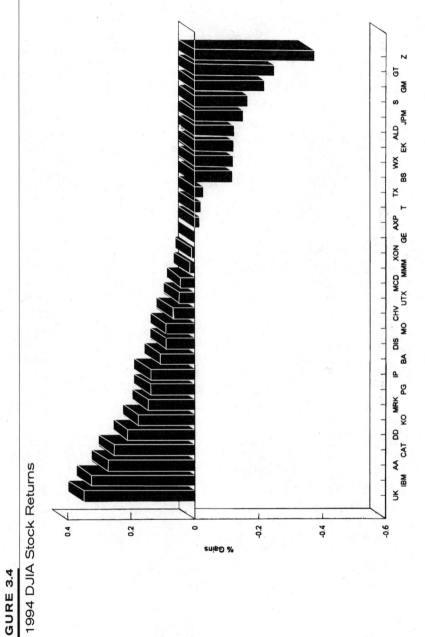

TABLE 3.13

1994 Dow Jones Industrial Average Total Returns:
Alphabetical List

DJIA Stocks	12/31/93 Price	12/31/94 Price	1994 Dividend	1994 Total Return
AlliedSignal	$39.50	$34.00	$0.65	−12.28%
Alcoa	$69.38	$86.63	$1.60	27.17%
American Express	$30.88	$29.50	$0.95	−1.39%
AT&T	$52.50	$50.25	$1.32	−1.77%
Bethlehem Steel	$20.38	$18.00	$0.00	−11.68%
Boeing	$43.25	$46.75	$1.00	10.40%
Caterpillar	$44.50	$55.13	$0.45	24.90%
Chevron	$43.57	$44.63	$1.85	6.69%
Coca-Cola	$44.63	$51.50	$0.78	17.14%
Disney	$42.63	$46.00	$0.29	8.58%
DuPont	$48.25	$56.13	$1.82	20.10%
Eastman Kodak	$56.25	$47.75	$1.70	−12.09%
Exxon	$63.13	$60.75	$2.91	0.84%
General Electric	$52.45	$51.00	$1.44	−0.02%
General Motors	$54.88	$42.13	$0.80	−21.77%
Goodyear Tire	$45.75	$33.63	$0.75	−24.85%
IBM	$56.50	$73.50	$1.00	31.86%
International Paper	$67.75	$75.38	$1.68	13.74%
McDonald's	$28.50	$29.25	$0.23	3.45%
Merck	$34.38	$38.13	$1.14	14.22%
MMM	$54.38	$53.38	$1.76	1.40%
Philip Morris	$55.63	$57.50	$2.86	8.50%
J. P. Morgan	$69.38	$56.13	$2.79	−15.08%
Procter & Gamble	$55.63	$62.00	$1.32	13.82%
Sears	$57.00	$46.00	$1.60	−16.49%
Texaco	$64.75	$59.88	$3.20	−2.58%
Union Carbide	$22.38	$29.38	$0.75	34.63%
United Technologies	$62.00	$62.88	$1.90	4.48%
Westinghouse	$14.13	$12.25	$0.20	−11.89%
Woolworth	$25.38	$15.00	$0.88	−37.43%
DJIA	3754.09	3834.44		2.14%

TABLE 3.14

1994 Dow Jones Industrial Average Total Returns:
Ranked by Performance

DJIA Stocks	12/31/93 Price	12/31/94 Price	1994 Dividend	1994 Total Return
1 Union Carbide	$22.38	$29.38	$0.75	34.63%
2 IBM	$56.50	$73.50	$1.00	31.86%
3 Alcoa	$69.38	$86.63	$1.60	27.17%
4 Caterpillar	$44.50	$55.13	$0.45	24.90%
5 DuPont	$48.25	$56.13	$1.82	20.10%
6 Coca-Cola	$44.63	$51.50	$0.78	17.14%
7 Merck	$34.38	$38.13	$1.14	14.22%
8 Procter & Gamble	$55.63	$62.00	$1.32	13.82%
9 International Paper	$67.75	$75.38	$1.68	13.74%
10 Boeing	$43.25	$46.75	$1.00	10.40%
11 Disney	$42.63	$46.00	$0.29	8.58%
12 Philip Morris	$55.63	$57.50	$2.86	8.50%
13 Chevron	$43.57	$44.63	$1.85	6.69%
14 United Technologies	$62.00	$62.88	$1.90	4.48%
15 McDonald's	$28.50	$29.25	$0.23	3.45%
16 MMM	$54.38	$53.38	$1.76	1.40%
17 Exxon	$63.13	$60.75	$2.91	0.84%
18 General Electric	$52.45	$51.00	$1.44	−0.02%
19 American Express	$30.88	$29.50	$0.95	−1.39%
20 AT&T	$52.50	$50.25	$1.32	−1.77%
21 Texaco	$64.75	$59.88	$3.20	−2.58%
22 Bethlehem Steel	$20.38	$18.00	$0.00	−11.68%
23 Westinghouse	$14.13	$12.25	$0.20	−11.89%
24 Eastman Kodak	$56.25	$47.75	$1.70	−12.09%
25 Allied Signal	$39.50	$34.00	$0.65	−12.28%
26 J. P. Morgan	$69.38	$56.13	$2.79	−15.08%
27 Sears	$57.00	$46.00	$1.60	−16.49%
28 General Motors	$54.88	$42.13	$0.80	−21.77%
29 Goodyear Tire	$45.75	$33.63	$0.75	−24.85%
30 Woolworth	$25.38	$15.00	$0.88	−37.43%

1995

Over 400 stocks had dropped 40 percent or more in 1994, causing many investors to drop out of the market entirely. Meanwhile, the Dow Industrials began the year at 3834, and there were those on Wall Street who wondered if it would ever reach 4000. Indeed, after most savvy prognosticators had failed to predict a poor year in 1994, many predicted a sharply lower Dow with tremendous downside risk. As fear of another miserable year in stocks ran rampant on the Street, the Dow did what it does best in 1995: it surprised everyone with a spectacular 36.48 percent total gain (see Tables 3.15, 3.16, and 3.17 and Figures 3.5 and 3.6).

Led by third-place finisher Philip Morris, benchmark's selections posted a 37.81 percent rise. Only Caterpillar disappointed benchmark investors with its subpar 8.74 percent return.

1995 Benchmark Recommendations	12-31-94 Price	12-31-95 Price	1995 Dividend	1995 Total Return
American Express	$29.50	$41.38	$0.90	43.32%
Caterpillar	$55.13	$58.75	$1.20	8.74%
DuPont	$56.13	$69.88	$1.60	27.35%
Eastman Kodak	$47.75	$67.00	$1.60	43.66%
Goodyear Tire	$33.63	$45.38	$0.95	37.76%
IBM	$73.50	$91.38	$0.50	25.01%
Philip Morris	$57.50	$90.25	$3.48	63.01%
Sears*	$46.00	$39.00	$31.67	53.63%
Benchmark picks				37.81%
DJIA's total return				36.48%

*Spun off .927035 shares of Allstate for every share of Sears owned.

TABLE 3.15

Benchmark's 1995 Dow Jones Industrial Average Monitor

DJIA Stocks	12/31/94 Price	Historical Market/ Book Low	High	ROE Ratio	1995 Book Value	Downside Target	Upside Target
AlliedSignal	$34.00	1.68	2.42	1.45	$12.85	$31.30	$45.09
Alcoa	$86.63	1.02	1.46	0.70	$43.65	$31.17	$44.61
American Express	$29.50	1.65	2.54	1.31	$15.30	$33.07	$50.91
AT&T	$50.25	2.52	3.43	1.57	$12.75	$50.44	$68.66
Bethlehem Steel	$18.00	0.98	1.77	2.06	$ 8.00	$16.15	$29.17
Boeing	$47.00	1.42	2.09	0.51	$29.20	$21.15	$31.12
Caterpillar	$55.13	1.41	2.13	2.05	$19.70	$56.94	$86.02
Chevron	$44.63	1.19	1.64	1.32	$23.85	$37.46	$51.63
Coca-Cola	$51.50	6.73	9.69	1.26	$ 5.50	$46.64	$67.15
Disney	$46.00	3.19	4.80	0.96	$13.30	$40.73	$61.29
DuPont	$56.13	1.58	2.18	1.73	$20.70	$56.58	$78.07
Eastman Kodak	$47.75	2.06	2.91	1.78	$13.95	$51.15	$72.26
Exxon	$60.75	1.66	2.12	0.99	$29.10	$47.82	$61.08
General Electric	$51.00	2.25	3.07	1.08	$18.05	$43.86	$59.85
General Motors	$42.13	0.93	1.45	2.00	$14.05	$26.13	$40.75
Goodyear Tire	$33.63	1.25	2.03	1.73	$21.40	$46.28	$75.15
IBM	$73.50	1.52	2.23	1.35	$39.50	$81.05	$118.91
International Paper	$75.38	0.95	1.34	0.93	$55.20	$48.77	$68.79
McDonald's	$29.25	2.48	3.50	0.94	$10.30	$24.01	$33.89
Merck	$38.13	4.54	7.05	0.70	$10.65	$33.85	$52.56
MMM	$53.38	2.60	3.37	1.09	$16.90	$47.89	$62.08
Philip Morris	$57.50	3.15	4.73	1.19	$16.70	$62.60	$94.00
J. P. Morgan	$56.13	1.17	1.74	0.91	$56.85	$60.53	$90.02
Procter & Gamble	$62.00	3.30	4.40	1.33	$12.35	$54.20	$72.27
Sears	$46.00	0.96	1.44	1.44	$34.75	$48.04	$72.06
Texaco	$59.88	1.17	1.53	1.07	$34.15	$42.75	$55.91
Union Carbide	$29.38	1.49	2.66	1.25	$11.25	$20.95	$37.41
United Technologies	$62.88	1.34	1.92	1.23	$30.60	$50.43	$72.26
Westinghouse	$12.25	1.90	3.08	1.00	$ 3.55	$6.75	$10.93
Woolworth	$15.00	1.33	2.19	0.75	$11.20	$11.17	$18.40
DJIA	3834.44	1.98	2.90	1.26	$21.51	4426.23	6473.98

TABLE 3.16

1995 Dow Jones Industrial Average Total Returns:
Alphabetical List

DJIA Stocks	12/31/94 Price	12/31/95 Price	1995 Dividend	1995 Total Return
AlliedSignal	$34.00	$47.50	$0.78	42.00%
Alcoa	$43.32	$52.88	$0.90	24.16%
American Express	$29.50	$41.38	$0.90	43.32%
AT&T	$50.25	$64.75	$1.32	31.48%
Bethlehem Steel	$18.00	$13.88	$0.00	−22.89%
Boeing	$47.00	$78.38	$1.00	68.89%
Caterpillar	$55.13	$58.75	$1.20	8.74%
Chevron	$44.63	$52.38	$1.93	21.68%
Coca-Cola	$51.50	$74.25	$0.88	45.88%
Disney	$46.00	$58.88	$0.35	28.75%
DuPont	$56.13	$69.88	$2.03	28.11%
Eastman Kodak	$47.75	$67.00	$1.60	43.66%
Exxon	$60.75	$81.13	$3.00	38.49%
General Electric	$51.00	$72.00	$1.64	44.39%
General Motors	$42.13	$52.88	$1.10	28.13%
Goodyear Tire	$33.63	$45.38	$0.95	37.76%
IBM	$73.50	$91.38	$1.00	25.69%
International Paper	$37.69	$37.88	$0.92	2.95%
J. P. Morgan	$56.13	$80.25	$3.00	48.32%
McDonald's	$29.25	$45.13	$0.26	55.18%
Merck	$38.13	$65.63	$1.24	75.37%
MMM	$53.38	$66.38	$1.88	27.88%
Philip Morris	$57.50	$90.25	$3.48	63.00%
Procter & Gamble	$62.00	$83.00	$1.50	36.29%
Sears	$46.00	$39.00	$1.43	N/A
Texaco	$59.88	$78.50	$3.20	36.44%
Union Carbide	$29.38	$37.50	$0.75	30.19%
United Technologies	$62.88	$94.88	$2.05	54.15%
Westinghouse	$12.25	$16.38	$0.20	35.35%
Woolworth	$15.00	$13.00	$0.15	−12.33%
DJIA	3834.44	5117.92		36.48%

TABLE 3.17

1995 Dow Jones Industrial Average Total Returns:
Ranked by Performance

DJIA Stocks	12/31/94 Price	12/31/95 Price	1995 Dividend	1995 Total Return
1 Merck	$38.13	$65.63	$1.24	75.37%
2 Boeing	$47.00	$78.38	$1.00	68.89%
3 Philip Morris	$57.50	$90.25	$3.48	63.00%
4 McDonald's	$29.25	$45.13	$0.26	55.18%
5 United Technologies	$62.88	$94.88	$2.05	54.15%
6 J. P. Morgan	$56.13	$80.25	$3.00	48.32%
7 Coca-Cola	$51.50	$74.25	$0.88	45.88%
8 General Electric	$51.00	$72.00	$1.64	44.39%
9 Eastman Kodak	$47.75	$67.00	$1.60	43.66%
10 American Express	$29.50	$41.38	$0.90	43.32%
11 AlliedSignal	$34.00	$47.50	$0.78	42.00%
12 Exxon	$60.75	$81.13	$3.00	38.49%
13 Goodyear Tire	$33.63	$45.38	$0.95	37.76%
14 Texaco	$59.88	$78.50	$3.20	36.44%
15 Procter & Gamble	$62.00	$83.00	$1.50	36.29%
16 Westinghouse	$12.25	$16.38	$0.20	35.35%
17 AT&T	$50.25	$64.75	$1.32	31.48%
18 Union Carbide	$29.38	$37.50	$0.75	30.19%
19 Disney	$46.00	$58.88	$0.35	28.75%
20 General Motors	$42.13	$52.88	$1.10	28.13%
21 DuPont	$56.13	$69.88	$2.03	28.11%
22 MMM	$53.38	$66.38	$1.88	27.88%
23 IBM	$73.50	$91.38	$1.00	25.69%
24 Alcoa	$43.32	$52.88	$0.90	24.16%
25 Chevron	$44.63	$52.38	$1.93	21.68%
26 Caterpillar	$55.13	$58.75	$1.20	8.74%
27 International Paper	$37.69	$37.88	$0.92	2.95%
28 Woolworth	$15.00	$13.00	$0.15	−12.33%
29 Bethlehem Steel	$18.00	$13.88	$0.00	−22.89%
30 Sears	$46.00	$39.00	$1.43	N/A

FIGURE 3.5

1995 DJIA Stock Returns

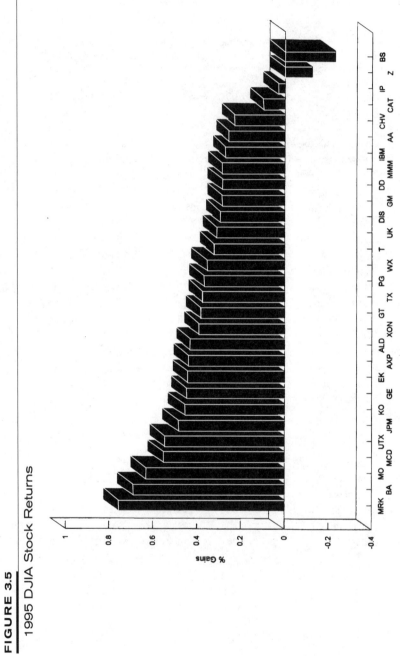

FIGURE 3.6

1995 Dow Jones Industrials

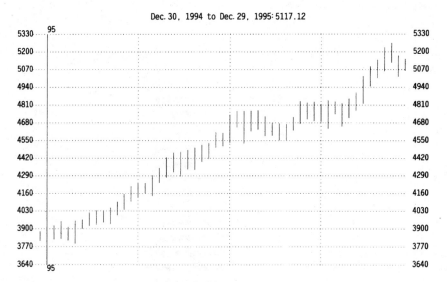

Dec. 30, 1994 to Dec. 29, 1995: 5117.12

1996

When a famous market forecaster announced that he was no longer going to make individual stock recommendations in one of his widely followed newsletters, he admitted that he was tired. That certainly wasn't the case with the Dow, which posted a vibrant 28.57 percent total return in 1996 thanks to surprisingly stronger corporate profits and lower interest rates (see Figures 3.7 and 3.8). At the same time, benchmark investing's picks surged ahead of the Dow with a 45.14 percent tally (see Tables 3.18, 3.19, and 3.20).

1996 Benchmark Recommendations	12-31-95 Price	12-31-96 Price	1996 Dividend	1996 Total Return
Alcoa	$52.88	$63.75	$1.33	23.07%
IBM	$91.38	$151.50	$1.30	67.21%
Benchmark picks				45.14%
DJIA's total return				28.57%

IBM finished as the second-best performing stock in the Dow in 1996, following years of underperformance, while Alcoa earned a

FIGURE 3.7

1996 DJIA Stock Returns

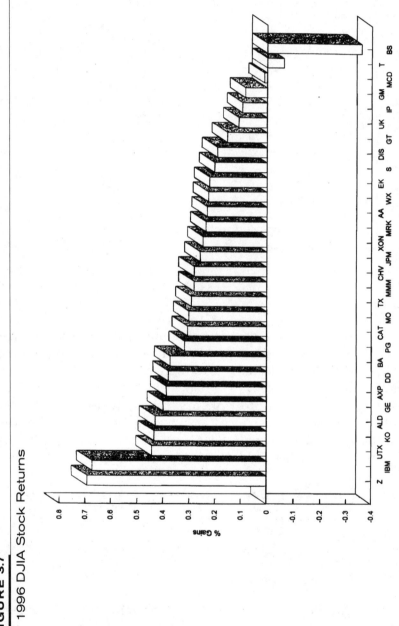

FIGURE 3.8

1996 Dow Jones Industrials

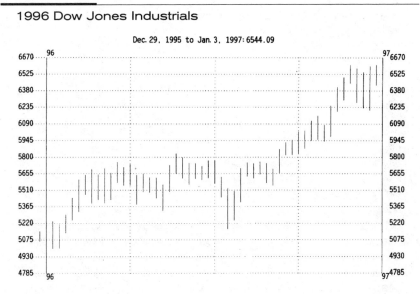

Dec. 29, 1995 to Jan. 3, 1997: 6544.09

respectable 23.07 percent total return. It was the sixth year in a row that benchmark investing beat the Dow in the 1990s, going six for six in impressive real-time investing (see Tables 3.21 and 3.22).

TABLE 3.18

Benchmark's 1996 Dow Jones Industrial Average Monitor

DJIA Stocks	12/31/95 Price	Historical Market/ Book Low	Historical Market/ Book High	ROE Ratio	1996 Book Value	Downside Target	Upside Target
AlliedSignal	$47.50	1.87	2.72	1.26	$15.40	$36.29	$52.78
Alcoa	$52.88	1.08	1.59	2.46	$28.95	$76.91	$113.24
American Express	$41.38	1.72	2.65	1.24	$16.95	$36.15	$55.70
AT&T	$64.75	2.77	3.82	1.43	$14.00	$55.46	$76.48
Bethlehem Steel	$13.88	1.05	1.86	1.39	$ 8.60	$12.55	$22.23
Boeing	$78.38	1.45	2.16	0.66	$30.00	$28.71	$42.77
Caterpillar	$58.75	1.62	2.46	1.46	$22.95	$54.28	$82.43
Chevron	$52.38	1.31	1.78	1.36	$24.85	$44.27	$60.16
Coca-Cola	$74.25	7.64	11.12	1.40	$ 5.40	$57.76	$84.07
Disney	$58.88	3.33	4.91	0.97	$15.30	$49.42	$72.87
DuPont	$69.88	1.79	2.46	2.04	$18.85	$68.83	$94.60
Eastman Kodak	$67.00	2.24	3.21	1.57	$16.70	$58.73	$84.16
Exxon	$81.13	1.75	2.26	1.09	$32.20	$61.42	$79.32
General Electric	$72.00	2.40	3.24	1.21	$18.10	$52.56	$70.96
General Motors	$52.88	1.01	1.58	1.60	$18.35	$29.65	$46.39
Goodyear Tire	$45.38	1.34	2.14	1.43	$25.20	$48.29	$77.12
IBM	$91.38	1.50	2.24	2.08	$46.80	$146.02	$218.05
International Paper	$37.88	1.00	1.41	1.56	$32.80	$51.17	$72.15
McDonald's	$45.13	2.55	3.70	0.97	$12.05	$29.81	$43.25
Merck	$65.63	4.66	7.28	0.75	$11.20	$39.14	$61.15
MMM	$66.38	2.67	3.46	1.00	$18.90	$50.46	$65.39
Philip Morris	$90.25	3.25	4.93	1.38	$17.30	$77.59	$117.70
J. P. Morgan	$80.25	1.19	1.77	0.97	$51.25	$59.16	$87.99
Procter & Gamble	$83.00	3.65	4.86	1.22	$15.30	$68.13	$90.72
Sears	$39.00	1.03	1.62	1.85	$12.60	$24.01	$37.76
Texaco	$78.50	1.34	1.75	1.18	$33.80	$53.44	$69.80
Union Carbide	$37.50	1.63	2.86	1.44	$23.25	$54.57	$95.75
United Technologies	$94.88	1.43	2.08	1.22	$34.65	$60.45	$87.93
Westinghouse	$16.38	2.04	3.26	0.69	$ 3.85	$5.42	$8.66
Woolworth	$13.00	1.35	2.20	0.55	$11.00	$8.17	$13.31
DJIA	5117.12	2.12	3.11	1.31	$21.22	5131.25	7526.80

TABLE 3.19

1996 Dow Jones Industrial Average Total Returns: Alphabetical List

DJIA Stocks	12/31/95 Price	12/31/96 Price	1996 Dividend	1996 Total Return
AlliedSignal	$47.50	$67.00	$0.90	42.95%
Alcoa	$52.88	$63.75	$1.33	23.07%
American Express	$41.38	$56.50	$0.90	38.71%
*AT&T	$64.75	$43.38	$1.71	−6.30%
Bethlehem Steel	$13.88	$8.88	$0.00	−36.02%
Boeing	$78.38	$106.50	$1.09	37.27%
Caterpillar	$58.75	$75.25	$1.50	30.64%
Chevron	$52.38	$65.00	$2.08	28.06%
Coca-Cola	$37.13	$52.63	$0.63	43.43%
Disney	$58.88	$69.75	$0.42	19.17%
DuPont	$69.88	$94.13	$2.23	37.89%
Eastman Kodak	$67.00	$80.25	$1.60	22.16%
Exxon	$81.13	$98.00	$3.12	24.64%
General Electric	$72.00	$98.88	$1.90	39.97%
General Motors	$52.88	$55.75	$1.60	8.45%
Goodyear Tire	$45.38	$51.38	$1.00	15.43%
IBM	$91.38	$151.50	$1.30	67.21%
International Paper	$37.88	$40.50	$1.00	9.56%
J. P. Morgan	$80.25	$97.63	$3.31	25.78%
McDonald's	$45.13	$45.38	$0.29	1.20%
Merck	$65.63	$79.63	$1.48	23.59%
MMM	$66.38	$83.00	$2.02	28.08%
Philip Morris	$90.25	$113.00	$4.40	30.08%
Procter & Gamble	$83.00	$107.63	$1.70	31.72%
Sears	$39.00	$46.00	$0.92	20.31%
Texaco	$78.50	$98.13	$3.25	29.15%
Union Carbide	$37.50	$40.88	$0.75	11.01%
United Technologies	$47.44	$66.25	$2.20	44.29%
Westinghouse	$16.38	$19.88	$0.20	22.59%
Woolworth	$13.00	$22.00	$0.00	69.23%
DJIA	5118	6448		26.01%

* Spun off Lucent and NCR in 1996.

TABLE 3.20

1996 Dow Jones Industrial Average Total Returns:
Ranked by Performance

DJIA Stocks		12/31/95 Price	12/31/96 Price	1996 Dividend	1996 Total Return
1	Woolworth	$13.00	$22.00	$0.00	69.23%
2	IBM	$91.38	$151.50	$1.30	67.21%
3	United Technologies	$47.44	$66.25	$2.20	44.29%
4	Coca-Cola	$37.13	$52.63	$0.63	43.43%
5	AlliedSignal	$47.50	$67.00	$0.90	42.95%
6	General Electric	$72.00	$98.88	$1.90	39.97%
7	American Express	$41.38	$56.50	$0.90	38.71%
8	DuPont	$69.88	$94.13	$2.23	37.89%
9	Boeing	$78.38	$106.50	$1.09	37.27%
10	Procter & Gamble	$83.00	$107.63	$1.70	31.72%
11	Caterpillar	$58.75	$75.25	$1.50	30.64%
12	Philip Morris	$90.25	$113.00	$4.40	30.08%
13	Texaco	$78.50	$98.13	$3.25	29.15%
14	MMM	$66.38	$83.00	$2.02	28.08%
15	Chevron	$52.38	$65.00	$2.08	28.06%
16	J. P. Morgan	$80.25	$97.63	$3.31	25.78%
17	Exxon	$81.13	$98.00	$3.12	24.64%
18	Merck	$65.63	$79.63	$1.48	23.59%
19	Alcoa	$52.88	$63.75	$1.33	23.07%
20	Westinghouse	$16.38	$19.88	$0.20	22.59%
21	Eastman Kodak	$67.00	$80.25	$1.60	22.16%
22	Sears	$39.00	$46.00	$0.92	20.31%
23	Disney	$58.88	$69.75	$0.42	19.17%
24	Goodyear Tire	$45.38	$51.38	$1.00	15.43%
25	Union Carbide	$37.50	$40.88	$0.75	11.01%
26	International Paper	$37.88	$40.50	$1.00	9.56%
27	General Motors	$52.88	$55.75	$1.60	8.45%
28	McDonald's	$45.13	$45.38	$0.29	1.20%
29	*AT&T	$64.75	$43.38	$1.71	−6.30%
30	Bethlehem Steel	$13.88	$8.88	$0.00	−36.02%

* Spun off Lucent and NCR in 1996.

TABLE 3.21

Year-by-Year Comparisons of Benchmark Investing's Results

Year	Benchmark	DJIA	Difference
1991	25.69%	23.93%	+1.76%
1992	14.92%	7.34%	+7.58%
1993	38.04%	16.72%	+21.32%
1994	11.36%	4.95%	+6.41%
1995	37.81%	36.48%	+1.33%
1996	45.14%	28.57%	+19.57%
Cumulative gain	344.12%	185.94%	
Annual compound rate	28.21%	19.14%	
Average annual percent	28.83%	19.67%	

TABLE 3.22

Benchmark Investing's Performance: 1991–1996

1991 Purchases	12/31/90 Price	12/31/91 Price	1991 Dividend	1991 Total Return
American Express	$20.63	$20.50	$0.94	3.93%
AT&T	$30.13	$39.13	$1.32	34.25%
Boeing	$45.38	$47.75	$1.00	7.43%
Sears	$25.38	$37.88	$2.00	57.13%
Benchmark picks				25.69%
DJIA's total return				23.93%

1992 Purchases	12/31/91 Price	12/31/92 Price	1992 Dividend	1992 Total Return
AT&T	$39.13	$51.00	$1.32	33.71%
Caterpillar	$43.88	$53.63	$0.60	23.59%
Eastman Kodak	$48.25	$40.50	$1.70	−12.54%
Benchmark picks				14.92%
DJIA's total return				7.34%

Continued

TABLE 3.22

Concluded

1993 Purchases	12/31/92 Price	12/31/93 Price	1993 Dividend	1993 Total Return
American Express	$24.88	$30.88	$1.00	28.14%
Caterpillar	$53.63	$89.00	$0.60	67.07%
Eastman Kodak	$40.50	$56.25	$2.00	43.83%
IBM	$50.38	$56.50	$0.50	13.14%
Benchmark picks				38.04%
DJIA's total return				16.72%

1994 Purchases	12/31/93 Price	12/31/94 Price	1994 Dividend	1994 Total Return
Merck	$34.38	$38.13	$1.14	14.22%
Philip Morris	$55.63	$57.50	$2.86	8.50%
Benchmark picks				11.36%
DJIA's total return				4.95%

1995 Purchases	12/31/94 Price	12/31/95 Price	1995 Dividend	1995 Total Return
American Express	$29.50	$41.38	$0.90	43.32%
Caterpillar	$55.13	$58.75	$1.20	8.74%
DuPont	$56.13	$69.88	$1.60	27.35%
Eastman Kodak	$47.75	$67.00	$1.60	43.66%
Goodyear Tire	$33.63	$45.38	$0.95	37.76%
IBM	$73.50	$91.38	$0.50	25.01%
Philip Morris	$57.50	$90.25	$3.48	63.01%
*Sears	$46.00	$39.00	$31.67	53.63%
Benchmark picks				37.81%
DJIA's total return				36.48%

1996 Purchases	12/31/95 Price	12/31/96 Price	1996 Dividend	1996 Total Return
Alcoa	$52.88	$63.75	$1.33	23.07%
IBM	$91.38	$151.50	$1.30	67.21%
Benchmark picks				45.14%
DJIA's total return				28.57%

*Spun off .927035 shares of Allstate for every share of Sears owned.

CHAPTER 4

The Benchmark
Investing Formula

Buy when everyone else is selling, and hold until everyone else is buying. This is more than a catchy slogan. It is the very essence of successful investment.

J. Paul Getty

$\mathbf{A}$t the peak of the Japanese stock market in 1991, Yale economist Robert Shiller found that 14 percent of Japanese investors expected a crash. However, after the Japanese market crashed, the figure *increased* to 32 percent. "One of the biggest errors in human judgment is to pay attention to the crowd," Shiller told *The Wall Street Journal.*[1] He went on to say that this helped explain the crash of 1987, when U.S. stocks fell nearly 23 percent on no news in one day. It also explains much day-to-day behavior.

Wall Street is manic-depressive. It swoons and sways from uncontrolled, excessive enthusiasm to unbounded, forlorn pessimism. This type of up-and-down behavior exists because of the inability of investors to recall the lessons of history. To accurately assess the future, we need to know the past, which teaches that it is far better to be fearful when others are greedy, and greedy only when others are fearful. There's no other field where the past has so significantly repeated itself as in the stock market. Those who fail to

---

1   Roger Lowenstein, "Sure, Markets Are Rational, Just Like Life," *The Wall Street Journal,* June 13, 1996, p. C1.

respect history are doomed to repeat it, according to Santayana. Key players and events may change, but human nature remains the same along with the basic dynamics of investing. If we refuse to learn the lessons of history, the past will return to endanger us.

Charles Ellis, managing partner of Greenwich Associates, conducted an intriguing historical study of comparative results of perfect market timing versus perfect stock selection. In the period 1940 to 1973, Ellis first assumed that he was fully invested in the Dow Jones Industrial Average at every bottom and completely in cash at every top, a goal any investor would be thrilled to achieve. This perfect market-timing strategy resulted in his original $1000 investment climbing to $85,000.

Ellis then took another approach. He assumed that he would remain fully invested in stocks but would always be in the best group. Over the 33-year period his $1000 grew to an incredible $4.2 billion.

Certainly, perfect market timing is impossible. The point is that value investors should spend their time trying to find the right stocks in which to invest rather than trying to avoid the next bear market. It means that benchmark investing has more validity as a method of increasing net worth than all the frenzied market-timing methods put together. It means that investors should never be out of the market, even a bear market. Is this reasonable? So long as undervalued companies with superior potential for appreciation can be bought, yes. It's reasonable because benchmark investing relies upon history as a guide. It's a vastly superior method of investing than putting money in and out of the market on whims and notions.

THE PHILOSOPHY BEHIND
BENCHMARK INVESTING

Benchmark investing exists because the stock market has a way of invariably overvaluing prospects of highly regarded companies and just as consistently undervaluing companies that appear to have poor prospects. Although all stocks have "intrinsic" value that accurately reflects their underlying fundamentals, they rarely sell at that level. And it must be remembered that this value is dynamic, not static. Rarely, however, do stocks sell at a level that reflects their true worth. Instead, they sell at levels that reflect fear (downside target price) or greed (upside target price). This pattern affords the benchmark investor the great advantage of buying financially strong Dow companies that are currently out of favor.

Real-time experience has proved that most undervalued and unloved companies have enjoyed a resurgence of renewed enthusiasm and higher market prices. Excesses in the stock market have provided the benchmark investor with opportunities from 1973 to 1997—through feast and famine—and I suspect the pattern would have held during most of this century as well. The reward for benchmark investors is to identify undervalued stocks and to earn superior returns from the market's subsequent upward revaluation to a price consistent with upside target prices.

Benchmark investing simply attempts to find out what range a particular stock should trade in, using its past as a road map. It provides a consistent and risk-averse method to identify the best bargains in the stock market.

The challenge most investors face is to know when a stock is priced fairly. Should they buy McDonald's, for example, when it trades at twice its book value? Or is IBM a bargain at 11 times trailing earnings? Had the benchmark formula been available in 1987, investors would have realized that the stock market was extremely overvalued by comparing the Dow Industrial stocks with their own historical ratios.

Investors don't need exotic market indicators to know when a stock's too expensive to purchase or to decipher the health of the market. All investors would have needed in 1987 was the proper use of history (benchmarks) to guide them to high-quality stocks at a discount. They would have realized that Goodyear Tire was the only Dow stock close to trading at undervalued prices and that the remainder were trading at astonishingly high levels. Everyone knows that markets collapse when stocks are at their most expensive. And 1987's market was incredibly expensive, a fact anyone using the benchmark formula would have realized. Benchmark investors would have avoided most of the erosion that subsequently followed in the Dow during the fourth quarter of 1987. Just as important, they would have known to invest in the tremendous bargains created by the October slaughter for superior long-term gains.

Benchmark investing finds a probable upside and downside range of a stock by using its most recent 10-year price history and making adjustments on the basis of return on equity (ROE) ratio. Longer-term yardsticks are employed because the period must be long enough to absorb and equalize the distortions of business cycles. Also, it's more impressive to find a continued pattern over a longer period of time rather than a single instance of profitability over a short period.

On Wall Street a great deal is constantly said about earnings per share, but the adjusted ROE ratio is the key to the success of the benchmark formula. Investors eagerly buy a stock whenever a company loudly reports record quarterly earnings. The fact is that investors are misled into believing that the company has done a superior job when it may not have done such a good job after all. That's because companies continually add to their capital base by retaining a portion of each year's earnings not used for dividends or capital spending. As a result, growth in earnings should not even be a consideration for benchmark investors. Earnings do not provide investors with a clear understanding of true growth. Instead, investors should focus on a company's return on equity, the ratio of operating earnings to shareholder equity.

Return on equity is a truer measure of a company's performance than earnings per share because it takes into account a company's growing capital base. As a result, return on equity has been the catalyst for the benchmark investing formula since its inception.

It is a waste of time to compare a mature oil company with a young, high-flying technology company. Although many on Wall Street do so, such a comparison tells nothing about either firm's true value. Another widely used analytical method on Wall Street, the relative value approach, attempts to determine the relative value of an individual company by comparing it with the prevailing level for the overall stock market. High-paid brokerage analysts publish daily reports similar to the following: "We continue to believe that XYZ Corp. will trade at a 25 percent premium to the market . . ."

This relative value approach can prove hazardous, even though at first glance it appears to be a good valuation tool. For example, in August 1987 the market was at a cyclical peak. If, at that time, investors had purchased a stock on the basis of broad market levels, they would have suffered a significant decline when the market crashed two months later.

In contrast, when comparing a company with itself, benchmark investors can quickly figure out its intrinsic value. For instance, a mature Dow company that for the past 10 years has traded between 1.5 and 3.1 market-to-book value would be considered relatively cheap if it traded at 1.3 times book.

Benchmark investors have the adjusted ROE ratio to fine-tune valuations even further. Suppose a company that has averaged a 10 percent return on equity for the past 10 years suddenly begins earning 20 percent returns on equity. Remember, this is far more significant than earnings rising by a similar amount, because the company's expanding asset base (book value) is also rising, making it more difficult for return on equity to increase. Rather than valuing the company as if it were earning a 10 percent return on equity, the market should add a 100 percent premium (20 percent divided by 10 percent) to its past valuation. Very often, however, the market is slow to recognize this disparity, providing benchmark investors with an incredible opportunity to purchase the stock at a bargain price.

For example, Coca-Cola saw its return on equity climb steadily from 1978 to 1994. During those 16 years, Coke's return on equity averaged 29.73 percent. In 1994, Coke's return on equity had risen to 45.5 percent, giving it a 1.53 adjusted ROE ratio. In other words, it deserved a higher valuation than in the past because of its above-average return on equity.

As a result of comparing Coke with itself and not Pepsi or any other stock, benchmark investing's formula clearly identified the world's largest soft drink company as a bargain at $40 a share in 1994. Over the next two years, Coke climbed more than 250 percent higher.

Any number of factors could be at work to account for a rise in a company's return on equity, but it really doesn't matter. What's important is that the company is now worth more than what it has historically traded for. Until the market recognizes this by bidding the company's shares up, the stock will be a bargain. The true value investor relishes buying a company at pennies on the dollar. Of course, the opposite is also true. If a company's return on equity falls below its 10-year average, its valuation should be adjusted lower. Doing so helps benchmark investors avoid overvalued stocks that appear to be trading at normal levels.

The following definitions are condensed descriptions of the variables used in the benchmark investing formula.

- *Downside target.* The downside target is the absolute low price that the stock should hit over the next 3 to 12 months,

based on the benchmark approach of considering only
historical, fundamental analysis. Stocks trading at or below
their downside target should have the most potential for
price appreciation. It should be noted that stocks do fall
below their downside target prices—sometimes much
lower—because of the vagaries of markets.

- *Upside target.* The upside target is the absolute high price
  that the stock should reach over the next 3 to 12 months.
  Stocks trading at or above their upside target price would
  have the least potential for capital gains. Stocks at or near
  their upside target should not necessarily be sold because
  of their overvaluation (see Chapter 7). These stocks very
  often reach higher highs as a result of investor expectations. However, benchmark investors would avoid
  adding new capital to such stocks.

- *Book value.* The calculation of a stock's book value is not
  meant to show the true value of its shares; many stocks sell
  at high multiples or fractions of book value. Therefore,
  book value is not widely used for direct valuation. Instead,
  it is useful in calculating the return on equity.

- *Market-to-book value ratio.* Market to book represents the
  market price per share divided by the book value per
  share, a highly useful valuation tool.

$$\frac{\text{Price per share}}{\text{Book value per share}}$$

BENCHMARK INVESTING'S FORMULA

All the historical data necessary to complete the benchmark formula
may be found in the *Value Line Investment Survey,* which is preferred
for its consistency and clarity. In fact, Warren Buffett continues to
read the weekly publication religiously. The formula is a seven-step
process that begins by finding a stock's historical average return on
equity for the past 10 years.

Step 1: Calculate the average return on equity for the
previous 10 years by adding the last 10-years' percentage
earned net worth as reported near the bottom of the
financials in *Value Line.*

Step 2: Find the adjusted ROE ratio. Divide the current year's
return on equity by the company's 10-year average found in

step 1. For example, if a company's return on equity for the current year is 30 percent and its average for the past 10 years was 15 percent, its ROE ratio is 2.0 (30/15 = 2.0).

$$\frac{\text{Current year's return on equity}}{\text{10-year average return on equity}}$$

Step 3: Calculate the stock's average book value for the previous 10 years.

Step 4: Calculate the stock's average yearly low price.

Step 5: Divide the average yearly low price by the average book value to calculate the stock's low market-to-book multiplier.

$$\frac{\text{Average yearly low price}}{\text{Average book value}}$$

Remember, it doesn't matter whether this number is high or low compared with other Dow stocks. All that matters is how a stock ranks with its own past ratios.

Step 6: Find the high market-to-book multiple by repeating steps 4 and 5.

$$\frac{\text{Average yearly high price}}{\text{Average book value}}$$

Step 7: Find the stock's upside and downside benchmarks—the final, critical step. To figure out where the stock's downside, or bargain, price should be, multiply the low market-to-book ratio by the relative ROE ratio by the current year's book value.

Low market-to-book × Adjusted ROE ratio × Book value
= Downside target price.

When you find a stock trading near or below this price, you have found a potential bargain.

In order to find the stock's upside price, replace the low market-to-book ratio with the high market-to-book ratio and perform the same math.

High market-to-book × Adjusted ROE ratio × Book value
= Upside price target

This is the price at which you might want to consider selling. Chapter 7 covers this topic in greater depth.

That's the benchmark formula. Disarmingly simple. Easy to duplicate. Consistent in its performance. It is reassuring to know that one of Warren Buffett's keynote views on investing is that an investor's financial success is in direct proportion to the degree to which he or she understands the investment. This separates true investors from speculators who buy and sell at the whims of the Wall Street rumor mill. The first question Buffett asks is whether the business is simple and understandable. To this, we might add that the valuation method must be just as accessible. Even novice investors will agree that, after a reasonable amount of practice, benchmark investing's strategy is simple and understandable.

Without a tool to judge a stock's true value, we're all potential victims of wavering emotions. Benchmark investing provides independent investors with such a dynamic and useful valuation tool. The challenge for most will be to trust this tool in all kinds of market environments.

NOTES AND EXCEPTIONS

Mere cheapness of a stock is rarely enough to achieve results that are consistently superior and obtained without needless risk. In other words, simply because a stock is trading below its downside price target is no reason to rush in and buy it. It's essential that you apply strict safeguards to protect yourself against so-called value traps.

Once price targets are established, the primary screen that benchmark investing uses to avoid the money-losing investments is to test whether a company's year-over-year earnings increase exceeds 10 percent. This happens to be an arbitrary number that has worked extraordinarily well in preventing investments in value traps. So, if a stock's earnings increase is less than 10 percent, you should avoid investing in the company. Here's why.

In the January 1, 1993, benchmark investing monitor of the Dow Industrials, Boeing appeared to be an attractive bargain, since it was trading at more than $12 below its downside target price. However, its estimated earnings gain over the next 12 months stood at just 6.12 percent, well below the 10 percent bogey mentioned above. Had benchmark investors ignored this red flag and invested in Boeing, they would have suffered inferior results unnecessarily.

This sounds awfully simplistic. But that's all right, because if it weren't simple enough for the novice to use—if benchmark investing required advanced calculus or a supercomputer program that only quant scientists knew how to use—it would be worthless.

Now suppose that a company's stock is cheap, that it's trading below its downside target. And suppose that its earnings increase is higher than 10 percent. The final screen that benchmark investors should use to determine whether a value trap is looming is to forecast the company's expected trading ranges for the next three to five years, using *Value Line's* estimates.

International Paper was trading well below its downside target at the beginning of 1991, and *Value Line* projected year-over-year earnings gains of 29.85 percent—well above our 10 percent bogey. But I didn't recommend International Paper because of *Value Line's* three- to five-year forecasts, which showed that the company's return on equity would drop back to 9, thus lowering the stock's long-term price targets to unattractive levels. With that in mind, International Paper no longer appeared to be such a bargain.

Investors will sometimes find companies that are widely undervalued or overpriced. They must learn to take advantage of these opportunities, because the benchmark formula has proved to be accurate over the years. One final caution: skip over the years when the book value or return on equity has been at a deficit. Do not use those years in your calculations. It is best to avoid companies that have erratic ROE ratios.

BENCHMARK INVESTING'S TENETS

Benchmark investing's long-term goal is to maximize the average annual rate of gain of the shares held in its recommended portfolio of solid Dow companies. These companies should generate cashflow and consistently earn above-average returns on equity.

Over the years, benchmark investing has proved successful in its quest by adhering to certain key doctrines. Most professional money managers are quick to restructure their portfolios by buying and selling Wall Street's latest "flavor of the month." Benchmark's portfolio, on the other hand, prefers to hold onto companies for the long term. That is, it's preferable to hold companies indefinitely as long as there is potential for above-average appreciation. More important, it's better to postpone paying taxes on capital gains in order to improve performance results. Long-term holders have a clear advantage over short-term traders because of the tax on capital gains. Consider an investor who buys a $1 stock that doubles every year. If that investor sells at the end of the first year, he or she will have a net gain of $.72 after paying capital gains taxes of 28 percent. If the investor continues to buy stocks that double each year, pay taxes annually, and reinvest what's left after taxes, at the end of 20 years the investor will have $47,130 after paying taxes of $39,414.

The case for long-term investing can be made by comparing the value of a $1 investment that is held for the same period (without selling and paying taxes) and that doubles each year. At the end of 20 years, a long-term investor will have $1,048,576. That's quite a compelling argument for long-term investing.

In comparison to the preferred methods of institutional money managers, benchmark's style may seem prudish, even outdated. Professional managers diversify their portfolios indexlike among the major industry groups in order to protect themselves from being out of fashion with the market. But benchmark investing's only strategy is to buy solid companies, and it doesn't include chasing after them at elevated prices. Instead, you should wait until expectations are low and these first-class Dow companies are on sale. You're looking to buy good companies that might not be viewed as good companies, those with transitory problems. Perfectly good companies in the broad market are discarded every day for reasons that don't make much sense. In fact, over a three-year period, most companies will show up on the 52-week new low list.

When making an investment, you need to consider a number of factors. *The most important consideration is valuation.* That is where the benchmark investor should begin. A world-class company can enjoy competitive advantages built in to ward off potential competitors; but if the stock is trading at historically high levels of valuation, the benchmark investor should avoid it. Ben Graham's first rule of investing was not to lose money, and I couldn't agree more. That's why benchmark investing focuses on purchasing only those companies that are trading below their downside target prices.

Think back to the outset of 1991. Stock prices had been faltering with the threat of war with Saddam Hussein. After the Iraqis invaded Kuwait in August 1990, the Dow fell 14 percent on huge volume. It could have been worse, considering the threat to oil stability and the potential for nuclear warfare. What did the stock market foresee for 1991? Wall Street was consumed with worry over the debt binge created by Drexel, plunging real estate prices, higher oil prices, and inflation caused by the threat of war with Iraq. For any benchmark investor who had the foresight to look beyond the market's typical worries, the Dow was ridiculously undervalued. Needless to say, the market did the unthinkable in 1991 by gaining 23.93 percent. And although benchmark investing failed to pick the top six Dow stocks that year, it did enjoy a 25.69 percent total return with its picks.

By investing in out-of-favor Dow companies, benchmark investors are able to limit their potential for downside risk. They do so by taking advantage of the suppressed anxieties of mass hysteria, that threshold where people begin to panic and lose control of their rational selves. Lurking in the back of every investor's mind is the fear that the stock market will melt down at a moment's notice.

On the other hand, benchmark investors need to realize that buying during panics is rational. They must understand that it is imperative to win the long war of nerves within themselves and buy good companies already beaten down—companies that tend to hold up better in declining markets. They must do so because there are few guarantees in the stock market except that difficult markets will occur, and that mass hysteria will erupt at these times. Down markets always have occurred and always will. Because such downturns cannot be predicted, benchmark investors must plan for and accept them as inevitable. They must also learn to ignore their inner fears to join in the hysteria by comprehending one very important thing: risk is diminished, not enhanced, by panic.

Benchmark investors will then be able to mitigate the down markets by focusing on undervalued companies in which others have low expectations. Consistently buying into fear and selling into euphoric, rampant greed will make money. It sounds easy. In practice, people seldom do it. When everyone else is afraid, most investors also tend to be afraid.

Benchmark investing's long holding period, in combination with a focus on a specific company's fundamentals, eliminates the use of market timing, earnings momentum, or other short-term fads. Benchmark investors are buying when the consensus is selling. They're selling when the consensus is buying, anchoring their decisions on fundamental considerations. Regardless of what the market does in any given year, benchmark investing will serve investors well over time.

The quintessential rule for the benchmark investor is to buy low and to sell high. Thus, valuation levels are the first and foremost considerations in benchmark investing.

ABOVE-AVERAGE RETURN ON EQUITY

A rising tide lifts all boats. Rising return on equity is no exception. When a company's return on equity continues to rise, as Coca-Cola's did from 1986 to 1996, it clearly shows that management is accomplishing its task by employing its capital in all the right places. Good business decisions by management will result in rewarding economic consequences. Benchmark investors should be on the lookout for companies with rising ROE ratios. Just as important, they should avoid companies whose return on equity is falling.

Buying a company without favorable long-term prospects is like buying the Empire State Building without an elevator. If a company is not expected to double its value in five years, it should be overlooked for those that will.

Economic strength is most often found in businesses that are in strong demand. These enterprises have little or no competition and present a high barrier to entry to prevent future competitors from crossing their turf. These companies also enjoy greater pricing flexibility, which allows them almost foolproof prosperity even in times of poor management. Many of the Dow stocks—American Express, Coca-Cola, Philip Morris, and Merck, to name a few— are franchises with economic goodwill.

Great companies make terrible investments if management can't convert sales into profits. It's not surprising, therefore, to see that lower profit margins result in lower gains in valuation; the opposite also applies. As a result, the benchmark investor should look for companies that constantly attack higher expenses and, as a result, enjoy higher profit margins. It's no accident that at the time of this writing Coca-Cola, General Electric, and Merck have the highest profit margins among the Dow stocks.

When asked what the secret to Wal-Mart's retail success was, founder Sam Walton replied, "Buying at the right price." No one held corporate overhead expenses as low as the legendary Walton, which explains why he was the richest man in America before his death in 1993.

TRENDS AND MANAGEMENT'S ROLE

The best returns are achieved by companies that have consistently superior returns on equity and profit margins. Exceptional returns rarely follow where businesses undergo major changes in product mix or earnings (see Table 4.1).

Coca-Cola enjoyed an incredible gain in return on equity, rising steadily from 18.8 percent in 1986 to 43 percent in 1996. At the same time, Coke's share price rose from a split-adjusted $3.51 to $53.88 during that period. To put Coke's gain in perspective, a $10,000 investment on January 1, 1986, would have grown to $153,025 without counting dividends. Coke's management concentrated (no pun intended) on selling more soft drinks to the world while seeing its net profits double from 9 percent to 18 percent.

Meanwhile, Westinghouse experienced a major reorganization of its business product. As a result, the stock actually lost value over the same period. A $10,000 investment in Westinghouse on January 1, 1986 would have been worth only $8363 by 1996 without counting dividends.

Benchmark investors should scour the Dow for managers who act like owners rather than managers. Look for those rare managers

TABLE 4.1

Fluctuations in Return on Equity

Year	Westinghouse	Coca-Cola
1996	3.0%	43.0%
1995	NMF	46.5%
1994	17.7%	39.3%
1993	30.4%	37.7%
1992	16.1%	38.4%
1991	14.1%	30.6%
1990	25.7%	32.2%
1989	21.0%	30.2%
1988	21.7%	28.2%
1987	20.7%	23.8%
1986	22.3%	18.8%

who actively cut costs to improve profits, disperse capital in the most efficient and intelligent manner, and are willing to take shrewd risks and be active rather than reactive. Seek out management that is totally committed to protecting shareholders and enhancing their investment. Maximizing shareholder value should be management's top priority. Honesty, candor, and competence are also highly sought traits in management.

Nothing gets Wall Street's attention like an announced share buyback program. Indeed, share buybacks are in vogue on Wall Street these days as a way for management to increase shareholder value. Companies nowadays "reward" their shareholders at a record rate by announcing buybacks to support their stock prices. However, if a company has a high historical valuation, management does a great disservice to its shareholders.

Investors automatically cheer buybacks, in the mistaken belief that buybacks contribute to some self-fulfilling prophecy of higher stock prices. The fact remains that repurchasing expensive stock won't add value. It might be better for management to invest excess cashflow into Treasury bills than to reinvest in inflated shares.

Top-quality management also strives to lower debt-to-equity ratios. The practical importance of low debt levels to safeguard an investment cannot be overstated. Efficient management is best characterized by little or no debt levels. Highly leveraged companies are vulnerable during inevitable economic slowdowns. It is best for management to err on the side of quality rather than risk the financial well-being of its shareholders by increasing the risk that comes with added debt.

BUFFETT'S BENCHMARK

Not surprisingly, benchmark investing works best for most investors whenever they're working with a limited number of stocks like the Dow Industrials. That's because considerable time and effort are required to input and maintain all the data necessary for the benchmark formula. But what about investors who want to follow a larger universe, such as the S&P 500 or Russell 1000? Anyone using benchmark's strategy with much larger groups such as these must invest an enormous amount of labor hours in the task. When I began testing benchmark investing by following over 1500 stocks, I had the generous help of a good friend, a computer expert from General Electric named Jim Morman. I also had two college undergraduates from a local university downloading the enormous amount of data every week.

Few people have access to such qualified talent or the time and resources to undertake such a huge task. Fortunately, I soon discovered that superior results could be found by simply following the 30 Dow stocks. But for those investors who wish to follow a larger group of stocks, there is a much less time-consuming alternative: the benchmark used by Warren Buffett.

This valuable tool requires little time to implement and is extremely intuitive and easy to learn. Buffett has used it for more than 40 years as one important component in making his investment decisions. One can only guess that he relies on this benchmark as a quick screen, since he still religiously follows the huge universe of stocks in *Value Line* every week.

Buffett's benchmark is nothing more than the "discounted cashflow valuation" formula he borrowed from John Burr Williams.[2] In using this screen, Buffett finds the value of a company by discovering what cashflow is expected to occur over the life of the business. "So valued," says Buffett, "all businesses, from manufacturers of buggy whips to operators of cellular telephones, become economic equals." [3]

Anyone can find out if a company is undervalued or overpriced by using this screen. All the investor has to do is (1) find a company's cashflow per share, (2) subtract capital spending per share from cashflow, (3) multiply that sum by the outstanding common shares, (4) divide that number by an appropriate discount rate (Buffett uses the rate of the long-term U.S. Treasury bond as the divisor), and (5) compare intrinsic value with market value.

It's easy enough to compare intrinsic value against current market value to see if a stock is valued fairly or not. The following example helps detail how Buffett's benchmark works.

In 1991, AlliedSignal's cashflow was $6.85 per share, while capital spending totaled $3.75 per share. Its "net" cashflow was $415 million as figured by multiplying $3.1 ($6.85 – $3.75) times outstanding shares. Finally, Allied's intrinsic value was $5.1 billion, found by

---

2 John Burr Williams, *The Theory of Investment Value* (North-Holland, 1938).

3 Robert Hagstrom, *The Warren Buffett Way* (New York: John Wiley & Sons, 1994), pp. 93–94.

dividing the net cashflow of $415 million by 8.1 percent, roughly the 30-year Treasury bond rate.

At the beginning of 1991, AlliedSignal's market value was $3.6 billion. According to Buffett's benchmark, Allied was trading below its intrinsic value at roughly 70 cents on the dollar. As a result, Allied was attractive to value investors who used this screen. When benchmark investing's formula also found Allied trading at historically undervalued levels, the benchmark investor realized that AlliedSignal was an intriguing investment possibility.

To review Buffett's benchmark:

1. Find a company's cashflow per share.
2. Subtract capital spending per share from cashflow.
3. Multiply "net" cashflow by its outstanding shares.
4. Divide by discount rate to find intrinsic value.
5. Compare intrinsic value with market value.

It must be stressed that this is only one part of a lengthy process that Buffett has used throughout his brilliant investing career. Buffett also places great emphasis on other business considerations. Therefore, Buffett's benchmark should in no way be considered his sole decision-making criterion, but only one facet. Still, Buffett's quick screening tool is very helpful for searching through large numbers of stocks. Investors may choose to use it as a preliminary screening method before performing more time-consuming research.

SUMMARY

To review the necessary steps to evaluate a stock's valuation levels using benchmark's formula, investors should:

1. Find the average return on equity for the previous 10 years.
2. Divide the current year's return on equity by its 10-year average return on equity to find the adjusted ROE ratio.
3. Find the average book value for the previous 10 years. Also, find the average low and high stock prices for the same period.
4. Calculate the stock's average yearly low price.

5. Find the average low *and* high market-to-book values for the previous 10 years by dividing the average low and high prices by the average book value from step 3.

6. Find the *downside target* by first multiplying the stock's low market-to-book average multiple by the adjusted ROE ratio. Then multiply that number by its current book value.

7. Find the *upside target* by first multiplying the stock's high market-to-book average multiple by the adjusted ROE ratio. Then multiply that number by its current book value.

Here is an example of the calculations for IBM stock:

10-year average return on equity	16.52%
Current return on equity (ROE)	24.50%
Adjusted ROE ratio:	1.48
10-year average book value	$47.25
10-year average low stock price	$78.44
Average low market-to-book ratio	1.66
10-year average high stock price	$116.24
Average high market-to-book ratio	2.46
Current book value (BV)	$46.30

Downside target price = 1.66 (low mkt/book) × 1.48 (ROE ratio) × $46.30 (BV) = $113.74

Upside target price = 2.46 (high mkt/book) × 1.48 (ROE ratio) × $46.30 (BV) = $168.56

CHAPTER 5

Benchmark Investing's Real-Time Results: 1991-1996

If we dare to penetrate, penetrate into the essence of things, then we would find the answer.

Albert Einstein*

The job of selecting winning stocks should never be taken lightly. That's because no one will ever know all there is to know about the stock market. And no one can expect to be right all the time. I've spent most of my adult life trying to understand and measure the stock market, and I realize that no one is smarter than the market all the time. Even with the consistency of benchmark investing, I have not been right all the time, as you will see. Nevertheless, I believe benchmark investing is a far superior method of investing for the vast majority of investors who are looking for a reliable, albeit imperfect, way to beat the market with less risk.

I began using benchmark investing in the summer of 1988 with the help of a couple of local college students who downloaded mountains of data for me three nights a week. Of course, I couldn't have followed the 1500-plus companies found in *Value Line* had it not been for the help of my good friend Jim Morman, a General Electric computer expert who programmed the entire operation.

---

* PBS, "A Science Odyssey," "Mysteries of the Universe" episode, January 12, 1998.

Nevertheless, after more than two years and thousands of hours of sorting through the *Value Line* companies, I realized that I could more easily achieve my goal of beating the stock market while limiting my database to the blue-chip stocks found in the Dow Jones Industrial Average. So I switched from 1500 *Value Line* stocks to 30 Dow stocks at the beginning of 1991. As a result, only those stocks bought and recommended since 1991 will be included in this chapter, to give you greater insight into benchmark investing's method, mistakes and all.

Sticking with only undervalued companies from the Dow has surely penalized my results, but part of the attraction of benchmark investing lies in the fact that there are only 30 stocks to monitor and understand versus hundreds or possibly thousands. Of course, the benchmark formula can be used with any company with a 10-year operating history, but I still recommend sticking with the world-class leaders in the Dow. As one Indianapolis 500 winner proclaimed, to finish first you must first finish. It's a feat made easier with benchmark investing's decidedly diminished equity universe. After all, Albert Einstein's dictum was: *Don't make things simple. Make them simpler.*

That's not to say benchmark investing can't be used with other companies. Investors can use the benchmark formula on thousands of stocks if they so desire. For example, benchmark investing recommended 3Com at the beginning of 1990 at a split-adjusted $3.38, Microsoft in 1994 at $20.16, Intel at $28 at the outset of 1996, and Arrow Electronics at $21.19 in August 1996. Anyone using benchmark investing could have scooped up those companies at incredible bargain levels and been handsomely rewarded during the succeeding years. It's been my experience, however, that limiting the universe to the Dow Industrial stocks provides adequate investment opportunities. The following real-time examples will give you the benefit of the information and results I've acquired, and are probably the best way to familiarize you with precisely how my stock-picking method works. So let's look at the stocks I recommended and bought at the beginning of each year since 1991. If you're looking for a simple, reliable, and workable system for beating the market, here it is.

ALLIEDSIGNAL (ALD)

Value of $10,000 Invested on January 1, 1991: $66,675 as of
December 31, 1997
(assumes annual reinvestment of dividends at year-end prices)

January 1	1991	1992	1993	1994	1995	1996	1997	1998
Price	$27.00	$43.88	$60.50	$79.00	$34.00	$47.50	$67.00	$38.81
Dividends	1.60	1.00	1.16	0.65	0.78	0.90	1.04	
Shares reinvested	13	6	5	15	13	11	22	
Year-end shares	383	389	809	824	837	848	1718	
Splits				2-1			2-1	

In January 1991 I recommended down-and-out AlliedSignal at
a split-adjusted $6.75 (see Figure 5.1). Had I known what I know
today, the probability is that I would *not* have bought the stock,
since its year-over-year earnings growth was under 10 percent. I
would have missed a huge winner. That just goes to show you that
sometimes it pays to be lucky. By the next year, Allied had soared

FIGURE 5.1

AlliedSignal, 1991–1997

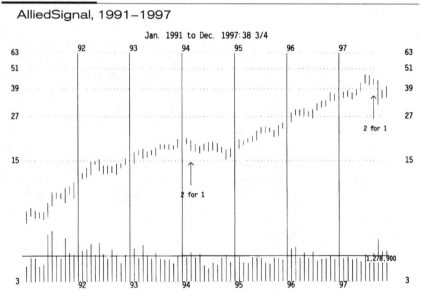

68.44 percent higher, turning in the fourth-highest performance among the Dow Industrials in 1991. From there, it continued to climb fairly steadily. On the seventh anniversary of my recommendation, Allied had vaulted 567 percent. Had you invested $10,000 in AlliedSignal in 1991 and reinvested all dividends into more shares, you would have started 1998 with 1718 shares worth $66,675. The stock rewarded investors with annual compounded returns of 31.1 percent during that period, while the Dow posted a still-impressive 19.89 percent average.

But why was AlliedSignal such an attractive investment opportunity at the beginning of 1991? Because even the most conservative calculation of the company's value indicated that Allied was a bargain. Benchmark investing's formula calculated a downside target of $27.29 and an upside target of $41.36, which represented a potential upside gain of 53 percent. Warren Buffett's discounted cashflow method of valuation (see Chapter 4) also indicated that Allied was a great bargain, trading at just 70 cents on the dollar.

When I recommended AlliedSignal, its 1991 return on equity was 13.5 percent, slightly higher than the previous 10-year average of 12.75 percent. But two items were encouraging concerning its return on equity. First, analysts expected a severe economic slowdown in the United States, if not an outright recession. Second, *Value Line*'s Marc Gerstein forecasted much higher returns on equity for the next two to four years. If he proved correct—Gerstein was actually very conservative in his estimates—Allied's future held potential *annual* gains of 22 to 43 percent for the benchmark investor.

At the time I recommended AlliedSignal, the conglomerate had annual sales of $11.8 billion. Sales topped $14 billion in 1997, while return on equity rose from 13.5 percent in 1991 to 24 percent. In 1991, Allied was the world's leading manufacturer of auxiliary power units for commercial transports and high-performance military aircraft. It was also the world's leading maker of passenger car and light truck brakes and aircraft wheels and brakes. But its principal business included aerospace components for commercial and military markets.

AlliedSignal was created in September 1985 following the merger of Allied Corporation and the Signal Companies, a diversified organization originally involved in oil and gas activities. The company began operating after World War I, when Germany controlled much of the world's chemical industry, causing shortages of such commodities as dyes and drugs. In response, *Washington Post* publisher Eugene Meyer and scientist William Nichols organized the Allied Chemical & Dye Corporation, incorporating in New York on December 17, 1920, after acquiring all the capital stock of five existing companies: the General Chemical Company, the Solvay Process Company, Semet-Solvay, the Barrett Company, and the National Aniline & Chemical Company.

As one of the 30 original companies included in the expanded Dow Industrial index in 1928, Allied opened a synthetic ammonia plant only to become the world's leading producer. Net earnings totaled $29 million at the beginning of the Great Depression. Ten years later, gross sales improved to $167 million. After World War II, Allied began manufacturing other products, including nylon and refrigerants. Sales had climbed to $1.2 billion by 1970. A decade later, sales had substantially improved to $5.5 billion. Just after the merger, the new company enjoyed sales of $11.79 billion, but Allied's progress then began to falter while all its major business segments felt pressure from a slowing economy. Sales and margins began to tumble. As a result, Allied's shares fell to $27.00 (unadjusted) by the end of 1990 from its 1986 peak of $55.50.

The company is coasting more smoothly nowadays. Having curbed its involvement in the automotive industry, the New Jersey–based company is focusing on its higher-margined specialty chemical business. Allied makes communications equipment, data and voice recorders, engines, and radar systems for aircraft along with high-tech equipment for missiles, spacecraft, and underwater applications. Engineered Materials produces nylon and polyester carpet fibers. It's also the number-one producer of hydrofluoric acid in the world and the third-largest maker of nylon in the United States. Other chemical products include refrigerants, solvents, and agricultural, photographic, and pharmaceutical agents. AlliedSignal's automotive division manufactures airbags, FRAM filters, master cylinders, Autolite spark plugs, turbochargers, and other vehicle components.

In 1993, the company signed a deal with the Russian government to help convert weapons-grade uranium from Russia's surplus missiles. The following year Allied purchased Ford Motor Company's British spark plug operations and Textron's Lycoming Turbine Engine Division. It completed construction of a turbocharger plant in China, enabling it to serve that country's booming market for diesel engines in 1995. Allied also bought a 96 percent stake in German specialty chemicals manufacturer Riedel-de Haen AG. Besides selling off its low-margin brake business to Robert Bosch in 1996, AlliedSignal formed a joint venture with India's JBM Group to manufacture up to 1 million seat belts annually at a plant in New Delhi.

Chairman Lawrence A. Bossidy turned AlliedSignal into a lean, mean, manufacturing machine following his arrival in June 1991, when he replaced Edward Hennessey, Jr., as chief executive officer. The General Electric veteran who had served as head of GE Capital and vice chairman to Jack Welch led Allied toward greater profitability in numerous ways. In seven years, the relentlessly cost-conscious Bossidy eliminated 36,000 jobs. He freed Allied from its skidding hydraulic and antilock brake business in 1996 by selling out to German manufacturer Robert Bosch. When Bossidy arrived, he found a sprawling, decentralized corporation that was spending too much money. Since then, he has cut capital spending from 70 percent of cashflow to 43 percent. Expectations are that capital spending will fall below 30 percent of cashflow over the next few years. Bossidy also moved Allied out of commodity chemicals and into specialty chemicals, where profit margins are higher. In 1991, 87 percent of its businesses were cyclical in nature and related to the mature commodities arena; by 1997 that figure had dropped to just 35 percent after Bossidy began focusing on higher growth areas. In 1995, Allied sold its 50 percent share in Paxon Polymer LP to Exxon Chemical. And in 1997, the company shed its seat belt and air bag operations to Breed Technologies for $710 million.

Net profit margins nearly tripled from 1991 to 1997, again thanks to Bossidy's keen eye on the bottom line. He saw employment drop from 107,000 to 82,000 in his first two years. Each remaining employee went through an 80-hour "total quality" training program focusing on such disciplines as teamwork and diagnostic skills. Purchasing was centralized to lower costs and reduce defects. Productivity improved as defects in manufacturing were cut by 50 percent.

In spite of its low valuation at the beginning of 1991, Allied had shown an uncanny ability to produce consistent returns on equity (see Table 5.1). Only twice, in 1982 and 1985, did return on equity fall below double digits as it posted a 12.75 percent annual average.

TABLE 5.1

AlliedSignal's Return on Equity: 1980–1990

Year	Return on Equity
1980	15.0%
1981	14.0%
1982	6.6%
1983	13.1%
1984	14.4%
1985	6.9%
1986	15.0%
1987	12.3%
1988	14.2%
1989	14.8%
1990	13.7%

Bossidy's arrival at AlliedSignal was a godsend for the company and its shareholders. In fact, Allied's stock soared 10 percent on the day his hiring was announced. Although he faced negative cashflow, projected earnings declines, lower bond ratings, and environmental and tax liabilities, Bossidy created wealth for shareholders by giving the company a direction, by cutting costs and raising margins. At the same time, he sloughed off low-margin businesses and focused on improving the remaining divisions. "Starting in 1991, Bossidy took charge of ailing AlliedSignal, motivated the troops, cut the fat, set lofty financial targets and, of most importance to investors, met those targets," wrote Jaqueline Doherty.[1]

The benchmark investor would have had no idea that any of the positive events were about to take place for Allied at the beginning of 1991. The only advantage the benchmark investor enjoyed was that the stock was historically undervalued in comparison to itself. Although prospects for the company were unappealing for the average investor, benchmark investors knew a bargain when they saw one. *Whenever the benchmark formula signals undervaluation, investors should become alert to the possibility of a bargain stock.* When other

---

1   Jaqueline Doherty, "Mixed Signals," *Barron's*, December 29, 1997, p. 29.

formulas such as the discounted cashflow method confirm the original findings, investors should not hesitate to invest in these bargain stocks. The key is to be patient enough to stand on the sidelines with cash while waiting for such bargains to emerge.

For an AlliedSignal annual report, call 973-455-2000 or visit the World Wide Web at: http://www.alliedsignal.com.

Alcoa (AA)

Value of $10,000 Invested on January 1, 1996: $13,653 as of December 31, 1997

(assumes annual reinvestment of dividends at year-end prices)

January 1	1996	1997	1998
Beginning price	$52.88	$63.75	$70.38
Dividends	1.33	0.97	
Shares reinvested	3	2	
Year-end shares	192	194	

Aluminum Company of America is the largest aluminum producer in the world, with annual shipments totaling more than 2.84 million metric tons a year. Annual sales top $13 billion. The Pittsburgh-based company has 23 business units with 178 operating and sales locations in 28 countries, including Japan, Australia, and various nations of South America and Europe.

I first recommended Alcoa at the beginning of 1996 at a price of $52.88 (see Figure 5.2). It was one of only two bargain stocks in the Dow to be found following the rousing 36.48 percent rise in the index in 1995. I wasn't crazy about the cyclical nature of the aluminum business. More important, the company looked dirt cheap, since its return on equity had risen dramatically from the previous five years, matching levels not seen since Alcoa's boom years of 1988 and 1989. As a result, Alcoa enjoyed a healthy adjusted ROE ratio of 2.05. With such a high relative ROE ratio, the benchmark formula showed the stock to be undervalued at any price under $76.91. At $52.88, Alcoa certainly appeared to be a bargain.

Other measures of valuation also showed Alcoa to be cheap. According to the discounted cashflow method, the stock was trading at 80 cents on the dollar. Meanwhile, the longer-term earnings evaluations confirmed benchmark's findings. As noted, my only concern was the cyclical nature of its product. A weakening of the

FIGURE 5.2

Aluminum Company of America, 1996–1997

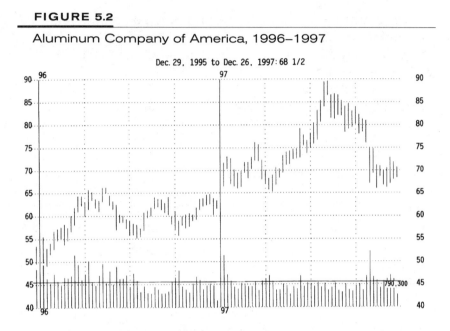

Dec. 29, 1995 to Dec. 26, 1997: 68 1/2

U.S. or European economy is always a critical threat to any commodity-type business like Alcoa. But *Value Line*'s Andrew Byrne had indicated that his long-term projections for Alcoa might prove conservative, a comforting thought as I recommended the company for purchase.

The aluminum industry has been notoriously cyclical. Historically, it has experienced either boom or bust times. To lessen the impact on market cycles and the economy, Alcoa modernized by closing older, inefficient plants, reduced its workforce, streamlined operations, and placed more emphasis on less volatile markets such as the aerospace and beverage industries. Alcoa also invested in low-cost foreign countries, which further helped lower production costs. As a result, Alcoa became leaner and more focused on realizing higher profit margins.

At the beginning of 1996, the oversupply of primary aluminum had been sharply reduced by rising customer demand. Internationally, Latin America and Asia offered substantial growth potential for fabricated products in the beverage industry. In addition, the company had entered into several joint ventures in China and around the world to expand its global presence. This greater international position would help reduce Alcoa's cyclical nature and provide additional sources of revenue. Stability and higher earnings would be the end result if Alcoa achieved its president's stated goals. Also, the company's plans for $80 million in cost reductions and share buybacks would likely improve the bottom line and shore up future growth prospects.

Ever since biblical times, people have been using alum. It's one of the aluminum compounds found in nature, although its chemical identity was not discovered until 1746. In 1855, French chemist Henri Sainte-Claire Deville exhibited an aluminum ingot at the Paris Exposition. It wasn't until 1886 that American Charles Martin Hall developed a method to smelt aluminum inexpensively. Hall's discovery of the electrolytic method of aluminum production brought the metal into wide commercial use and became the foundation of aluminum production.

In 1888, Hall formed the Pittsburgh Reduction Company. The company changed its name to the Aluminum Company of America in 1907. Three years later, Alcoa introduced aluminum foil and found other applications for aluminum in the fledgling airline and automobile industries.

In 1928, Alcoa transferred most of its foreign properties to its Canadian subsidiary, Aluminum Ltd, which later became Alcan, presently its largest competitor. After Hall's smelting patent expired in 1912, the U.S. government and Alcoa debated antitrust issues in court for years. Finally, a 1946 federal ruling forced the company to sell many operations built during World War II as well as its Canadian subsidiary to Alcan.

In the competitive aluminum industry of the 1960s, Alcoa relied largely on its laboratories to devise lower-cost production methods, especially in beverage cans. Over the next decade, Alcoa began offering products such as aerospace components. In the 1980s, it doubled its research and development spending and invested heavily in acquisitions and plant modernization.

Chairman and chief executive officer Paul O'Neill, a former president of International Paper, arrived in 1987 and shifted the company's focus back to aluminum. Sales and earnings set records in 1988 and 1989 but plunged afterward to a low of 40 cents a share in 1993, reflecting a weak global economy and record-low aluminum prices.

O'Neill set two goals for Alcoa: to increase aluminum sales worldwide and to expand overseas operations in an effort to shed its cyclical nature. The company also has its sights on battling the steel industry for a larger share of the auto market. Aluminum ranks as one of the most important industrial metals available today. It is also one of the lightest metals in the world and is capable of being cast, rolled, stamped, drawn, machined, or extruded. In addition, it is corrosion resistant and heat reflective, and an excellent electrical conductor. Aluminum is more widely used than any other metal except steel and iron.

Pure aluminum metal is used in electronic components, reflectors, utensils, and fine jewelry. It is also converted into a powder that can be mixed with other substances to produce metallic paints, rocket propellants, flares, and solders. Aluminum-copper alloys are employed extensively as structural components of buildings, aircraft, space satellites, railroad cars, and boats. The growing emphasis on greater fuel economy has stimulated the widespread use of these high-strength, low-weight alloys in the manufacturing of autos.

During Alcoa's boom years in the late 1980s, management prepared for the next down cycle. The company absorbed costs to make plants more efficient. Management used its strong cashflow to improve its financial condition. Alcoa's long-term debt to total capitalization ratio declined from 39 percent in 1987 to 25 percent in 1988. In addition, Alcoa spent heavily to modernize its facilities. Longer-term growth for Alcoa will result from the secular trend toward increased use of aluminum in autos, an upturn in aerospace demand, and worldwide expansion, especially in the Pacific Rim.

Here is an example of a benchmark selection that failed to beat the Dow in its first two years, trailing the index 37.44 percent to 51.43 percent. However, so long as its long-term appreciation potential remains attractive, I will recommend holding onto the stock. Time will tell whether it was a worthy selection.

For an Alcoa annual report, call 412-553-3042. Alcoa's Internet address is: http://www.shareholder.com/Alcoa.

AMERICAN EXPRESS (AXP)

Value of $10,000 Invested on January 1, 1991: $52,300 as of Decmber 31, 1997
(assumes annual reinvestment of dividends at year-end prices)

January 1	1991	1992	1993	1994	1995	1996	1997	1998
Price	$20.63	$20.50	$24.88	$30.88	$29.50	$41.38	$56.50	$89.25
Dividends	0.94	1.00	1.00	0.95	0.90	0.90	0.90	
Shares reinvested	22	20	17	17	12	9	5	
Year-end shares	506	526	543	560	572	581	586	

This and the following example clearly demonstrate why you must have patience when you practice benchmark investing. On January 1, 1991, I recommended buying shares of American Express at $20.63 (see Figure 5.3). Boy, did I err on that call. A year later, the stock traded lower at $20.50 a share. With dividends included, my recommendation trailed the Dow 3.93 percent to 23.93 percent. This is a good example of where you can be "right" and still lose in investing.

FIGURE 5.3

American Express, 1991–1997

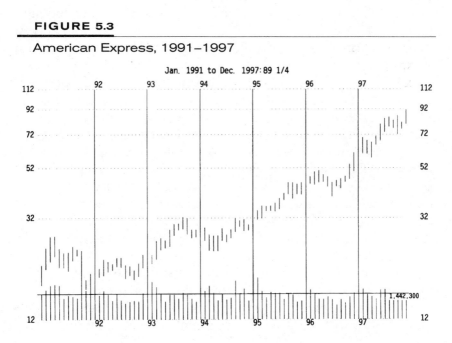

Fortunately, American Express sprung to life beginning in 1992 and beat the Dow in five of the next six years.

American Express is a blue-chip stock that had fallen from its 1989 peak of $39.38 to $20.63 at the beginning of 1991, mainly as a result of huge losses incurred in the financial services area. Even though losses were climbing and revenues had fallen, the company's adjusted return on equity remained above its 10-year average of 16.44 percent. As a result, American Express was a bargain according to benchmark investing at any price below $26.75.

If everything had been rosy at the New York City–based company, the stock wouldn't have become unloved and undervalued. Anyone buying a franchise like American Express after it has fallen to incredibly low valuations has to have firm convictions that the giant will eventually turn around as it did following the infamous salad oil scandal of 1963. As 1991 progressed, the company's financial condition worsened to the point where its credit rating was downgraded in the fall. But in early 1992 the company raised a much-needed $975 million through the sale of its ownership in First Data, its fast-growing information services business. Meanwhile, its IDS money management business had been maintaining a 20 percent growth pace, and Wall Street reacted favorably to Harvey Golub's decisiveness as new CEO and the subsequent sale of Shearson. Golub would later spin off Lehman Brothers so the company could once again focus on its franchise Travel Related Services.

Most people think of American Express as the credit card you shouldn't leave home without, thanks to its ubiquitous television advertising. There are over 30 million such cards around the world today. In fact, Travel Related Services, which includes credit and charge cards and traveler's checks, accounted for over 70 percent of American Express Company's $17 billion in revenue in 1996. The company has had an important impact on American society as millions rely on its traveler's checks before starting their vacations. Its two other principal subsidiaries are American Express Financial Advisers (AEFA) and American Express Bank. AEFA provides financial planning services and products to a variety of individuals, businesses, and institutions, including insurance, money management, tax preparation, and investment products. American Express Bank supplies banking services to 37 countries. The company operates an extensive worldwide travel agency, with locations in 160 countries, and helps companies manage their travel operations. It also publishes lifestyle and travel magazines.

When the American Express Company was formed on March 18, 1850, by Henry "Stuttering" Wells and his two main competitors, it did what its name implied. The newly formed company delivered goods and communications over vast distances. The express business had existed for only 15 years, but it was already a vital component of the American transportation and communication system. As the U.S. population grew and relocated into the interior of the country, the need arose for an express service. Railroads handled bulk freight, the U.S. Postal Service carried the mail, and the express carried everything else. The three systems fought over the same business at times, but the express was specifically designed to carry items that required both rapid transport and safe delivery. American Express invented the COD system, which enabled merchants shipping goods to have the express company collect the money from customers. In 1864, the company started a postal money order form that soon became popular because it could be bought and cashed almost anywhere.

In 1891, American Express introduced its traveler's check, a form of letter of credit, which is now accepted around the world. The American Express charge card was first introduced in 1958. Its users had no credit limits and had to pay off balances each month.

James Robinson III, the company's flamboyant chief executive officer from 1977 to 1993, hoped to turn American Express into a financial services supermarket. To achieve his grand vision, Robinson bought brokerage firm Shearson Loeb Rhoades, the Boston Company, Balcor Real Estate, once powerful investment banker Lehman Brothers, Investors Diversified Services, and brokerage firm E. F. Hutton during the 1980s. Robinson predicted that the typical consumer could have a stockbroker in California, a banker in New York, an insurance agent in Maryland, and a real estate agent jetting back and forth from Chicago to Boston. All on the American Express Card, of course.

But Robinson's grand dream never materialized. By 1990, American Express lost over $800 million after restructuring charges. Worse yet, there appeared to be no end in sight for the losses. American Express also introduced Optima in 1987, its first revolving credit card to compete with MasterCard and Visa. The company had previously scorned credit cards and had no experience with the underwriting involved. As a result, Optima was another money loser. In 1989, American Express suffered an embarrassing public relations fiasco when it issued a public apology for having investigated and spread rumors about Edmond Safra, a former chairman of American Express Bank. In connection with this settlement, the company paid $8 million to Safra's favorite charities. This action sparked a shareholder suit against management.

With the losses in the financial services area came a steep drop in earnings in the early 1990s. In addition, the company's mainstay travel services were allowed to drift, and the fee-heavy American Express card lost market share. Golub was brought in to replace Robinson with the goal of restoring stability in 1993. The former IBM executive cut costs and restructured the company so that its segments worked together. Golub sold Shearson Lehman to Sandy Weill at Travelers in 1994 and later that same year spun off Lehman Brothers.

Golub was then free to train his sights on reclaiming the company's share of the charge card market. American Express revived the Optima card and introduced several cobranded cards in an effort to crack the revolving credit market. Wal-Mart began accepting American Express in all its 3000 retail stores in 1995. A year later, Golub lobbied heavily to get banks to offer the American Express card. The company also announced it would join with software leader Microsoft in 1996 to start an online corporate travel booking service. American Express even began aggressively competing in the discount brokerage arena.

Warren Buffett bought 10 percent of American Express in 1995 and sought permission to increase his interest to 17 percent. Known to support superior managers like Golub, the Omaha billionaire agreed to vote with the board so long as Golub remained chief executive officer.

Charge cards began gradually replacing cash during the early 1990s as more and more outlets such as gas stations and grocery stores began to accept them. Moreover, beginning in 1990, credit card transaction volume began to rise at a double-digit rate, and the trend appears to be long term. Therefore, the future is promising for American Express.

Although Golub slashed costs and sold off unprofitable units, he wasn't afraid to tackle problems at the company's premier Travel Related Services as well. He spearheaded efforts to expand internationally as well as into smaller U.S. corporate businesses. In addition, he began buying back 20 million shares at attractive levels, further improving the company's bottom line.

The company's profitability improved despite incurring higher marketing expenses and maintaining higher reserves against losses. The combination of Golub's cost-cutting efforts and laserlike management helped turn American Express back to its profitable ways once again. Currently, about one-third of the company's total profits come from overseas, but the company plans to boost that total to one-half over the next several years. Tiger Woods, whose name is known throughout the world, signed a long-term contract—a move that will likely help the company realize its global dreams of worldwide higher revenue and profits.

American Express is an excellent example for benchmark investors to review because it shows the danger of a value trap. It also clearly demonstrates the importance of patience and belief in the method of benchmark investing. Even though the stock was undervalued at the beginning of 1991, it took more than a year to realize any significant gains. Had you exercised patience and discipline and held onto American Express, you would have averaged 26.66 percent annual compound returns from 1991 to 1997, good enough to far outpace the Dow's 19.89 percent average during the same period.

For an American Express annual report, call 212-640-2000. AXP's Internet address is: http://www.americanexpress.com.

AT&T CORPORATION (T)

Value of $10,000 Invested on January 1, 1991: $34,077 as of December 31, 1997

(assumes annual reinvestment of dividends at year-end prices)

January 1	1991	1992	1993	1994	1995	1996	1997	1998
Price	$30.13	$39.13	$51.00	$52.50	$50.25	$64.75	$43.38	$61.31
Dividends	1.32	1.32	1.32	1.32	1.32	1.71	1.32	
Shares reinvested	11	8	8	9	7	156	27	
Year-end shares	342	350	358	367	374	528	555	
Spin-offs						.99 shares of Lucent & NCR		

As interesting as AT&T's past has been, its future looks even more compelling.

In 1882, Alexander Graham Bell made the first utterance on the telephone when he said, "Mr. Watson, come here. I want you." With those words Bell ushered in the new telecommunications era. Even so, President Grover Cleveland told Bell that his new invention was interesting but impractical and would never be used. Today, the company that Bell founded is AT&T, a $53 billion powerhouse with 80 million residential customers and offices in more than 200 countries around the world.

I first recommended the telecommunications giant at the outset of 1991, when it was trading roughly 10 percent below its downside price target (see Figure 5.4). AT&T's shares quickly rose an impressive 67.96 percent in 1991 and 1992. But the next two years would test my faith in my valuation of the company, as it posted an anemic 3.76 percent total return while the Dow climbed 21.67 percent. AT&T has been the best example of why a benchmark investor sometimes needs *extraordinary* patience.

FIGURE 5.4

AT&T, 1991–1997

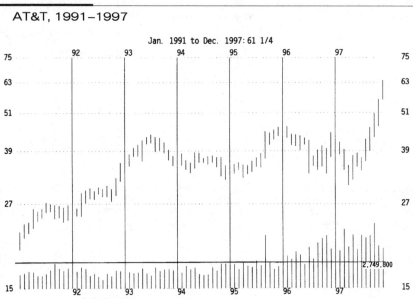

In retrospect, I wish I could tell you that my research said to sell the long-distance company at the beginning of 1993. It didn't. Nor would I have told you to buy AT&T at that time. This illustrates an important point of benchmark investing, which is that you should focus solely on a company's current valuation, cashflow, and earnings when buying. But when deciding whether or not to sell, you should consider longer-term forecasts. This strategy helps you avoid selling stocks too soon. In this example, however, it also keeps you holding stocks that you wouldn't buy. In other words, sometimes benchmark investing prevents you from selling stocks that should be sold. Nonetheless, it is my strong conviction that investors will still be better served by focusing on the long term with the full knowledge that there will be stocks that underperform from time to time as AT&T did in 1993 and 1994.

Despite the lousy years, you would have seen a hypothetical $10,000 investment rise to $34,077 between 1991 and the end of 1997. That's still not a bad mistake to make, but during that same period a $10,000 investment in the Dow would have risen to $35,600.

AT&T has gone through monumental changes in the last few years. Just as several other Dow stocks spun off or divested themselves of noncore business in the 1990s, AT&T spun off NCR and Lucent, its computer products and services and network products and R&D unit in late 1996. Under the direction of new CEO Michael Armstrong, the long-distance king also sold its Universal card to Citicorp for $4 billion in late 1997. Two months later, in early January 1998, AT&T announced the buyout of Teleport Communications Group for $11.3 billion, a move that would give the company instant access to 60 major U.S. local phone markets. AT&T would then focus on its telecom services, which include cellular service, online and Internet access, and paging, video, and electronic commerce services. It also provides wireless services, air-to-ground telephone services, messaging, electronic mail, and toll-free and 800 calling.

The company expanded internationally, making communications infrastructure sales in China, the Philippines, Saudi Arabia, and other countries. It also formed a new venture with European partner Unisource N.V. to boost its telecommunication market share in Europe.

American Telephone & Telegraph was incorporated in New York on March 3, 1885. The parent company of the "Bell System" owned only long-distance lines connecting local Bell companies until 1930, when the company acquired the successor to the other Bell company in existence.

Financier J. P. Morgan and his allies gained control of AT&T and installed Theodore Vail as president in 1907. AT&T won control of Western Union in 1909; however, the Wilson administration threatened antitrust action. In the 1913 Kingsbury Commitment, AT&T agreed to sell Western Union, buy no more independent phone companies without regulatory approval, and grant independents access to its networks.

By 1940, sales eclipsed $1.1 billion. In 1949, the Justice Department sued to force AT&T to sell Western Electric. A 1956 settlement allowed AT&T to keep its prize but prohibited it from entering nonregulated businesses. FCC rulings stripped AT&T of its telephone equipment monopoly in 1968 and allowed specialized carriers such as tiny MCI to hook their microwave systems to the phone network in 1969.

A government suit led to the settlement that, in 1984, spun off the seven regional Bell companies. AT&T kept long-distance services and Western Electric. After the breakup, then-CEO Robert Allen cut jobs to remain competitive.

The company formally adopted the name AT&T Corp in 1994, then soon thereafter acquired the nation's number-one cellular service provider, McCaw Cellular, for $11.5 billion. It also bought online service Interchange Network Company from Ziff-Davis Publishing that year. In 1995, AT&T agreed to pay $3.3 billion for the 48 percent of cellular communications company LIN Broadcasting that it did not already own. The following year, AT&T joined forces with BBN Planet, the leading provider of managed Internet access and security services to U.S. corporations and institutions, to launch WorldNet, an Internet access service.

By the middle of 1997, AT&T's 3 million shareholders were unhappy. That's because the company had badly trailed the Dow in the midst of a roaring bull market. In addition, the company was losing market share to bitter rivals in its core long-distance market while also suffering from poor management that continued to make strategic blunders. If that weren't bad enough, the Telecommunications Act of 1996 had torn down competitive barriers that AT&T had long enjoyed. In the previous years since the court-appointed breakup of Ma Bell, AT&T had seen its share of the long-distance market drop form 90 percent to just 54 percent. The prospect of more competition had knocked the shares down 28 percent while the Dow had climbed 26 percent by mid-1997.

That's when AT&T named C. Michael Armstrong of Hughes Electronics as successor to retiring chairman Robert E. Allen. At Hughes, Armstrong had wasted little time in turning around a money-losing operation. He did it by cutting costs, laying off 25 percent of the workforce, selling unprofitable and unneeded assets, and pushing heavily into new technologies where Hughes had a niche. At Hughes, the former IBM European Division head emphasized the importance of customers and what they needed.

The Detroit native was hired in late October 1997. AT&T's shares rose more than 50 percent in the next two months thanks to the hard line that Armstrong took on costs. He immediately froze all hiring, set stringent new guidelines that tied managers' compensation to the success of the company, and redirected more than $2 billion in local phone services spending. All of AT&T's current expenses were under review at the end of 1997 in an effort to reduce costs and plow the savings back into new networks and services that could correct the company's weak revenue growth. Armstrong was expected to spend heavily to acquire local phone services assets (like Teleport), expand AT&T's Internet and wireless business, and establish a foothold in overseas markets where barriers to competition were falling.

Interestingly, Armstrong also instituted requirements for top managers and board directors to own hefty amounts of company stock. Until then, directors hadn't had to own stock. Another bright spot for AT&T in 1997 was its effective use of national advertising. In fact, *USA TODAY* chose AT&T's ads starring actor Paul Reiser as the biggest winner of the year.[2]

For AT&T's annual report, call 212-387-5400 or visit the World Wide Web at: http://www.att.net.

---

2 Dottie Enrico and Melanie Wells, "Ad Industry's 1997 Stars," *USA TODAY*, December 22, 1997, p. 6B.

THE BOEING COMPANY (BA)

Value of $10,000 Invested on January 1, 1991: $24,421 as of December 31, 1997
(assumes annual reinvestment of dividends at year-end prices)

January 1	1991	1992	1993	1994	1995	1996	1997	1998
Price	$45.38	$47.75	$40.13	$43.25	$46.75	$78.38	$106.50	$48.94
Dividends	1.00	1.00	1.00	1.00	1.00	1.09	0.56	
Shares reinvested	4	5	5	5	5	3	5	
Year-end shares	224	229	234	239	244	247	499	
Splits							2-1	

During its history, the world's largest commercial aircraft maker has ridden the winds of economic change. At the beginning of 1991, those winds were not kind to Boeing. Worldwide airline traffic was down. The airline industry saw several carriers go bankrupt or close to bankruptcy after decades of feasting on a deep-pocketed military and enjoying an indifferent and regulated environment.

It was in this atmosphere that I recommended Boeing at a split-adjusted $22.69 on January 1, 1991 (see Figure 5-5). The Seattle-based corporation appeared to be undervalued relative to its own historical ratios. It had fallen from a peak of $61.88 in 1990. The stock had historically traded from a low market-to-book value of 1.23 to as high as 2.00 times book during the previous 10 years, while averaging 13.52 percent returns on equity. As a result, its adjusted ROE ratio stood at a premium of 1.56. Boeing appeared undervalued at any price below $47.97.

Unfortunately, Boeing's shares trailed the Dow badly in 1991 and were pummeled in 1992, dropping as low as $34.13 before closing the year at $40.13—down 13.86 percent (see Figure 5.5). Only Merck, Westinghouse, and IBM lost more money than Boeing in 1992. The following year, Boeing showed meager improvement, rising 10.27 percent. In 1994, Boeing posted another incremental gain of 10.40 percent, leaving benchmark investors barely ahead of Treasury bills on their Boeing investment.

At this point, benchmark investors could have sold out, or they could have held onto their shares and waited for the market's reappraisal of the company. According to the benchmark formula,

FIGURE 5.5

Boeing, 1991–1997

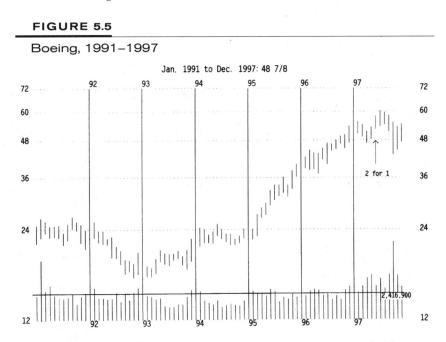

Boeing remained undervalued on a long-term basis. But could the formula be wrong? After all, the stock had been a major disappointment. For those investors who remained committed to the stock, Boeing finally rewarded them in 1995 and 1996 with excellent gains.

When considering investment returns, perhaps we should always humbly keep in mind the old fable of the tortoise and the hare. As the tale points out, the race is won by the plodding, ever-persistent tortoise, which doesn't let distractions slow it down.

By the time 1992 rolled around, stocks in the Dow had enjoyed a great rise to a year-end high of 3200. Many of the larger stocks such as AlliedSignal, Merck, Philip Morris, and Coca-Cola had enjoyed tremendous gains in 1991. But the dominant global producer of commercial jets had struggled as a result of myriad problems. It appeared that the high-profile company was flying into a heavy financial fog that incensed the bears on Wall Street but created a wonderful buying opportunity for the benchmark investor.

These high-quality shares had exceptional potential for capital gains for the benchmark investor. Worldwide traffic growth was projected to increase at a rate of 7.2 percent. And a corporate survey revealed that 6500 aircraft would be needed to serve that growth and another 4200 would be needed as replacements. Since Boeing had historically captured 60 percent of the world commercial aircraft market, the future looked profitable.

In addition, Boeing bought out McDonnell Douglas and the defense division of Rockwell International in mid-1997, allowing the company to realize economies of scale as well as take advantage of reduced worldwide competition. Along with that, the company was expected to nearly double monthly production to 26 airliners in 1997, since almost one-third of the world's commercial aircraft fleet was nearing the age of 20 (major airlines typically retire their planes between ages 20 and 30). Moreover, Boeing accomplished these impressive production gains while reducing its employee count by 50,000, thus cutting costs substantially and improving profit margins long after it had seen the rest of American industry implement such moves with success more than a decade earlier. Further reason for optimism regarding Boeing is the fact that the company projected that the world's airlines would need $1.1 trillion of new aircraft by 2016—a projection that translates to 16,000 new planes, almost one and a half times the number in existence today.

The only question is whether Boeing can satisfy demand. With an $88 billion backlog of orders, Boeing is in the midst of the fastest production increase in the history of civil aviation. And company plans call for the jet maker to produce 47 planes a month by late 1998.

Boeing manufactures the 737, 747, 757, 767, and 777, which represent a variety of passenger and cargo designs and range capabilities. Its 737 is the best-selling jetliner in commercial aviation history. Although commercial aircraft products and services account for more than 70 percent of Boeing's revenues, the company also makes military aircraft and helicopters, is the primary contractor of the space station, and works on MX missiles and the B-2 and F-22 planes.

The company was founded just before World War I by Bill Boeing, who built his first airplane in 1916. His Seattle factory, at first called Pacific Aero Products Company, changed its name to Boeing Airplane Company the following year. During World War I, Boeing built training planes for the U.S. Navy. After the war, when military sales evaporated, Boeing began the first international airmail service. The company introduced the first all-metal airliner in 1933. During World War II, Boeing was the leading producer of bombers, including the B-29 that dropped the atomic bomb on Hiroshima. Between 1935 and 1965, Boeing pioneered commercial jet aircraft. Its 707 was the first passenger jet service carrier, flying between London and New York in 1958. In the 1960s, Boeing built the first stage of the rockets used in the Apollo space program.

In 1995, Boeing was the second-leading Dow stock, gaining 68.89 percent and trailing only Merck, another benchmark selection. Boeing rose another 37.27 percent in 1996 before losing 8.1 percent in 1997. Still, it had provided the benchmark investor with an average of 13.60 percent compound annual returns between 1991 and 1997, showing that sometimes investors will be called upon to demonstrate incredible patience and conviction in the strategy. At the same time, the company announced that it would proceed with the long-anticipated acquisition of its rival, McDonnell Douglas, making the combined company the world's largest aerospace-military manufacturer.

Critics pointed out that the merger would leave only two worldwide commercial aircraft manufacturers—Boeing and Airbus, a consortium of European companies. But the new Boeing will find numerous competitors in areas like military electronics, helicopters and missiles, and information technology. Still, the new Boeing is a world leader and national asset that flies most of the world's travelers and accounts for the largest positive element of the nation's international balance of payments.

A hypothetical $10,000 investment in Boeing at the beginning of 1991 would have turned into $24,421 with dividends reinvested by the end of 1997, while a similar investment in the Dow would have risen to $35,598.

For Boeing's annual report, call 206-655-2121. Boeing's Internet address is: http://www.boeing.com.

CATERPILLAR (CAT)

Value of $10,000 Invested on January 1, 1992: $47,384 as of December 31, 1997
(assumes annual reinvestment of dividends at year-end prices)

January 1	1992	1993	1994	1995	1996	1997	1998
Price	$43.88	$53.63	$89.00	$55.13	$58.75	$75.25	$48.50
Dividends	0.60	0.60	0.64	1.20	1.50	0.90	

January 1	1992	1993	1994	1995	1996	1997	1998
Shares reinvested	2	1	1	9	9	17	
Year-end shares	229	230	231	471	480	977	
Splits			2-1			2-1	

On January 1, 1992, I recommended Caterpillar, the world's largest manufacturer of earth-moving and construction machinery (see Figure 5.6). Once again I had found a world-class bargain stock trading well below its downside price target. By now you should realize that the technique for finding an undervalued stock is very straightforward. You simply find a company trading at historically low valuation levels, invest, and wait patiently. Caterpillar met those criteria at the start of 1992 after losing $136 million in 1991. To make matters worse, the company had been struck by the United Auto Workers in a bitter feud over health care and wages. Not surprisingly, Caterpillar's shares were selling at an all-time low: 1.08 times book value. This was too good a bargain for me to ignore, despite the choppy inconsistency of earnings and recent sales.

FIGURE 5.6

Caterpillar, 1992–1997

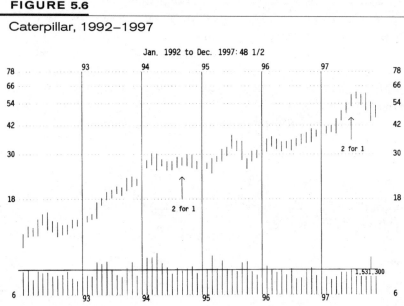

On February 14, 1992, *Value Line's* Mark Leach wrote: "CAT stands to benefit mightily when the economy finally does recover, and that knowledge underlies our projection that *these shares may well triple in value by 1995–97."* Leach's prediction was right on the mark, as Caterpillar more than tripled by the end of 1997 (see Figure 5.6), averaging an impressive 29.60 percent compound annual return while the Dow gained 19.23 percent.

When the economy is in the doldrums, professional money managers begin to think about investing in cyclical companies like Caterpillar that perform well whenever the economy perks back up. The most important question to ask about a cyclical company is whether the possibility exists for superior appreciation of its shares. In other words, will you, the benchmark investor, be rewarded for your investment? Clearly, the answer must be in the affirmative before you invest in such an up-and-down enterprise.

Caterpillar's worldwide machinery sales reached $16 billion in 1995 and topped $18 billion two years later. These products account for over three-fourths of sales and are used in the construction, mining, materials handling, forest products, and farming industries. The Peoria, Illinois, company also makes natural gas and diesel engines and turbines, has manufacturing operations in 13 countries, and sells through its network of independent dealers.

Cofounders Benjamin Holt and Daniel Best helped revolutionize farming in 1904, when they modified the agricultural tractor by substituting a gas engine for steam and replacing iron wheels with crawler tracks. This improved the tractor's mobility over dirt by making it lighter and distributing its weight more evenly. Agriculture entered a new era.

In 1915, the British adapted Holt's "caterpillar" design to the armored tank. The caterpillar's efficiency surprised Holt and spurred the development of earth-moving and construction equipment. Holt merged with another California company, Best Tractor, in 1925. In 1928 the new organization, named Caterpillar Tractor Company, moved to its present headquarters in Peoria while maintaining corporate offices in San Leandro, California.

During the 1930s, Caterpillar expanded into foreign markets. Sales volume more than tripled during World War II when the company supplied the military with earth-moving equipment. Returning soldiers touted its durability and quality, and the company enjoyed continued high demand during the postwar years. Caterpillar emerged in solid first place in the industry, far ahead of International Harvester.

Sales increased steadily, reaching almost $9.2 billion by 1981. However, 50 consecutive years of profits ended when CAT ran up $953 million in losses between 1982 and 1984 as equipment demand fell and competition from foreign firms intensified. Caterpillar doubled its product line between 1984 and 1989. The "Plant with a Future" program, introduced in 1985, shifted production toward smaller equipment, cut the workforce, and enabled CAT to recoup lost market share. In 1990, CEO Donald Fites reorganized Caterpillar along product lines. The next year, the company clashed with the union over health benefits; a strike ensued, and Caterpillar reported its first annual loss since 1984. Most of the 12,500 striking employees had returned to work without a contract by May 1992, dealing the UAW a surprising blow.

In 1993, the firm completed a $1.8 billion modernization program that automated many of its factories, reduced the size of its labor force, and helped protect the company from organized labor. That investment paid off when almost two-thirds of Caterpillar's UAW employees at eight plants in Colorado, Illinois, and Pennsylvania went on strike in 1994 over unfair labor charges. Company management swiftly retaliated by hiring temporary, contract, and permanent workers and using its foreign factories to help fill orders. Caterpillar reported record sales and profits in 1994—and boasted that the strike had no impact. In 1995, another year of record earnings, both sides agreed to federally mediated contract talks, and late in the year the union called off the strike.

Another positive to consider was the fact that Caterpillar was a pure infrastructure play. America's roads, bridges, and highways appeared on the verge of breakdown as cash-strapped state and local governments had deferred construction projects. With the U.S. economy expected to rebound, spending would increase on these projects, and Caterpillar would enjoy the lion's share of business. Caterpillar was and is the leader in nearly every market in which it competes, and would be a direct beneficiary of renewed infrastructure spending.

Nearly every benchmark selection will first suffer a withering barrage of negative reports to send prices plummeting before it becomes attractive enough to purchase for the long term. The key, once again, is to find a purchase price so attractive that even a mediocre sell provides good results. It is rare to find a world-class Dow stock trading at low valuations when everything is rosy for the company.

Caterpillar was no exception when I saw the share price plummet to bargain levels. The company had lost money and was expected to lose more as its markets suffered through extended recessions worldwide. A major union was pitting an acrimonious battle with management and there was political uncertainty with a new American president. Investors would have been hard-pressed to find a less appealing stock when they could have invested instead in a sexy technology stock.

But remember, the time to buy is usually only after the stock has fallen significantly. The exception occurs whenever a company significantly improves its return on equity without the market rewarding the company with suitably higher share prices. In this case, however, Caterpillar had dropped 36 percent from its 1989 peak price of $69.00 a share. It would drop only another $2.00 in 1992 before rising 23.59 percent for the year versus the Dow's 7.34 percent rise. The point is that these are the classical elements of a great investment so long as the company is financially strong enough to weather the bad times.

For Caterpillar's annual report, call 309-675-1000 or visit the World Wide Web at: http://www.cat.com.

Coca-Cola (KO)

Value of $10,000 Invested on July 1, 1994: $33,878 as of December 31, 1997
(assumes annual reinvestment of dividends at year-end prices)

	7/1 1994	1995	1996	1997	1998
Price	$40.63	$51.50	$74.25	$52.63	$66.69
Dividends	0.58	0.88	1.00	0.56	
Shares reinvested	2	2	4	4	
Year-end sales	248	250	504	508	
Splits			2-1		

Price tells nothing about value. By the summer of 1994, Coke's stock
had been stuck in a tight trading range for two and a half years after
an impressive fivefold run-up since 1988. In technical Wall Street
jargon, the stock had consolidated its gains by trading in a relatively
narrow trading range. To the average Wall Street investor, Coca-
Cola was overvalued. The thinking was, "How could Coke continue
to grow at its robust pace?"

But I began recommending the stock at a split-adjusted $20.31
a share on July 1, 1994 (see Figure 5.7), when Coke's ROE ratio
climbed to 1.53 percent, moving its downside target to $39.99.
Hardly an extreme undervaluation, but it was enough for a company
that was easily expected to double over the next four years according
to the benchmark investing formula.

Coke's woldwide volume had just begun to rise in the first
quarter of 1994, up an impressive 7 percent overall. And its profits
had increased 15 percent that same quarter. The lion's share of
Coke's gains were coming from outside the United States, where the
company had done little or no business up to that point. Coca-Cola
had just completed the plant expansion necessary to begin to fully

FIGURE 5.7

Coca-Cola, 1994–1997

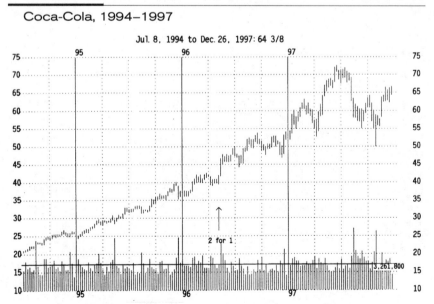

support growth in Eastern Europe and other largely untapped markets, including China and India. The average Chinese citizen drank three Cokes a year, versus the average American's consumption of 125 a year.

At the same time, Coke had aggressively been buying back its shares. In 1994 alone, the company bought back 25 million shares, a clear signal to the investment community that management was bullish on its future.

The "real thing" is a fabulous global franchise that has handsomely rewarded benchmark investors since I recommended it. Marketed like nothing before or since, Coca-Cola enjoys the world's best-known corporate identity. According to the company, Coca-Cola is actually the second most famous expression in the world after "OK." Not bad for a business that was invented by an Atlanta pharmacist from coca leaves and kola nuts in 1886. Only 400 Cokes were sold that year, but today Coke is the world's largest manufacturer, marketer, and distributor of carbonated soft drink concentrates and syrups. Since Coke spun its bottlers off its balance sheet in 1986, it has been a single-minded seller of beverage concentrate. Today, Coca-Cola seduces the world with its caramel-colored sugar water to the tune of $18.8 billion in 1997 sales. The company is also the global leader in juice drink products.

Coca-Cola dominates the global soft drink market, with 42 percent of the U.S. market and 47 percent of the rest of the world's. Four of its brands—Coca-Cola Classic, Diet Coke, Caffeine-Free Diet Coke, and Sprite—are among the 10 best-selling soft drinks in America, and Classic Coke is far and away the leader.

Druggist Asa Candler had bought the company for $2300 in 1891. By 1895, the soda fountain drink was available in all states, entering Canada and Mexico by 1898. Candler sold most U.S. bottling rights in 1899 to Benjamin Thomas and John Whitehead of Chattanooga for $1.00. With the backing of John Lupton, these men developed the regional franchise bottling system, creating over 1000 bottlers within 20 years. The bottlers used the contoured bottle designed by the C. J. Root Glass Company of Terre Haute, Indiana, in 1916.

Candler's family sold the company to Atlanta banker Ernest Woodruff for $25 million in 1919, the same year Coca-Cola went public. In 1923, Woodruff appointed his son Robert president. The younger Woodruff continued as chairman until 1942, and remained influential until his death in 1985 at the age of 95. Woodruff's contributions were in advertising and overseas expansion. During World War II, he decreed that every soldier would have access to a 5-cent bottle of Coke. With government assistance, Coca-Cola built 64 overseas bottling plants during the war.

Woodruff realized that Coke couldn't just be as good as the rest of the soft drinks on the market. To him, Coke had to be the best. "We wanted to promote Coca-Cola not just as a soft drink but as something bigger than just the answer to thirst," he once said.[3] He wanted to make it a thing apart. To reach that goal, he hired two of the most famous artists of the day—Norman Rockwell and N. C. Wyeth—to portray regular Americans drinking his product.

Coca-Cola bought Minute Maid in 1960 and introduced Sprite in 1961, TAB in 1963, and Diet Coke in 1982. Woodruff guided the company for over 60 years and throughout his career was a genius for finding the most talented people for the job. His genius became evident when he saw to it that he was succeeded in 1981 by his protégé, Roberto Goizueta. A Yale-educated chemical engineer from Cuba who gradually rose through the ranks, Goizueta was a spectacular choice as CEO. Goizueta and his wife fled Havana to the United States when Castro took over, arriving in Florida by boat with $40 and 100 shares of Coca-Cola—shares that would be worth more than $3 million at the time of his death in October 1997.

In fact, Goizueta was responsible for refocusing and rejuvenating the company. He introduced Diet Coke in 1982, the same year he bought Columbia Pictures for $665 million and began operations in Russia and China. Goizueta later sold Columbia to Sony in 1989 for $1.55 billion. Perhaps his most important accomplishment was to lash together hundreds of bottlers worldwide into a handful of large bottlers with sound financial backing. Many on Wall Street felt that Goizueta's strategy to build this powerful network of bottlers was the real "secret formula" behind Coke's success under his reign. One dollar invested in Coke on the day Goizueta took over in 1981 was worth $65 on the day he died, an increase unmatched over that period.

Coke introduced POWERaDE, its 1990 entry in the rapidly growing sports drink market, and entered Russia the next year. In 1993, Coke formed a joint venture with FEMSA, Mexico's largest beverage company. In 1995, Coke bought root beer maker Barg's, its

---

3   John Merline, "Coca-Cola's Robert Woodruff," *Investor's Business Daily*, January 16, 1997, p. 1.

first purchase of an American beverage maker in more than three decades.

Coca-Cola soft drinks are sold in nearly 200 countries around the world. Although the company's juice and juice drink products are sold primarily in the United States and Canada, it owns 40 manufacturing plants around the world. Since mid-1994, Coke averaged a stunning 41.12 percent annual compounded return. A $10,000 investment in the company would have grown to $33,878 by the end of 1997.

For Coca-Cola's annual report, call 404-676-2121 or visit the World Wide Web at: http://www.coca-cola.com.

EASTMAN KODAK COMPANY (EK)

Value of $10,000 Invested on January 1, 1991: $23,272 as of December 31, 1997

(assumes annual reinvestment of dividends at year-end prices)

January 1	1991	1992	1993	1994	1995	1996	1997	1998
Price	$41.63	$48.25	$40.50	$56.25	$47.75	$67.00	$80.25	$60.56
Dividends	2.00	2.00	2.00	1.70	1.60	1.60	1.76	
Shares reinvested	9	12	9	9	6	8		
Year-end shares	249	261	270	279	285	290	298	

It would have taken a lot of nerve for anyone to buy Eastman Kodak at the beginning of 1991, and nerve is a typical requirement of becoming a benchmark investor (see Figure 5.8). As usual, here was a world-class company with $19 billion in sales trading 41 percent below its recent highs even though it was expecting to rack up record sales in 1991. The reasons? Worries over a $909 million jury award to Polaroid, a faltering economy in the United States, and nearly two decades of stagnation under inbred management.

No, things were far from picture-perfect at the world's producer of photographic products. But with the dark cloud of the Polaroid case dissipated—some on Wall Street reckoned the jury award could have reached $2 billion—the stock was very attractive to me. After all, its downside price target was $51.44, so the stock was already trading at distressed levels. Or as Benjamin Graham liked to find, there was a "margin of safety" built into the price of the stock.

FIGURE 5.8

Eastman Kodak, 1991–1997

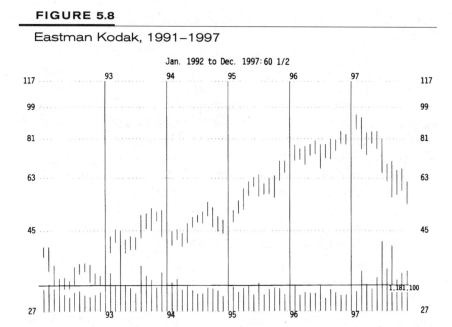

Of course, with perfect hindsight I would not have recommended Kodak in 1991 because it failed my year-over-year earnings projections. Nor was it cheap according to Buffett's cashflow benchmark, trading at a premium rather than the desired discount. Nonetheless, Kodak gained a respectable 20.71 percent in 1991 despite an unexpectedly weak final fourth quarter.

In fact, 1991's restructuring charges—required because of poor management decisions—were the company's fifth write-off in six years. The negative charges began to unnerve Wall Street even more than the Polaroid fiasco. Another write-off damaged Kodak's third quarter earnings and sent the stock reeling to an 11.92 percent loss in 1992. The bottom-line problem with Eastman Kodak, according to Wall Street, was reminiscent of the strategic failures at Xerox when it failed to capitalize on its leading word processing system and graphical user interface to completely miss the PC market.

So firebrand George Fisher was recruited as Kodak's new chairman in 1993. As chairman at Motorola, Fisher had confounded the skeptics by winning with pagers and cellular phones, two new technologies that he had to stick his neck out to support and that became consumer hits. The move was widely cheered on Wall Street. Shares of Kodak rocketed 43.83 percent that year largely as the result of the arrival of the first outsider for a senior executive spot in 20 years.

Fisher brought with him a new focus for the company to reduce debt, improve returns, and aggressively pursue growth. In fact, he saw to it that Kodak began a new program that pegged more of its executive pay to performance and required its top managers to invest one to four times their base salaries in company stock. Further developments included divestitures of Eastman Chemical and its noncore businesses, which had generated 23 percent of the company's profits in 1993. A large portion of the $7.86 billion in divestitures was used to reduce debt further—from $6.8 billion in 1993 to just $660 *million* by 1994. In fact, the interest savings more than offset the loss of the drug business contributions. Other positives included Kodak taking over complete ownership of Qualex, the nation's largest wholesale photo finisher, in August 1994.

After Kodak won a product-dumping action against Fuji Films in 1994, Fuji was almost driven out of the United States, allowing the American company to win back U.S. market share from its intensely competitive Japanese rival. In 1995, Kodak began concentrating on developing countries such as China, the former Soviet Union, India, Indonesia, Vietnam, and Eastern Europe. Research indicated that there were 56 million households in China alone that had the ability to adopt photography. Imagine, 10 million Chinese weddings a year to photograph. Meanwhile, Fisher was also backing speedy development of Kodak's digital photography business for the future. He intensified Kodak's move into digital imaging by teaming with Microsoft in 1996 to produce a new imaging technology for computers.

At the end of 1996, Kodak announced that it had bought back 12 million shares, a move that contributed to higher earnings. And when Fisher quelled rumors of leaving the company by signing an extension of his original five-year contract in 1997, the new contract included more performance-oriented clauses tied to the market price of Kodak shares, which spelled good tidings for shareholders.

George Eastman founded the company over a century ago and coined the name Kodak. After developing a method for dry-plate photography, Eastman established the Eastman Dry Plate and Film Company in 1884 in Rochester, New York. The company settled on the name Kodak in 1892 after Eastman tried many combinations of letters starting and ending with *k*, which he thought was a "strong, incisive sort of letter."

In 1888, the company introduced its first camera, a small, easy-to-use device that sold for $25 and was loaded with enough film for 100 pictures. To develop the film, owners mailed the camera to Kodak, which returned it with the pictures and more film. The user-friendly Brownie camera followed in 1900. In 1923, Kodak introduced a home-movie camera, projector, and film.

Kodak continued to dominate the photography industry with the introduction of its Kodachrome color film in 1935 and the Brownie handheld movie camera in 1951. The Instamatic, introduced in 1963, became Kodak's greatest success. The camera, with the film in a foolproof cartridge, eliminated the need for loading in the dark. By 1976, Kodak had sold an estimated 60 million Instamatics, 50 million more cameras than all its competitors combined.

Subsequent introductions have included the Kodak instant camera and the disk camera. In the 1980s, Kodak diversified into electronic publishing, batteries, floppy disks, pharmaceuticals, and do-it-yourself and household products. Each of the ventures had been sold off by 1994 as the company refocused on its photography business.

Kodak entered a joint research and development project with four Japanese photo giants (Canon, Nikon, Minolta, and Fuji Photo) in 1992 to examine silver-halide photographic systems. That same year Kodak introduced the Photo CD, a compact disk capable of storing photographs. At a price of $20 per disk and $500 for the player, the Photo CD failed as a consumer product but became popular among desktop publishers and other small businesses. Kodak relaunched its Photo CD directly to the desktop publishing market in 1995 and said it would license, for free, its machine standards for converting photos into CDs. That year the company stepped up the pressure on Fuji by lodging a trade complaint against Japan, charging that Fuji had engaged in decades of unfair trade practices in selling film in Japan, the world's second-largest market.

In early 1996, Kodak announced plans to sell its copier division to Danka Business Systems, which struggled with stiff competition and poor earnings. It also agreed to operate drugstore chain Eckerd's seven regional photo-processing labs, a move that raised Kodak's share of the wholesale development market to 80 percent. That year the company won a U.S. Commerce Department grant to develop an optical disk system with one terabyte of storage, 40 times more than current systems. Also in 1996 the U.S. government asked the World Trade Organization to resolve Kodak's dispute with Fuji and the Japanese government.

Kodak is shooting for a big share of the developing technologies that recently have reinvigorated the imaging market. One is the Advanced Photo System (APS), which Kodak developed with Canon, Fuji, Minolta, and Nikon. Kodak has introduced a line of innovative APS cameras and drop-in film with improved color, marketed under the Advantix name, and related products for photo finishers. Digital imaging is another outlet that's clicking for the company, especially with the growing sophistication of PC users. Top software programs—including Adobe's Pagemaker and Photoshop, Corel's CorelDraw, and Microsoft's Windows 95—incorporate Kodak's color management system. The firm is making breakthroughs in several other technologies, including CD storage, document management, applied imaging (e.g., thermal printers), and advanced medical imaging (the company is a leader in X-ray films).

Emerging markets in Asia, Eastern Europe, Latin America, and Russia also present photo opportunities for Kodak. Recent company expansions have included an office in Moscow, where Kodak opened its first movie theater, and a motion picture film finishing plant in India. But the success of Eastman Kodak will depend on its focus on customers and growth in a marketplace moving at warp speed. On November 11, 1997, Fisher announced new plans to cut $1 billion in costs while eliminating 10,000 jobs. In addition, he announced plans to concentrate on digitial print stations in retail stores where people get their film developed. The 13,000 kiosks will let consumers access photos from the Internet, manipulate them, and print them.

A hypothetical $10,000 investment in Eastman Kodak would have reached $18,046 by the end of 1997, while a similar investment in the Dow would have climbed to $35,598.

For Eastman Kodak's annual report, call 716-724-5492 or visit the World Wide Web at: http://www.kodak.com.

GENERAL ELECTRIC (GE)

Value of $10,000 Invested on January 1, 1991: $58,777 as of December 31, 1997

(assumes annual reinvestment of dividends at year-end prices)

January 1	1991	1992	1993	1994	1995	1996	1997	1998
Price	$57.38	$76.50	$85.50	$104.88	$51.00	$72.00	$98.88	$73.38
Dividends	2.04	2.32	2.60	3.00	1.70	1.90	1.08	
Shares reinvested	4	4	4	10	9	7	5	
Year-end shares	178	182	186	382	391	398	801	
Splits				2-1			2-1	

Investors had been especially hard on the shares of the world's largest diversified industrial company during the second half of 1990. The shares had plummeted from a high of $75.50 to $50.25 in that period. Without question, the reason the shares were so distressed was Wall Street's shortsighted concern over leveraged buyout real estate loans included in GE Capital's portfolio.

That's how I came to recommend General Electric at the beginning of 1991 (see Figure 5.9). Though it was trading slightly above its downside target, it was close enough to be a recommendation. *(Note:* I did not include either GE or Coca-Cola in my overall performance record because they weren't trading below their downside targets.) It also helped that the shares were trading at 63 cents on the dollar according to the cashflow valuation used by Warren Buffett. And GE's long-term valuation projections showed potential for annual growth in the 14–29 percent range. Thus, I gladly scooped up shares of the Fairfield, Connecticut, giant at $57.38 on January 1, 1991. By the end of 1997, the shares had averaged compound annual gains of 28.79 percent. A $10,000 investment at the beginning of 1991 would have grown to $58,777 by the end of 1997.

The main reason for the phenomenal increase (see Figure 5.9) is that I was able to buy a fantastic company while it was temporarily suffering from a short-term problem. Of course, General Electric is no ordinary company. And its larger-than-life Jack Welch is no ordinary CEO. Calling upon his extraordinary energy and legendary toughness and problem-solving abilities, Welch created a new kind of company, one that infused the speed, hunger, and urgency of a

FIGURE 5.9

General Electric, 1991–1997

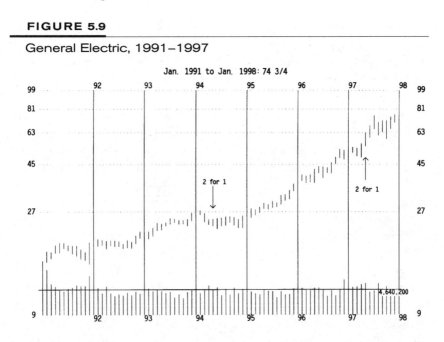

Jan. 1991 to Jan. 1998: 74 3/4

small company into a corporate colossus. Despite an increasingly competitive global environment for its products and services, GE's partnership with Welch has resulted in one of the best investments of the 1990s.

The company is one of the largest and most diversified industrial complexes in the world. Its businesses include jet aircraft engines, home appliances, television broadcasting, lighting, industrial materials such as plastics, power generation, medical systems, and computer services. GE Capital Services, which offers consumer and specialized financing and property and casualty reinsurance, also provides $19 billion in revenues. The conglomerate is among the world's 10 largest industrial firms, with a market value of $120 billion, the highest-valued company in America.

What makes Welch so unique is his corporate focus on people to bring out the ingenuity and energies of GE personnel. He's pushing the corporate envelope into the next century by focusing on fast-growing emerging global markets, new products, and quality improvements in the manufacturing and services divisions. GE has been building plants, forming joint ventures, and making acquisitions outside the United States as it moves to globalize its business. Welch is also speeding up new product development, to help expand the market shares of business segments. He hopes to improve margins by cutting waste and increasing yields.

GE is approaching its longstanding goal of having each of its segments be a leader in its industry. The National Broadcasting Company (NBC) enjoyed its most profitable period ever, with strong ratings leading to higher advertising revenues. NBC televised the 1996 Summer Olympic Games to a record U.S. audience of 209 million viewers, an achievement that positioned the network for strong ratings not only for its new fall schedule, but also for its upcoming broadcasts of the 2000 through 2008 Olympics. NBC also launched MSNBC, a 24-hour news and information channel that is currently distributed to 24 million cable households.

GE's aircraft engines segment continued its strong market position by winning more than half the world's orders for commercial aircraft engines in 1996. Its lighting business developed a global presence, and its plastics unit achieved record growth by supplying the computer and consumer electronics industries. In addition, GE's home appliance business made a serious bid to replace Whirlpool as the manufacturer of Sears' Kenmore brand.

Meanwhile, GE Capital Services continued its expansion into the market for insurance and annuity products with the acquisition of First Colony; the company also expanded its auto leasing operations in acquiring Marubeni Systems in Japan. GE may be spread across several industries and continents, but the company is bucking the trend toward downsizing and spin-offs. The company has declared that it wants to get bigger, and that its only spin-off will be lots of cash.

General Electric was incorporated in 1892 in New York, the result of a merger between the Thomson-Houston Company and the Edison General Electric Company. Charles Coffin was GE's first president, and light bulb inventor Thomas Edison, who left the company in 1894, was one of its directors. GE's financial strength and focus on research led to the company's success. Products included elevators, trolleys, motors, light bulbs, and toasters and other appliances under the GE and Hotpoint labels. In the 1920s, holding 1.2 million shares of Radio Corporation of America (RCA), GE joined AT&T and Westinghouse in a radio broadcasting joint venture. Sales had climbed to $337 million by the end of the Roaring

Twenties, but GE was forced to sell off its RCA holdings in 1930 because of an antitrust ruling. Fifty-six years later, GE acquired RCA, which also owned NBC, for $6.4 billion.

From 1940 to 1952 annual sales increased sixfold. GE entered the computer industry in 1956 but sold the business in 1970 to Honeywell because of operating losses. By 1980, GE's revenues had reached $25 billion from sales of plastics, consumer electronics, nuclear reactors, and jet engines. Between 1980 and 1989, GE sold operations that accounted for 25 percent of its 1980 sales and focused on such high-performance ventures as medical equipment, financial services, and industrial plastics and ceramics.

During the early 1990s, GE expanded its lighting business, entering the European and Japanese markets through acquisitions. The company bought mutual fund wholesaler GNA in 1993 for $525 million and gained SEC permission for GE Investment Management, which runs GE's pension assets, to sell mutual funds to the public. GE sold scandal-plagued Kidder Peabody to Paine Webber in 1994 for a package valued at $670 million.

While GE agreed to sell its struggling GEnie online service in 1996, NBC and software giant Microsoft formed MSNBC. That year GE and United Technologies' Pratt & Whitney subsidiary agreed to form a joint venture to build engines for a new Boeing jumbo jet. Looking ahead toward the millennium, GE expected to sustain double-digit growth by moving more into servicing services and globalizing its business. Indeed, most of GE's businesses are forging ahead. As if to highlight the point, GE's board of directors approved an additional $6 billion share repurchase in 1997 after buying back 292 million shares since 1991.

General Electric is a company intent on getting bigger, not smaller. A company with a legendary past—it's the only surviving original member of the Dow Jones Industrial Average—General Electric looks like it will continue to hum powerfully ahead into the future.

For GE's annual report, call 203-373-2211 or visit the World Wide Web at: http://www.ge.com.

INTERNATIONAL BUSINESS MACHINES (IBM)

Value of $10,000 Invested on January 1, 1993: $43,839 as of
December 31, 1997
(assumes annual reinvestment of dividends at year-end prices)

January 1	1993	1994	1995	1996	1997	1998
Price	$50.38	$56.50	$73.50	$91.38	$151.50	$104.63
Dividends	1.58	1.00	1.00	1.30	0.77	
Shares reinvested	5	2	2	1	3	
Year-end shares	203	205	207	208	419	
Splits					2-1	

Would Big Blue survive?

Those were the kinds of questions being asked about IBM when I recommended it on January 1, 1993 (see Figure 5.10). After all, the shares had plunged nearly 55 percent in the two previous years, setting lows not seen since 1975. Prospects couldn't have been worse for the one-time king of Wall Street. Its main market was eroding far faster than the company anticipated. Customers were turning away in droves from IBM's expensive mainframe systems for less costly platforms from its competitors. Pricing pressures for all the company's products were expected to continue because manufacturers were cutting prices just to maintain their share of the market.

I remember IBM as being one of the most difficult stock recommendations I ever made because of the incredible negative events for the once-proud corporation. It took a real leap of faith in benchmark investing for me to tell people I was recommending the stock after we'd seen it drop from international prominence as the world's largest supplier of technology to almost an afterthought on Wall Street. Heads would turn scornfully when I said to buy IBM. "You're kidding, aren't you?" was a normal reply. People thought I was off my rocker on this call, and I wasn't so sure they weren't right. But I stuck to my guns, knowing also that IBM was trading at 57 cents on the dollar according to its cashflow valuation. Now I look back upon that call with subdued pride, because IBM turned around with a surprising vengeance. By the end of 1997, the stock had quadrupled. In just five

FIGURE 5.10

International Business Machines, 1993–1997

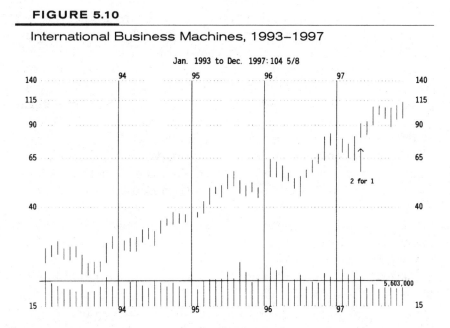

Jan. 1993 to Dec. 1997: 104 5/8

years, $10,000 invested would have grown to $43,839, while a similiar investment in the Dow would have risen to just $26,761 during that same period.

Four months after I began recommending the company, IBM named former RJR Nabisco head Louis Gerstner, Jr., as chairman and chief executive officer, the first leader of IBM who had not worked his way up through the ranks. No stranger to turmoil at RJR, Gerstner brought with him a fresh vision as the company began a remarkable turnaround. He immediately increased the independence of his individual business units, and jettisoned those that showed little promise. He cut over 100,000 jobs in four years and retired over 50 percent of IBM's long-term debt. In essence, Gerstner stabilized IBM first, then strengthened the company.

By 1995, IBM reported record revenues that topped $70 billion for the first time. Just as important, revenue growth rose 12 percent for the first time in more than a decade. That same year, IBM had $7.7 billion in cash after spending $5.7 billion to repurchase IBM stock and $2.9 billion to acquire Lotus. In just two years, Gerstner saw IBM's market value climb an incredible $27 billion.

IBM remains in a position to surprise Wall Street. Since rallying from its 1993 lows, the company now has four product cycles beginning early stages—PCs, UNIX servers and workstations, minicomputers, and mainframes. In other words, IBM is ready to continue to roar. Today, Big Blue retains its status as the world's largest supplier of advanced information processing technology and communication systems and services. It enjoyed record revenues of $78 billion in 1997, with foreign sales accounting for 48 percent.

The company has executed an impressive, though occasionally bumpy, turnaround since 1992, when it was losing billions of dollars. But major problems, such as excess staff, unused capacity, plants in expensive countries, and overpriced products, appear to be a thing of the past. After a 40 percent reduction in employment, IBM has also lowered costs by opening plants in low-cost countries such as Singapore, Australia, and Mexico.

To a large degree, IBM went through a trying period following the enormous success of its 360 mainframe computer in 1970. The 360 generated billions of dollars in cash that remained unspent until the late 1970s, when a plant expansion program began. Just as IBM began its expensive growth phase, the market shifted toward the PC. If anything, the success of its initial PC entry in 1981 lulled IBM into the belief that it could cope with rapidly evolving technology. Management reacted slowly to excess staff levels beginning in 1986, and was unwilling to cut capital spending plans. IBM began to seriously change after 1989, beginning with employee reductions and attempting to segment its many business into self-dependent entities. Division heads were required to think like independent, profit-conscious businesspeople.

Today, things are much rosier. International Business Machines is the world's largest provider of computer hardware, software, and services. Only a few years ago analysts made dire forecasts for IBM's mainframe and midrange computers. But with customers such as airlines, insurance companies, and banks depending on mainframes, and with the booming Internet business calling on "big servers," that segment has surprised skeptics.

Software is another stable revenue source for IBM. Its $12.7 billion in 1995 revenue ranked it ahead of IBM's PC business and dwarfed its mainframe business. More important, its 65 percent gross margins were miles ahead of any other segment. And software represents a growth opportunity for the future. But most of IBM's software sales involve programs for the company's larger main-frame and minicomputer (AS/400) systems. Sixty-seven percent of its revenues come from monthly license fees on operating systems. Highly profitable, these license fees represent a steady stream of income and earnings. And they increase as customers upgrade their systems. Now IBM wants to be a player in the enterprise software market. To further that end, it acquired spreadsheet publisher Lotus in 1995 and systems management software maker Tivoli Systems a year later.

IBM deemphasized the high-competition, low-margin PC and storage markets. And, with its OS/2 operating system a disappointment, it is looking to the interdependent areas of big computers, semiconductors, software, and service for momentum.

Big Blue, so-called after the color of its corporate logo, led America into the computer age. For many years, IBM was *the* computer industry. The company incorporated on June 16, 1911, when Charles Flint formed the Computing-Tabulating-Recording Company. In 1914, Flint recruited National Cash Register's star salesman, 40-year-old Thomas Watson, to rescue the flagging business. Watson aggressively marketed C-T-R's Hollerith machine, a punch-card tabulator, and supplied tabulators to the U.S. government during World War I, tripling C-T-R's revenues to almost $15 million by 1920. Watson changed the name to International Business Machines on February 14, 1924. The company soon dominated the global market for tabulators, time clocks, and electric typewriters. Sales totaled $7.6 million in 1928, almost as much as now-defunct Nash earned that same year. IBM had become the largest office machine firm in America by 1940, with sales approaching $50 million.

IBM initially dismissed the potential of computers. Meanwhile, competitors were conducting research on electronic computing devices. When Remington Rand's UNIVAC began replacing IBM machines, IBM quickly responded under the leadership of Thomas Watson, Jr., who predicted that the future belonged to computers and introduced the 701, the first of several generations of IBM computers that would dominate the marketplace for the next 20 years. Using its superior R&D and marketing, IBM built a market share near 80 percent in the 1960s and 1970s.

The introduction of the IBM PC in 1981 kick-started the personal computer industry with its barrage of PC clones. The shift to smaller, open systems, along with greater competition in all of IBM's segments, caused wrenching change. After posting profits of $6.6 billion in 1984, IBM began a slow slide.

IBM acquired Lotus for $3.5 billion in 1995, with the aim of using its marketing prowess to make Lotus Notes the application of choice for tying far-flung networks together. In early 1996, the company agreed to acquire Tivoli Systems for $743 million to fill a void in its software strategy. After investing an estimated $1.2 billion, IBM and remaining partner Sears sold Prodigy to management and investors for $250 million. The company said it would participate with 10 banks to offer home banking services in 1997 in a joint venture tentatively called INET.

IBM's potential lies in the fact that its installed base of hardware and services alerts management to opportunities for novel uses of its products. The company boasted more U.S. patents than any other corporation in 1997, grabbing the top spot for the fifth consecutive year in an area dominated by Japanese businesses. And with four new product cycles just beginning, IBM should be in a position to give investors more revenue growth. Finally, the company has used its cashflow to buy back more than 60 million shares since 1994. Note, too, that the company's board of directors authorized another $3.5 billion stock buyback in 1997, all the more reason to continue holding the shares bought in 1993 when all looked bleak.

For IBM's annual report, call 914-765-1900. IBM's Internet address is: http://www.ibm.com.

MERCK (MRK)

Value of $10,000 Invested on January 1, 1994: $32,966 as of December 31, 1997
(assumes annual reinvestment of dividends at year-end prices)

January 1	1994	1995	1996	1997	1998
Price	$34.38	$38.13	$65.63	$79.63	$106.00
Dividends	1.03	1.14	1.24	1.74	
Shares reinvested	7	5	4	5	
Year-end shares	297	302	306	311	
Splits				2-1	

At the time I first recommended Merck in 1994, it was trading just above its downside price target after falling 38.62 percent in the previous two years thanks to President Clinton's efforts to curb drug company profits (see Figure 5.11).

This highlights the validity of having a long-term perspective when it comes to investing, because no one should buy a stock for the short run. I'm constantly amazed at people who worry about what a stock does in the first few months they own it. Whether the price rises, falls, or remains flat, investors should be far more concerned about the long-term prospects of the stock.

With that longer-term mind-set, I was able to look beyond the pain that had been inflicted on the Merck stock, realizing that the company had one of the most productive R&D programs in the industry and that it had a very broad product line, with an amazing 19 drugs contributing more than $100 million each. Merck also had two billion-dollar sellers in Vasotec and Mevacor, along with approval for additional indications and more potential blockbuster drugs in the final stages of FDA testing. So, even though Merck had

FIGURE 5.11

Merck & Co., 1994–1997

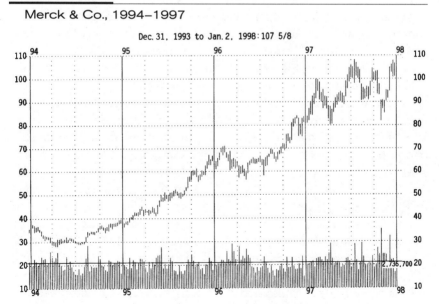

Dec. 31, 1993 to Jan. 2, 1998 : 107 5/8

back-to-back miserable years, it's important to note that spectacular returns were the result of its willingness to focus on the long term. Merck rewarded investors with 34.75 percent compound annual returns from 1994 to the end of 1997, while the Dow posted a 23.05 percent return.

Headquartered in Whitehouse Station, New Jersey, Merck has pledged to increase spending on research, concentrate on the managed-care market, and boost pharmaceutical production in an effort to retain its top position without needing a merger. Merck's products include antibiotics, anti-inflammatories, asthma treatments, cardiovascular drugs, endocrinologic medications, ophthalmic products, ulcer medicines, and vaccines. Its Vasotec hypertension and heart failure drug is the number one cardiovascular medication in the world, while Zocor outsells all other drugs used to lower cholesterol levels. Products in development include Singulair (for asthma), Maxalt (for migraine headaches), and Propecia (for baldness). Merck's Medco unit provides pharmacy benefit management for employer health plans. In a move that chairman Raymond Gilmartin called "one of Merck's greatest accomplishments," the company announced the release of its Crixivan AIDS drug in 1996.

Merck was started in 1887, when chemist Theodore Weicker came to America from Germany to set up an American branch of E. Merck AG of Germany. George Merck, grandson of the German company's founder, emigrated in 1891 and entered a partnership with Weicker. At first the firm imported and sold drugs and chemicals from Germany, but in 1903 it opened a plant in Rahway, New Jersey, to manufacture alkaloids. Weicker sold out to Merck in 1904 and bought a controlling interest in competitor Squibb. During World War I, Merck gave the U.S. government the 80 percent of company stock owned by family in Germany (George kept his shares). After the war, the stock was sold to the public.

In 1927, Merck merged with Powers-Weightman-Rosengarten of Philadelphia, a producer of the antimalarial quinine. At its first research lab, established in 1933, Merck scientists did pioneering work on vitamin B-12 and developed cortisone, the first steroid, in 1944. Five Merck scientists received Nobel prizes in the 1940s and 1950s. In 1953, Merck merged with pharmaceuticals producer Sharp & Dohme of Philadelphia, which brought with it a strong salesforce. Merck introduced the antihypertensive drug Diuril in 1958 and other drugs in the early 1960s, but for nearly 10 years there were few new drugs. John Horan, who took over as CEO in 1976, accelerated research and development to create new products.

Biochemist Roy Vagelos, who became CEO in 1985, continued the commitment to R&D. Merck introduced 10 major new drugs in the 1980s, including Mevacor for high cholesterol and Vasotec for high blood pressure. In 1993, Merck bought Medco Containment Services and instantly became one of the best-positioned, vertically integrated companies in the rapidly evolving health care industry, with access to information from a network of more than 40,000 drugstores. To attract more customers, in 1991 Medco introduced its Prescriber's Choice program, which informed doctors of generic or other less expensive equivalents of prescribed drugs. In 1994, Merck established subsidiaries in Cyprus, Germany, Holland, Peru, and South Korea and began a joint venture in China to make and sell its products. In 1995 and early 1996, Merck began marketing eight new drugs, including Cozaar (for reducing hypertension), Varivax, and Pepcid AC. Crivixan was already the leading protease inhibitor used in AIDS therapy by 1997, and Fosamax saw its potential double when it received FDA approval to be used as a preventive treatment for osteoporosis.

For Merck's annual report, call 908/423-1000. Merck's Internet address is: http://www.merck.com.

PHILIP MORRIS COMPANIES, INC. (MO)

Value of $10,000 Invested on January 1, 1994: $28,371 as of December 31, 1997
(assumes annual reinvestment of dividends at year-end prices)

January 1	1994	1995	1996	1997	1998
Price	$55.63	$57.50	$90.25	$113.00	$45.25
Dividends	2.86	3.48	4.41	1.60	
Shares reinvested	8	7	7	21	
Year-end shares	187	195	202	627	
Splits				3-1	

Benchmark investing's formula sniffed a bargain at the beginning of 1994 with Philip Morris shares trading at $55.63 (see Figure 5.12). In fact, the formula projected that the shares could climb as high as

FIGURE 5.12

Philip Morris, 1994–1997

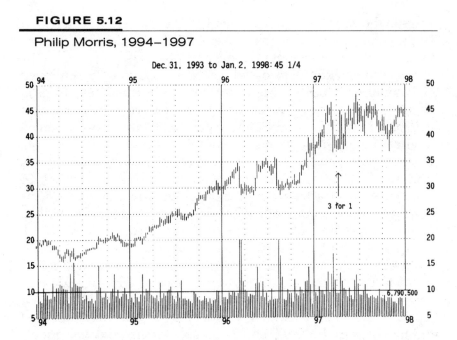

$80.52 over the next 12 months, nearly 45 percent higher without even considering the company's hefty annual dividend. Further, Buffett's benchmark indicated that Philip Morris was trading at 69 cents on the dollar. As a result, I recommended buying the most successful and profitable cigarette company in the world on January 1, 1994. Since that recommendation, Philip Morris more than doubled while averaging 29.78 percent compound annual gains. In just four years, a $10,000 investment would have climbed to $28,371.

Once again I had found a stock that investors were shying away from in large part because of their shortsighted focus on temporary problems. Ignoring the company's improving bottom line and its $2.5 billion in free cashflow, investors instead were worried that the Food and Drug Administration might classify nicotine as a drug. As a result, the stock was a great bargain at $55.63, with even more potential heading into the long term. Meanwhile, by lowering prices temporarily, Marlboro, its flagship brand of cigarettes, had quickly won back its top market share position after losing ground to generics a year earlier. By the fourth quarter of 1994, the company's entire cigarette line achieved record market shares in the United States.

A pair of important legal events took place in 1995. First, a West Virginia judge struck down 8 of 10 claims in the state's suit against the tobacco industry. At the same time, the Florida legislature voted in favor of repealing legislation that helped the state sue the tobacco industry for the cost of treating smoking-related illnesses. By early 1996, Philip Morris was on a roll in spite of the ever-present threat of tobacco litigation. International cigarette sales were enjoying double-digit gains. Its General Foods division continued to be a reliable profit generator, with a new focus on higher-margined products and cost cutting.

During the summer of 1997, the Clinton White House, state attorneys general, and the tobacco industry agreed upon a $368.5 billion settlement to be paid over 25 years. But the deal could take several years, if it happens at all. And of all the tobacco companies, Philip Morris probably has the most to gain from a settlement, despite the fact that the company would have to pay roughly half the settlement because of its market dominance.

Famous for the world's best-selling Marlboro cigarette, the company also markets a wide variety of powerful premium brands. Its Kraft food division sells such leading brands as Oscar Mayer, Jell-O, and Post cereals along with Philadelphia cream cheese, Maxwell House coffee, Tang, Kool Aid, Raisin Bran, and Tombstone pizza. It is the largest and most diversified food and beverage company in America. Moreover, its Miller Brewing Company is the second largest beer maker in America. Quite simply, Philip Morris is one of the richest and best-run companies in the world. The conglomerate's worldwide sales topped $69 billion in 1996 and climbed above $72 billion in 1997.

Philip Morris opened his London tobacco store in 1847. His heirs sold the company to William Thomson at the turn of the century. In 1902, Thomson introduced his company's cigarettes to the American marketplace. American investors purchased the rights to leading Philip Morris brands in 1919 and 10 years later began manufacturing cigarettes in Richmond, Virginia. Philip Morris & Company was incorporated on August 17, 1926, after acquiring Continental Tobacco Company. When the original members of the old Tobacco Trust raised their prices in 1930, Philip Morris countered by introducing inexpensive cigarettes popular with Depression-weary consumers. A popular ad campaign in 1933 featured bellhop Johnny Roventini chanting the slogan "Call for Philip Morris."

The company acquired Benson & Hedges and its president, Joseph Cullman III, in 1954. Cullman enlisted advertiser Leo Burnett, who created the hugely successful Marlboro Man. Under Cullman, Philip Morris experienced tremendous overseas expansion. In 1970, Philip Morris purchased Miller Brewing Company. With its typical aggressive marketing of Lite beer, Miller vaulted to the second spot among the world's beer makers by 1980.

Philip Morris paid $5.7 billion in 1986 for food and coffee giant General Foods, a member of the Dow Industrial index at the time of its takeover. In 1988, Philip Morris purchased Kraft for a staggering $13 billion. In 1990, the company strengthened its European position by acquiring Swiss-based coffee and confectionary company Jacobs Suchard AG for $4.1 billion. Three years later, Philip Morris bought out RJR Nabisco's North American cold cereal operation. It also bought a 20 percent interest in Molson, Canada's largest brewer, and all of Molson Breweries USA.

Also in 1993, Philip Morris cut the price on Marlboro cigarettes by 40 cents a pack to fend off low-priced competitors. The cut caused a 46 percent drop in domestic tobacco profits but boosted market share in the United States for Philip Morris brands. Amid price pressures and political attacks, CEO Michael Miles—the first nontobacco man in company history to be named chairman and CEO—stepped down in mid-1994, shortly after the board rejected a proposal to split Philip Morris into separate tobacco and food companies.

New CEO Geoffrey Bible led challenges in 1995 to the Environmental Protection Agency's findings on secondhand smoke as well as to smoking regulations in Florida and San Francisco. That summer, the company settled a $10 billion libel suit it had filed against Capital Cities/ABC over an ABC news story. In May 1996 the Castona case, which sought class-action status in order to recoup the cost of damages allegedly involving cigarettes, was decertified by a court of appeals in Florida. However, Philip Morris will continue to be sensitive to legal matters concerning tobacco.

In August 1996, Philip Morris was one of the most feared stocks in America. Legal matters were choking the tobacco business. A Florida jury had handed down a devastating verdict against Brown & Williamson Tobacco Company, causing related stocks to tumble. And the number of states suing the industry to recoup Medicaid money spent on treating smoke-related illnesses was gradually building. Investors panicked. Philip Morris shares dropped to 52-week lows. But four months later, the stock climbed 30 percent to new all-time highs on the heels of news that antismoking crusader David Kessler had announced his resignation from the Food and Drug Administration.

While the company appears headed toward continued prosperity, legal challenges will continue for the tobacco industry. Philip Morris enjoys powerful premium-name companies in new and established markets around the globe. What's more, the company is building on its already extensive global infrastructure to attempt to reach its two stated goals of increasing earnings by growing its business and significantly improving the price of the stock.

The company has used its considerable cashflow to buy back over 100 million shares since the beginning of 1990. It bought back $3 billion worth in 1997 alone.

Soon after Geoffrey Bible took over the reins of the company—following Michael Miles' unsuccessful attempt to split the food and tobacco businesses—the company's profit margins and market share points began to rise to former levels, thanks to aggressive marketing. In addition, Bible nearly doubled share buybacks to $2.1 billion a year. When considering the use of cashflow, Bible aimed to strike a balance between investing in the future growth of the company and taking steps to improve immediate returns. The company also aggressively increased dividends by double-digit rates in 1995, 1996, and 1997, thereby improving shareholder value significantly.

Benchmark investing may have been a year early on Philip Morris, given its below-par 8.50 percent first-year total return. However, subsequent years paid off enormously for the patient benchmark investor. This highlights the risk that benchmark investors must be willing to take whenever they invest in companies that are struggling at low valuations for one reason or another.

For the Philip Morris annual report, call 212-880-5000. At present, Philip Morris does not have an Internet address.

SEARS, ROEBUCK & COMPANY (S)

Value of $10,000 Invested on January 1, 1991: $38,962 as of
December 31, 1997
(assumes annual reinvestment of dividends at year-end prices)

January 1	1991	1992	1993	1994	1995	1996	1997	1998
Price	$25.38	$37.88	$45.50	$57.00	$46.00	$39.00	46.00	$45.25
Dividends	2.00	2.00	1.70	1.60	31.67	0.92	0.92	
Shares reinvested	20	18	13	15	372	16	17	
Year-end shares	414	432	444	459	831	847	864	
Spin-offs					.927035 shares of Allstate			

When I recommended Sears at the beginning of 1991, the stock had
frustrated Wall Street by posting losses in three of the four previous
years (see Figure 5.13). After hitting a high of $59.50 in 1987, Sears had
drifted as low as $22.00 in the fourth quarter of 1990. Talk about your
unloved and unwanted companies. On top of that, America was ex-
pecting a recession in 1991. So why did I buy Sears at that time?

FIGURE 5.13

Sears Roebuck, 1991–1997

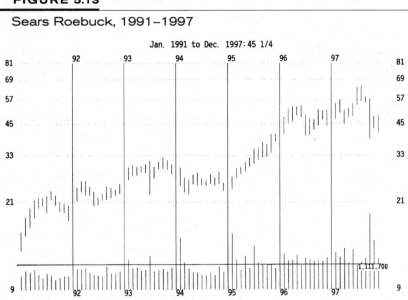

Jan. 1991 to Dec. 1997: 45 1/4

To me, Sears was a bargain just waiting to be plucked. While Wall Street was focusing on substantial catastrophe-related losses at Allstate and lower profits at Coldwell Banker—two noncore Sears businesses that were later jettisoned—I was looking at a stock that was trading below its downside price target and trading at a discount to its intrinsic value. Investors were handsomely rewarded by Sears in 1991, when the stock jumped up 57.13 percent. And for those who held on to the world's second-largest retailer until the end of 1997, the stock averaged 21.50 percent per year. During that same time span, the Dow Industrials rose only 19.89 percent.

As simple as it sounds, that's all you have to do to be successful as a benchmark investor. If you can calculate the raw data for relative ROE ratios and complete a handful of simple math steps, you can determine whether a company is trading at distressed levels. You don't have to be an analyst. No, let *Value Line*'s well-respected analysts do the numbers for you. Then, once you've found what appears to be a bargain, look at the company's cashflow valuation as Warren Buffett does.

If the company still appears to be cheap, notice what benchmark investing's formula projects two to four years out. By this time, if you still find the stock to be cheap, buy it and hold on regardless of whether it rises sharply or falls in the short run. That's really the hardest part of being a value investor: believing in yourself while ignoring the noise—good and bad—from Wall Street.

Sears embarked on an incredible resurgence in 1991 after the company began reducing costs and increasing its share of the retail trade by implementing its everyday-low-pricing policy. At the same time, Allstate posted high income gains in 1991 and benefited from lower catastrophe losses. Dean Witter also enjoyed big gains, thanks to lower interest rates and a strong stock market. Sears would later sell 20 percent of Dean Witter in an initial public offering, and the rest of the brokerage firm was spun off as a special dividend in 1993.

Coldwell Banker was also sold, and Sears' famous catalog operations were shut down in 1993 as the company continued to downsize and deleverage its balance sheet. Sears completed most of its divesting program in mid-1995, when it spun off Allstate to shareholders via a special tax-free dividend. At the same time, Arthur Martinez assumed the responsibilities of chairman and CEO after serving as the head of Sears' merchandising group. In four years, the company had positioned itself for the long run to concentrate on its primary business of retailing its core products such as Craftsman, Die Hard, and Kenmore as well as apparel.

Today, Sears is the world's second largest retailer, operating HomeLife, Sears, Western Auto, and other retail outlets. The company operates over 2300 department stores and specialty stores in the United States. Sears also has 161 stores in Canada and Mexico. Its credit operations, with more than 26 million active charge card holders, represent more than $3 billion in revenues, comprising about 60 percent of Sears' earnings power.

In 1886 Richard W. Sears, a railway agent in Minnesota, bought a shipment of watches being returned to the maker. He started the R. W. Sears Watch Company six months later, moved to Chicago, and in 1887 hired watchmaker Alvah C. Roebuck. Sears sold the watch business in 1889 and two years later formed another mail-order business that became Sears, Roebuck, and Company in 1893. The company issued its first general catalog in 1896, offering low prices and money-back guarantees to the farmers who were the principal customers of Sears.

Sears, Roebuck & Company was incorporated in New York on June 16, 1906, after succeeding an Illinois company of the same name. Anticipating the changes that the automobile would bring to rural life, Sears opened its first retail store in 1924—in my hometown of Evansville, Indiana—so that farmers could drive to town to buy merchandise. In 1925, Sears brought out a line of tires. By 1940, Sears was the nation's largest mail-order house with sales of $617 million. Its business was supplemented by a chain of 488 retail general merchandise stores.

After struggling through the high interest rates and low growth of the late 1970s, Sears decided to diversify into financial services and in 1981 acquired real estate firm Coldwell Banker and investment firm Dean Witter Reynolds. Under the Dean Witter umbrella, Sears launched the Discover card in 1985. As with American Express and General Electric, the financial operations never created any synergy for Sears and detracted from its core business.

In reaction to falling market share in the 1980s, Sears lurched from retail strategy to retail strategy, diversifying into auto supplies and repairs and neglecting its department stores. For example, the company cofounded the Prodigy online service in 1984 with IBM and CBS.

After retiring in 1995, CEO Edward Brennan was replaced by Martinez, chairman and CEO of Sears' merchandising group. Sears sold its 50 percent interest in Internet provider Prodigy Services Company in 1996.

More important, however, Sears was simply a retailer for the first time since 1931. The Chicago-based company had shed much of its weight, including its catalog division, Allstate Insurance, Dean Witter and Discover card, Homart shopping center developers, on-line service Prodigy, and the Sears Tower. Today Sears focuses on its core retail operations, a network of more than 800 mall-based department stores and 1500 freestanding stores. In the process of downsizing, Sears shut 113 stores and cut 50,000 jobs.

Hoping to lure consumers to "the softer side of Sears," the nation's number-two retailer has restructured its Home Group, moving its household merchandise out of mall-based stores and into its freestanding Homelife and Sears Hardware stores to make room for more apparel and accessories.

Over the next three years, Sears intends to build its apparel business from about 28 percent of store sales to 40 percent. The development of a high-quality private-label program is a top priority as a means to communicate a strong price-value image to Sears' customers. The company's commitment to its retail operations is paying off. With a concentration on apparel sales, same-store sales are climbing.

Sears currently operates more than 2600 fast-growing specialty stores that sell tires, hardware, automotive products, and home furnishings. Specialty sales are expected to emerge as Sears' growth engine in the future. As a result, the market has recognized Sears' favorable long-term prospects and is trading at premium levels that would prevent a serious benchmark investor from buying.

For the Sears annual report, call 847-286-2500. Sears' Internet address is: http://www.sears.com.

CHAPTER 6

Benchmark Investing's Long-Term Results: 1973-1996

Order and simplification are the first steps toward the mastery of a subject.

Thomas Mann

People are captivated by exciting new concepts on Wall Street. Who can resist the sizzle of a red-hot initial public offering like a Planet Hollywood trading at 100 times earnings, especially compared with a down-and-out Dow stock that's fallen on hard times? It happens all the time. For instance, in 1990 investors shied away from financial stocks like American Express. In 1992, they fled from Merck and other pharmaceuticals that were under attack by the Clintons. History has clearly shown, however, that investing in undervalued Dow stocks has provided superior results even during the worst markets.

Had investors bought only those undervalued Dow stocks identified by my benchmark investing method at the beginning of each year from 1973 until the end of 1996, they would have beaten the Dow in 23 out of those 24 years. On a cumulative basis, their returns would have been 17.5 times greater than the Dow's gains during that period.

The following analysis is what prompted me to go forward with testing benchmark investing. It's a coherent, understandable strategy that anyone can duplicate. The criteria for stock selection were simple: (1) the stock had to be trading at or below its historical downside target price; and (2) its year-to-year projected earnings gains had to be higher than 10 percent. It's interesting to note that benchmark investing's overall return would have been enhanced had I forgone the second criterion. However, I feel strongly that conservation of capital takes priority over gains, just as Benjamin Graham did. And in certain cases, the year-over-year bogey would have prevented regrettable losses. That's why I include it in all my investment considerations.

Benchmark investing is a mechanism that will help investors rein in their emotions so that they can begin investing on an objective basis. And it's no fluke. After all, I purposely began my back-testing in the bear market of 1973–1974, when the Dow lost 40 percent of its value. Although benchmark investors also would have lost money during that period, their losses would have amounted to only 8.35 percent.

Benchmark investing has been explicitly stated, historically tested, and rigorously implemented. This discipline will never deviate, much less go through a midlife breakdown or emotional crisis. Therefore, style drift is impossible with benchmark investing. Knowing how a stock selection strategy performs historically helps you understand, estimate, and control risk and return when planning your portfolio.

Multiyear performance results are vital to making informed investment decisions. Any strategy can work for a few quarters or even for a few years. Yet vulnerable strategies rarely do well for long. After they've enjoyed a profitable cycle, they almost always fall apart. But decades of profitable returns provide you with statistically reliable base rates for a strategy. Base rates are just like batting averages. They tell you what to expect from a strategy.

Benchmark investing's long-term results—which you can duplicate on your own—can help you form realistic expectations about anticipated performance. The results provide you with a framework for understanding *how* and when a strategy beats the market. For example, benchmark investing really has shined during subpar years for the Dow. Benchmark investing's best relative performance occurred in 1984, when it beat the Dow by 16.16 percent to 1.08 percent. In 1987, benchmark investing picked only one stock in a broadly overvalued market, but it gained 47.09 percent compared with the Dow's 6.02 percent gain.

Knowing that benchmark investing will probably shine during substandard years for the market, investors can have confidence in and stick with the strategy when it doesn't beat the Dow. In 1989, the

Dow beat benchmark investing 31.71 to 21.03 percent, but when the Dow lost 0.57 percent the next year benchmark investing clobbered the index with a 15.63 percent total return. This is particularly important when a strategy is underperforming the market and your emotions misguide you toward abandoning a system at exactly the wrong time.

Another interesting phenomenon of benchmark investing is that it rarely led to investing in the best-performing stock in a given year, and yet it still wildly outperformed the Dow with its consistent winners (see Table 6.1). The top Dow stock was a benchmark recommendation in only 11 of the 24 years in the period. More important, the strategy had several picks that lost, but none were ever the worst-performing Dow stock in any given year (see Table 6.2).

I would be remiss if I did not point out some of the huge winners that benchmark investing missed. For example, much to my regret, benchmark investing did not recommend Goodyear Tire in 1991, when it turned in a whopping 185.49 percent annual total return. Nor did my strategy select Allied Chemical in 1979, when it gained 80.07 percent, but it *did* recommend the renamed Allied Corp. in 1983, when it gained 79.61 percent.

Tables 6.3 through 6.50 list the top annual performing stocks in the Dow from 1973 to 1996. Benchmark investing's recommendations are denoted in **boldface** type.

TABLE 6.1

Benchmark Investing's Top Selections

Benchmark Picks	Year	Percent Gain	DJIA's Return
Woolworth	1975	147.33%	44.40%
Chrysler	1976	104.15%	22.72%
Sears	1982	95.23%	25.79%
General Motors	1975	95.22%	44.40%
Chevron	1980	82.87%	21.41%
United Technologies	1976	78.01%	22.72%
IBM	1996	67.21%	28.57%

TABLE 6.2

The Dow's Best and Worst Performers: 1973–1996

Year	Best Dow Stock	% Return	Worst Dow Stock	% Return
1973	Allied Chemical*	83.41%	Disney	−60.03%
1974	United Aircraft[†]	73.41%	Westinghouse	−56.73%
1975	Woolworth	147.33%	Merck	6.41%
1976	United Technologies	72.73%	Eastman Kodak	−17.01%
1977	Allied Chemical	15.86%	Bethlehem Steel	−43.96%
1978	Minnesota Mining	34.29%	Allied	−32.01%
1979	Allied Chemical	80.07%	Coca-Cola	−16.92%
1980	Standard Oil (Cal.)**	82.88%	Boeing	−10.08%
1981	AT&T	33.79%	Boeing	−45.85%
1982	Sears	95.20%	Caterpillar	−23.38%
1983	Allied Corp.*	79.61%	Disney	−14.90%
1984	Exxon	29.37%	Bethlehem Steel	−36.49%
1985	Union Carbide	102.08%	Bethlehem Steel	−9.00%
1986	Merck	82.93%	Bethlehem Steel	−60.00%
1987	Bethlehem Steel	168.00%	American Express	−56.95%
1988	Woolworth	54.52%	Eastman Kodak	−4.13%
1989	Coca-Cola	76.16%	Bethlehem Steel	−20.09%
1990	Philip Morris	27.87%	American Express	−38.00%
1991	Goodyear Tire	185.49%	Westinghouse	−31.93%
1992	Disney	50.89%	Westinghouse	−21.67%
1993	Caterpillar	67.07%	Woolworth	−37.48%
1994	Union Carbide	34.63%	Woolworth	−37.48%
1995	Merck	75.37%	Bethlehem Steel	−22.87%
1996	Woolworth	69.23%	Bethlehem Steel	−36.02%

* Allied Chemical and Allied Corp. are now named AlliedSignal.
** Standard Oil of California is now named Chevron.
† United Aircraft is now named United Technologies.

TABLE 6.3

Benchmark Investing's 1973 Dow Jones Industrial Monitor

DJIA Stocks	12/31/72 Price	Historical Market/ Book Low	High	ROE Ratio	1973 Book	Downside Target	Upside Target
Allied Chemical	$29.00	1.17	1.70	1.16	$29.45	$39.97	$58.08
Alcoa	$53.13	1.15	1.64	0.83	$39.24	$37.45	$53.41
American Brands	$42.13	1.56	2.13	1.00	$18.37	$28.66	$39.13
American Can	$31.63	1.03	1.45	0.95	$34.58	$33.84	$47.63
American Telephone	$52.75	1.14	1.43	1.08	$48.29	$59.45	$74.58
Anaconda	$19.50						
Bethlehem Steel	$29.38	0.61	0.85	1.30	$51.42	$40.78	$56.82
Chrysler	$41.00	0.77	1.30	0.93	$49.22	$35.25	$59.51
DuPont	$177.50	2.78	3.70	1.08	$70.02	$210.23	$279.80
Eastman Kodak	$148.38	5.43	7.62	1.00	$19.19	$104.20	$146.23
Exxon	$87.50	1.38	1.80	1.42	$29.58	$57.96	$75.61
General Electric	$72.88	3.07	4.21	1.15	$18.17	$64.15	$87.97
General Foods	$28.50	2.58	3.42	0.83	$15.81	$33.86	$44.88
General Motors	$81.13	2.24	2.94	1.08	$42.51	$102.84	$134.98
Goodyear Tire	$31.50	1.42	1.89	0.92	$23.46	$30.65	$40.79
International Harvester	$38.38	0.68	0.98	1.21	$46.21	$38.02	$54.80
International Nickel	$31.88	2.49	3.49	1.37	$16.35	$55.77	$78.17
International Paper	$41.88	1.24	1.70	1.49	$26.62	$49.18	$67.43
Johns-Manville	$31.25	1.22	1.81	1.09	$27.58	$36.68	$54.41
Owens-Illinois	$41.75	1.56	2.25	0.88	$22.82	$31.33	$45.18
Procter & Gamble	$111.50	3.23	4.58	1.03	$21.36	$71.06	$100.76
Sears	$116.00	2.88	3.82	1.00	$15.87	$45.71	$60.62
Standard Oil (Cal.)	$79.63	1.04	1.44	1.33	$33.22	$45.95	$63.62
Swift	$39.38	0.79	1.19	1.23	$28.52	$27.71	$41.74
Texaco	$37.50	1.50	2.01	1.13	$29.39	$49.82	$66.75
Union Carbide	$50.00	1.52	2.02	1.21	$34.56	$63.56	$84.47
United Aircraft	$44.50	0.89	1.93	1.08	$23.72	$22.80	$49.44
U.S. Steel	$30.50	0.56	0.78	1.41	$45.62	$36.02	$50.17
Westinghouse	$43.00	1.68	2.44	0.76	$22.36	$28.55	$41.46
Woolworth	$31.25	1.05	1.64	1.05	$29.54	$32.57	$50.87
DJIA	1020.01	1.68	2.35	1.10	31.48	1052.82	1474.73

TABLE 6.4

Benchmark Investing's 1974 Dow Jones Industrial Monitor

DJIA Stocks	12/31/73 Price	Historical Market/ Book Low	High	ROE Ratio	1974 Book	Downside Target	Upside Target
Allied Chemical	$49.00	1.14	1.70	1.60	$33.12	$60.41	$90.09
Alcoa	$48.50	1.11	1.61	1.28	$63.24	$89.85	$130.32
American Brands	$32.25	1.55	2.13	0.98	$19.69	$29.91	$41.10
American Can	$26.25	0.99	1.39	1.36	$38.91	$52.39	$73.56
American Telephone	$50.13	1.12	1.39	1.09	$50.16	$61.24	$76.00
Anaconda	$26.13						
Bethlehem Steel	$33.00	0.59	0.83	1.91	$57.03	$64.27	$90.41
Chrysler	$15.38	0.70	1.24	NMF	$44.08	$0.00	$0.00
DuPont	$159.00	2.68	3.59	0.71	$72.09	$137.17	$183.75
Eastman Kodak	$116.00	5.42	7.67	0.87	$21.12	$99.59	$140.93
Exxon	$94.13	1.38	1.79	1.52	$67.58	$141.76	$183.87
General Electric	$63.00	3.06	4.19	1.08	$19.89	$65.73	$90.01
General Foods	$23.75	2.42	3.21	0.68	$17.09	$28.12	$37.30
General Motors	$46.13	2.07	2.80	0.43	$41.93	$37.32	$50.48
Goodyear Tire	$15.25	1.29	1.81	0.75	$23.75	$22.98	$32.24
International Harvester	$25.75	0.66	0.96	1.22	$49.08	$39.52	$57.48
International Nickel	$35.25	2.37	3.32	1.55	$18.24	$67.00	$93.86
International Paper	$52.00	1.24	1.76	2.02	$29.08	$72.84	$103.39
Johns-Manville	$16.50	1.11	1.71	0.88	$30.04	$29.34	$45.20
Owens-Illinois	$30.88	1.41	2.05	0.93	$49.62	$65.07	$94.60
Procter & Gamble	$92.00	3.38	4.75	0.98	$23.15	$76.68	$107.76
Sears	$80.25	2.82	3.83	0.72	$33.10	$67.21	$91.28
Standard Oil (Cal.)	$35.00	1.01	1.43	1.33	$36.79	$49.42	$69.97
Swift	$24.88	0.76	1.18	1.49	$39.24	$44.44	$68.99
Texaco	$29.38	1.40	1.93	1.22	$32.90	$56.19	$77.47
Union Carbide	$34.13	1.43	1.95	1.82	$40.49	$105.38	$143.70
United Aircraft	$23.75	0.91	2.03	1.12	$24.10	$24.56	$54.79
U.S. Steel	$37.63	0.54	0.75	2.24	$79.77	$96.49	$134.01
Westinghouse	$25.38	1.59	2.39	0.14	$20.83	$4.64	$6.97
Woolworth	$18.38	0.98	1.57	0.71	$29.49	$20.52	$32.87
DJIA	850.86	1.66	2.35	1.17	37.91	1377.40	1949.94

TABLE 6.5

Benchmark Investing's 1975 Dow Jones Industrial Monitor

DJIA Stocks	12/31/74 Price	Historical Market/ Book Low	High	ROE Ratio	1975 Book	Downside Target	Upside Target
Allied Chemical	$28.38	1.09	1.69	1.13	$33.07	$40.73	$63.15
Alcoa	$29.88	1.05	1.56	0.45	$42.58	$20.12	$29.89
American Brands	$30.25	1.55	2.14	0.96	$21.99	$32.72	$45.18
American Can	$29.00	0.98	1.36	0.97	$41.93	$39.86	$55.31
American Telephone	$44.63	1.08	1.35	1.01	$51.43	$56.10	$70.12
Anaconda	$13.50						
Bethlehem Steel	$24.88	0.57	0.80	1.18	$59.82	$40.23	$56.47
Chrysler	$7.25	0.70	1.24	NMF*	$39.45	$0.00	$0.00
DuPont	$92.25	2.48	3.45	0.48	$73.41	$87.39	$121.57
Eastman Kodak	$62.88	4.99	7.34	0.80	$22.87	$91.30	$134.29
Esmark	**$27.88**	**0.73**	**1.14**	**1.75**	**$43.30**	**$55.32**	**$86.38**
Exxon	$64.63	1.31	1.74	1.06	$70.88	$98.42	$130.73
General Electric	$33.38	2.86	4.09	0.93	$21.72	$57.77	$82.62
General Foods	**$17.88**	**2.23**	**3.02**	**0.98**	**$18.95**	**$41.41**	**$56.08**
General Motors	**$30.75**	**1.87**	**2.57**	**0.56**	**$44.24**	**$46.33**	**$63.67**
Goodyear Tire	$12.88	1.19	1.68	0.77	$25.05	$22.95	$32.40
International Harvester	$19.75	0.62	0.92	0.68	$50.14	$21.14	$31.37
International Nickel	$21.50	2.19	3.17	0.85	$19.26	$35.85	$51.90
International Paper	$35.75	1.24	1.81	1.38	$32.01	$54.78	$79.95
Johns-Manville	$19.50	0.99	1.54	0.67	$30.81	$20.44	$31.79
Owens-Illinois	$33.75	1.30	1.89	0.91	$53.84	$63.69	$92.60
Procter & Gamble	$81.50	3.31	4.74	0.94	$25.27	$78.63	$112.59
Sears	$48.25	2.60	3.68	0.75	$33.40	$65.13	$92.18
Standard Oil (Cal.)	$22.25	0.94	1.37	1.02	$36.79	$35.27	$51.41
Texaco	$20.88	1.29	1.79	0.65	$38.16	$32.00	$44.40
Union Carbide	$41.38	1.34	1.84	1.11	$44.11	$65.61	$90.09
United Aircraft	$32.63	0.93	1.70	1.11	$27.22	$28.10	$51.36
U.S. Steel	$38.00	0.52	0.73	1.61	$85.92	$71.93	$100.98
Westinghouse	**$10.00**	**1.47**	**2.28**	**0.88**	**$21.88**	**$28.30**	**$43.90**
Woolworth	**$9.38**	**0.91**	**1.47**	**1.04**	**$31.36**	**$29.68**	**$47.94**
DJIA	616.24	1.56	2.21	0.95	39.34	1090.12	1552.22

TABLE 6.6

Benchmark Investing's 1976 Dow Jones Industrial Monitor

DJIA Stocks	12/31/75 Price	Historical Market/ Book		ROE Ratio	1976 Book	Downside Target	Upside Target
		Low	High				
Allied Chemical	$33.25	0.98	1.57	1.17	$35.83	$41.08	$65.82
Alcoa	$38.63	0.96	1.48	0.97	$45.31	$42.19	$65.05
American Brands	$38.63	1.56	2.17	0.79	$24.25	$29.89	$41.57
American Can	$31.38	0.92	1.26	1.16	$43.35	$46.26	$63.36
American Telephone	$50.88	1.01	1.27	1.14	$53.43	$61.52	$77.36
Anaconda	$17.13						
Bethlehem Steel	$32.88	0.52	0.76	0.78	$61.66	$25.01	$36.55
Chrysler	$10.13	0.72	1.33	1.28	$46.10	$42.49	$78.48
DuPont	$126.50	2.11	3.04	0.85	$77.61	$139.19	$200.54
Eastman Kodak	$106.13	4.63	6.87	0.81	$24.84	$93.16	$138.23
Esmark	$31.63	0.69	1.09	1.17	$33.43	$26.99	$42.63
Exxon	$88.75	1.21	1.66	1.02	$77.78	$96.00	$131.70
General Electric	$46.13	2.60	3.78	1.17	$22.78	$69.30	$100.75
General Foods	$27.63	1.94	2.72	1.07	$21.18	$43.97	$61.64
General Motors	$57.63	1.61	2.30	1.33	$48.79	$104.47	$149.25
Goodyear Tire	$21.75	1.06	1.54	0.59	$25.75	$16.10	$23.40
International Harvester	$22.38	0.57	0.86	1.63	$53.94	$50.12	$75.61
International Nickel	$25.25	1.98	2.91	0.89	$20.32	$35.81	$52.63
International Paper	$57.75	1.21	1.83	1.26	$36.99	$56.39	$85.29
Johns-Manville	$23.25	0.96	1.48	0.82	$31.37	$24.69	$38.07
Owens-Illinois	$51.88	1.14	1.68	0.97	$64.38	$71.19	$104.91
Procter & Gamble	$89.00	3.28	4.67	1.01	$28.14	$93.22	$132.73
Sears	$64.50	2.35	3.39	0.92	$37.16	$80.34	$115.89
Standard Oil (Cal.)	$29.38	0.86	1.27	1.08	$39.65	$36.83	$54.38
Texaco	$23.38	1.11	1.56	0.68	$32.88	$24.82	$34.88
Union Carbide	$61.13	1.19	1.69	1.17	$48.22	$67.14	$95.35
United Technologies	$46.38	1.02	1.94	1.20	$61.40	$75.15	$142.94
U.S. Steel	$65.00	0.49	0.73	1.06	$88.91	$46.18	$68.80
Westinghouse	$13.38	1.33	2.10	1.13	$23.55	$35.39	$55.88
Woolworth	$22.00	0.81	1.37	1.09	$33.39	$29.48	$49.86
DJIA	852.41	1.41	2.08	1.04	42.84	1084.15	1753.55

TABLE 6.7

Benchmark Investing's 1977 Dow Jones Industrial Monitor

DJIA Stocks	12/31/76 Price	Historical Market/ Book Low	High	ROE Ratio	1977 Book	Downside Target	Upside Target
Allied Corp.	$40.00	0.95	1.49	1.23	$38.67	$45.19	$70.87
Alcoa	$57.25	0.90	1.41	1.24	$49.22	$54.93	$86.06
American Brands	$45.75	1.60	2.19	0.99	$27.08	$42.89	$58.71
American Can	$39.00	0.86	1.09	1.22	$46.49	$48.78	$61.82
AT&T	$63.50	0.98	1.23	1.22	$55.94	$66.88	$83.94
Bethlehem Steel	$40.38	0.51	0.74	NMF	$49.90	$0.00	$0.00
Chrysler	$20.38	0.61	1.11	0.47	$47.88	$13.73	$24.98
DuPont	$135.13	1.95	2.74	1.00	$84.06	$163.92	$230.32
Eastman Kodak	$86.00	4.32	6.45	0.79	$26.74	$91.26	$136.25
Esmark	$35.75	0.76	1.17	0.88	$35.41	$23.68	$36.46
Exxon	$53.63	1.18	1.60	0.87	$41.30	$42.40	$57.49
General Electric	$55.38	2.47	3.55	1.19	$25.56	$75.13	$107.98
General Foods	$30.25	1.78	2.49	0.95	$23.00	$38.89	$54.41
General Motors	$78.50	1.51	2.10	1.38	$53.71	$111.92	$155.65
Goodyear Tire	$23.75	1.00	1.44	0.98	$27.32	$26.77	$38.55
Inco	$32.63	1.83	2.71	0.37	$20.30	$13.75	$20.35
International Harvester	$33.00	0.53	0.78	1.72	$57.75	$52.64	$77.48
International Paper	$68.88	1.28	1.91	1.04	$39.10	$52.05	$77.67
Johns-Manville	$33.50	0.92	1.41	1.47	$34.58	$46.77	$71.67
MMM	$56.63	4.15	6.38	1.03	$19.24	$82.24	$126.43
Owens-Illinois	$56.25	1.01	1.51	0.80	$68.00	$54.94	$82.14
Procter & Gamble	$93.63	3.25	4.56	1.04	$31.20	$105.46	$147.96
Sears	$69.00	2.22	3.17	1.03	$40.46	$92.52	$132.11
Standard Oil (Cal.)	$41.00	0.81	1.20	1.13	$43.18	$39.52	$58.55
Texaco	$27.75	1.01	1.42	0.73	$34.40	$25.36	$35.66
Union Carbide	$61.88	1.14	1.59	0.93	$49.99	$53.00	$73.92
United Technologies	$38.88	0.57	1.04	1.17	$34.22	$22.82	$41.64
U.S. Steel	$49.75	0.51	0.74	0.36	$57.48	$10.55	$15.31
Westinghouse	$17.63	1.23	1.92	1.30	$25.54	$40.84	$63.75
Woolworth	$25.75	0.78	1.30	0.89	$34.91	$24.23	$40.39
DJIA	1004.65	1.45	2.13	1.01	40.43	1148.58	1742.83

TABLE 6.8

Benchmark Investing's 1978 Dow Jones Industrial Monitor

DJIA Stocks	12/31/77 Price	Historical Market/ Book Low	High	ROE Ratio	1978 Book	Downside Target	Upside Target
Allied Chemical	$44.25	0.92	1.43	0.99	$41.33	$37.64	$58.51
Alcoa	$46.63	0.84	1.33	1.73	$55.50	$80.65	$127.70
American Brands	$43.00	1.67	2.23	1.23	$31.92	$65.57	$87.55
American Can	$38.34	0.81	1.09	1.21	$45.38	$44.48	$59.85
American Tel.	$60.50	0.96	1.19	1.29	$58.76	$72.77	$90.20
Bethlehem Steel	$21.13	0.49	0.72	1.24	$54.05	$32.84	$48.26
Chrysler	$12.63	0.45	0.72	NMF	$42.44	$0.00	$0.00
DuPont	$120.38	1.77	2.50	1.48	$93.63	$245.27	$346.43
Eastman Kodak	$51.13	3.86	5.93	1.02	$30.01	$118.16	$181.52
Esmark	$30.00	0.78	1.16	0.98	$31.19	$23.84	$35.46
Exxon	$48.13	1.16	1.57	0.96	$43.74	$48.71	$65.92
General Electric	$49.88	2.30	3.25	1.19	$28.14	$77.02	$108.83
General Foods	$31.50	1.63	2.29	1.19	$25.98	$50.39	$70.80
General Motors	$62.88	1.42	1.98	1.27	$59.96	$108.13	$150.78
Goodyear Tire	$17.25	0.92	1.32	1.02	$29.17	$27.37	$39.27
Inco	$17.13	1.62	2.48	0.32	$20.39	$10.57	$16.18
International Harvester	$30.75	0.50	0.75	1.38	$60.97	$42.07	$63.10
International Paper	$43.75	1.20	1.85	0.93	$41.26	$46.05	$70.99
Johns-Manville	$32.50	0.89	1.36	1.09	$38.33	$37.18	$56.82
MMM	$48.50	3.77	5.55	1.23	$21.86	$101.37	$149.23
Owens-Illinois	$23.88	0.91	1.35	0.94	$35.82	$30.64	$45.46
Procter & Gamble	$85.88	3.09	5.74	1.04	$33.82	$108.68	$201.89
Sears	$28.00	2.09	2.97	1.05	$21.92	$48.10	$68.36
Standard Oil (Cal.)	$38.88	0.80	1.17	1.12	$46.69	$41.83	$61.18
Texaco	$27.75	0.94	1.32	0.69	$34.61	$22.45	$31.52
Union Carbide	$41.00	1.03	1.47	0.88	$53.45	$48.45	$69.14
United Technologies	$35.88	0.85	1.41	1.24	$34.20	$36.05	$59.80
U.S. Steel	$31.50	0.50	0.75	0.63	$58.14	$18.31	$27.47
Westinghouse	$18.13	1.10	1.68	1.40	$27.46	$42.29	$64.59
Woolworth	$18.88	0.73	1.20	1.22	$36.55	$32.55	$53.51
DJIA	831.17	1.36	2.03	1.10	41.18	1282.48	1914.28

TABLE 6.9

Benchmark Investing's 1979 Dow Jones Industrial Monitor

DJIA Stocks	12/31/78 Price	Historical Market/ Book Low	High	ROE Ratio	1979 Book	Downside Target	Upside Target
Allied Chemical	$28.25	0.85	1.35	0.08	$38.83	$2.64	$4.19
Alcoa	$47.75	0.78	1.25	2.22	$67.52	$116.92	$187.37
American Brands	$50.38	1.69	2.30	1.49	$36.59	$92.14	$125.39
American Can	$35.88	0.76	1.02	1.19	$48.52	$43.88	$58.89
American Telephone	$60.50	0.94	1.16	1.23	$61.37	$70.96	$87.56
Bethlehem Steel	$19.63	0.46	0.68	1.37	$58.87	$37.10	$54.84
Chrysler	$8.63	0.44	0.81	NMF	$24.07	$0.00	$0.00
DuPont	$126.00	1.58	2.28	1.39	$104.76	$230.07	$332.01
Eastman Kodak	$58.63	3.39	5.18	1.03	$33.32	$116.34	$177.78
Esmark	$24.00	0.76	1.13	1.06	$33.81	$27.24	$40.50
Exxon	$49.13	1.11	1.50	1.33	$48.56	$71.69	$96.88
General Electric	$47.13	2.14	3.03	1.19	$31.45	$80.09	$113.40
General Foods	$32.13	1.47	2.04	1.17	$29.15	$50.14	$69.58
General Motors	$53.75	1.29	1.80	0.95	$64.63	$79.20	$110.52
Goodyear Tire	$16.13	0.83	1.19	0.66	$30.18	$16.53	$23.70
Inco	$15.75	1.42	2.20	0.61	$21.52	$18.64	$28.88
International Harvester	$36.25	0.47	0.73	2.22	$69.85	$72.88	$113.20
International Paper	$36.50	1.15	1.75	1.65	$53.38	$101.29	$154.13
Johns-Manville	$22.63	0.82	1.25	0.92	$40.17	$30.30	$46.20
MMM	$63.13	3.42	4.96	1.23	$25.16	$105.84	$153.50
Owens-Illinois	$17.88	0.81	1.17	1.06	$39.24	$33.69	$48.67
Procter & Gamble	$88.88	2.93	5.33	1.06	$39.10	$121.44	$220.91
Sears	$19.75	1.89	2.70	0.88	$23.53	$39.14	$55.91
Standard Oil (Cal.)	$46.88	0.77	1.12	1.57	$52.43	$63.38	$92.19
Texaco	$23.88	0.85	1.20	1.33	$39.22	$44.34	$62.60
Union Carbide	$34.00	0.94	1.35	1.11	$61.05	$63.70	$91.48
United Technologies	$38.88	0.88	1.44	1.18	$38.54	$40.02	$65.49
U.S. Steel	$21.25	0.47	0.73	NMF	$53.06	$0.00	$0.00
Westinghouse	$16.63	0.97	1.52	1.57	$26.46	$40.30	$63.14
Woolworth	$19.38	0.68	1.11	1.48	$42.00	$42.27	$69.00
DJIA	805.01	1.29	1.92	1.22	44.97	1285.52	2198.32

TABLE 6.10

Benchmark Investing's 1980 Dow Jones Industrial Monitor

DJIA Stocks	12/31/79 Price	Historical Market/ Book Low	High	ROE Ratio	1980 Book	Downside Target	Upside Target
Allied Chemical	$49.13	0.83	1.34	1.67	$45.80	$63.48	$102.49
Alcoa	$54.88	0.73	1.17	1.61	$78.60	$92.38	$148.06
American Brands	$67.88	1.73	2.36	1.44	$44.66	$111.26	$151.77
American Can	$35.38	0.71	0.94	0.77	$49.90	$27.28	$36.12
AT&T	$52.13	0.91	1.13	1.12	$63.40	$64.62	$80.24
Bethlehem Steel	$21.13	0.45	0.66	0.54	$60.03	$14.59	$21.39
DuPont	$40.38	1.48	2.09	0.96	$37.21	$52.87	$74.66
Eastman Kodak	$48.13	2.98	4.63	1.06	$37.35	$117.98	$183.31
Exxon	$55.13	1.08	1.44	1.48	$55.50	$88.71	$118.28
General Electric	$50.63	1.99	2.81	1.10	$36.00	$78.80	$111.28
General Foods	$33.38	1.31	1.84	1.08	$32.30	$45.70	$64.19
General Motors	$50.00	1.16	1.64	NMF	$67.60	$0.00	$0.00
Goodyear Tire	$12.88	0.73	1.07	0.93	$32.09	$21.79	$31.93
IBM	$64.38	2.97	4.12	1.11	$26.18	$86.31	$119.73
Inco	$23.75	1.25	1.99	0.95	$23.80	$28.26	$44.99
International Harvester	$39.13	0.46	0.71	NMF	$63.75	$0.00	$0.00
International Paper	$37.00	1.05	1.60	0.80	$57.02	$47.90	$72.99
Johns-Manville	$24.13	0.76	1.13	0.68	$40.29	$20.82	$30.96
Merck	$72.25	4.36	6.14	0.94	$24.96	$102.30	$144.06
MMM	$50.25	3.08	4.12	1.12	$28.08	$96.86	$129.57
Owens-Illinois	$20.25	0.69	1.00	1.00	$42.55	$29.36	$42.55
Procter & Gamble	$74.25	2.75	4.92	1.04	$43.56	$124.58	$222.89
Sears	$18.00	1.68	2.42	0.65	$24.38	$26.62	$38.35
Standard Oil (Cal.)	$56.38	0.77	1.11	1.66	$61.45	$78.55	$113.23
Texaco	$28.88	0.79	1.09	1.41	$46.64	$51.95	$71.68
Union Carbide	$42.00	0.87	1.24	1.11	$68.40	$66.05	$94.15
United Technologies	$43.00	0.89	1.40	1.27	$43.24	$48.87	$76.88
U.S. Steel	$17.50	0.46	0.72	1.25	$59.98	$34.49	$53.98
Westinghouse	$20.13	0.88	1.40	1.64	$29.80	$43.01	$68.42
Woolworth	$25.13	0.62	1.01	1.17	$45.20	$32.79	$53.41
DJIA	838.74	1.39	2.03	1.13	44.23	1257.05	2074.58

TABLE 6.11

Benchmark Investing's 1981 Dow Jones Industrial Monitor

DJIA Stocks	12/31/80 Price	Historical Market/ Book		ROE Ratio	1981 Book	Downside Target	Upside Target
		Low	High				
Allied Chemical	**$53.50**	**0.78**	**1.26**	**1.36**	**$55.31**	**$58.67**	**$94.78**
Alcoa	$59.63	0.72	1.11	0.83	$41.24	$24.65	$37.99
American Brands	$77.50	1.50	2.07	1.05	$62.95	$99.15	$136.82
American Can	$30.38	0.71	0.93	0.97	$52.76	$36.34	$47.59
AT&T	$47.88	0.87	1.03	1.09	$67.52	$64.03	$75.80
Bethlehem Steel	$26.38	0.41	0.61	0.87	$63.26	$22.56	$33.57
DuPont	**$42.00**	**1.25**	**1.85**	**0.77**	**$43.60**	**$41.97**	**$62.11**
Eastman Kodak	**$69.75**	**2.35**	**3.52**	**1.01**	**$41.67**	**$98.90**	**$148.15**
Exxon	$80.63	1.03	1.38	1.22	$32.84	$41.27	$55.29
General Electric	$61.25	1.87	2.59	1.04	$40.08	$77.95	$107.96
General Foods	**$30.25**	**1.14**	**1.58**	**1.11**	**$35.90**	**$45.43**	**$62.96**
General Motors	$45.00	0.94	1.41	0.11	$57.20	$5.91	$8.87
Goodyear Tire	**$16.00**	**0.52**	**0.84**	**1.14**	**$33.10**	**$19.62**	**$31.70**
IBM	$67.88	2.58	3.59	0.93	$30.66	$73.57	$102.36
Inco	$20.38	1.11	1.81	0.99	$26.70	$29.34	$47.84
International Harvester	$22.63	0.46	0.71	1.16	$57.00	$30.42	$46.95
International Paper	$42.00	0.95	1.50	1.10	$64.40	$67.30	$106.26
Johns-Manville	$24.75	0.63	0.98	0.37	$38.06	$8.87	$13.80
Merck	$84.75	3.74	5.11	0.84	$27.00	$84.82	$115.89
MMM	$59.00	2.61	3.73	1.03	$29.36	$78.93	$112.80
Owens-Illinois	$25.50	0.62	0.90	1.00	$43.95	$27.25	$39.56
Procter & Gamble	$68.88	2.50	3.30	1.00	$46.68	$116.70	$154.04
Sears	**$15.25**	**1.27**	**1.88**	**0.69**	**$23.77**	**$20.83**	**$30.83**
Standard Oil (Cal.)	$99.50	0.76	1.23	1.27	$37.13	$35.84	$58.00
Texaco	$48.00	0.69	1.01	1.27	$53.11	$46.54	$68.12
Union Carbide	**$50.25**	**0.76**	**1.13**	**0.89**	**$76.80**	**$51.95**	**$77.24**
United Technologies	$61.00	0.89	1.42	1.23	$47.14	$51.60	$82.33
U.S. Steel	**$24.75**	**0.31**	**0.48**	**2.59**	**$69.11**	**$55.49**	**$85.92**
Westinghouse	**$29.63**	**0.79**	**1.31**	**1.48**	**$33.08**	**$38.68**	**$64.14**
Woolworth	$24.75	0.46	0.76	0.58	$44.00	$11.74	$19.40
DJIA	963.99	1.17	1.70	1.03	45.85	974.22	1653.38

TABLE 6.12

Benchmark Investing's 1982 Dow Jones Industrial Monitor

DJIA Stocks	12/31/81 Price	Historical Market/ Book Low	High	ROE Ratio	1982 Book	Downside Target	Upside Target
Allied Corp	$43.88	0.77	1.24	0.62	$56.18	$26.82	$43.19
Alcoa	$25.63	0.69	1.08	NMF	$38.60	$0.00	$0.00
American Brands	$36.75	1.52	2.40	1.09	$23.88	$39.56	$62.47
American Can	$34.38	0.65	0.87	0.27	$43.24	$7.59	$10.16
American Telephone	$58.75	0.85	1.04	1.00	$69.07	$58.71	$71.83
Bethlehem Steel	$23.25	0.40	0.60	NMF	$28.31	$0.00	$0.00
DuPont	$37.25	1.19	1.77	0.65	$44.87	$34.71	$51.62
Eastman Kodak	$71.13	2.21	3.29	0.85	$45.56	$85.58	$127.41
Exxon	$31.25	1.00	1.35	0.88	$32.84	$28.90	$39.01
General Electric	**$57.38**	**1.71**	**2.33**	**1.01**	**$44.76**	**$77.30**	**$105.33**
General Foods	**$31.75**	**1.01**	**1.37**	**1.05**	**$36.06**	**$38.24**	**$51.87**
General Motors	$38.50	0.90	1.36	0.35	$57.63	$18.15	$27.43
Goodyear Tire	$19.00	0.52	0.81	0.96	$33.14	$16.54	$25.77
IBM	**$56.88**	**2.43**	**3.41**	**1.14**	**$33.13**	**$91.78**	**$128.79**
Inco	$14.25	0.73	1.04	NMF	$12.98	$0.00	$0.00
International Harvester	$7.13	0.46	0.72	1.01	$(24.92)	$(11.58)	$(18.12)
International Paper	$39.13	0.89	1.39	0.33	$64.94	$19.07	$29.79
Manville	$14.88	0.60	0.94	0.56	$36.70	$12.33	$19.32
Merck	$84.00	3.60	4.94	0.81	$29.70	$86.61	$118.84
MMM	$54.50	2.47	3.50	0.94	$30.30	$70.35	$99.69
Owens-Illinois	$29.63	0.52	0.74	0.29	$50.34	$7.59	$10.80
Procter & Gamble	**$80.38**	**2.33**	**4.12**	**1.07**	**$50.30**	**$125.40**	**$221.74**
Sears	**$16.13**	**1.18**	**1.75**	**0.88**	**$25.08**	**$26.04**	**$38.62**
Standard Oil (Cal.)	$42.88	0.80	1.26	0.69	$38.72	$21.37	$33.66
Texaco	$33.00	0.67	1.00	0.74	$55.12	$27.33	$40.79
U.S. Steel	$29.88	0.32	0.49	NMF	$58.11	$0.00	$0.00
Union Carbide	$51.38	0.74	1.08	0.44	$73.53	$23.94	$34.94
United Technologies	$41.75	0.89	1.42	1.04	$51.12	$47.32	$75.49
Westinghouse	$25.50	0.72	1.19	1.29	$36.32	$33.73	$55.75
Woolworth	$18.00	0.45	0.74	0.83	$31.56	$11.79	$19.38
DJIA	875.00	1.20	1.77	0.80	41.12	902.04	1330.51

TABLE 6.13

Benchmark Investing's 1983 Dow Jones Industrial Monitor

DJIA Stocks	12/31/82 Price	Historical Market/ Book Low	High	ROE Ratio	1983 Book	Downside Target	Upside Target
Allied Corp	$32.38	0.72	1.15	1.24	$44.67	$39.88	$63.70
Alcoa	$31.00	0.67	1.05	0.45	$39.06	$11.78	$18.46
American Brands	$45.88	1.01	1.40	1.13	$36.90	$42.11	$58.38
American Can	$30.88	0.63	0.84	0.86	$42.78	$23.18	$30.90
American Express	$64.25	1.40	2.28	0.72	$35.51	$35.79	$58.29
AT&T	$59.38	0.83	1.02	0.23	$65.00	$12.41	$15.25
Bethlehem Steel	$19.25	0.39	0.59	NMF	$23.53	$0.00	$0.00
DuPont	**$35.88**	**1.08**	**1.61**	**0.74**	**$47.03**	**$37.59**	**$56.03**
Eastman Kodak	$86.00	2.02	3.01	0.42	$30.29	$25.70	$38.29
Exxon	**$29.75**	**0.93**	**1.29**	**1.00**	**$34.80**	**$32.36**	**$44.89**
General Electric	$94.88	1.54	2.10	1.02	$49.56	$77.85	$106.16
General Foods	$39.63	0.95	1.35	1.04	$39.15	$38.68	$54.97
General Motors	**$62.38**	**0.84**	**1.30**	**1.33**	**$64.87**	**$72.47**	**$112.16**
Goodyear Tire	$35.00	0.51	0.83	1.30	$28.61	$18.97	$30.87
IBM	**$96.25**	**2.24**	**3.22**	**1.18**	**$38.02**	**$100.49**	**$144.46**
Inco	$11.75	0.80	1.39	NMF	$10.54	$0.00	$0.00
International Harvester	$4.25	0.45	0.67	NMF	$(28.96)	$0.00	$0.00
International Paper	$48.38	0.80	1.25	0.43	$66.76	$22.97	$35.88
Merck	$84.63	3.21	4.41	0.81	$33.00	$85.80	$117.88
Minnesota Mining	$75.00	2.26	3.25	0.95	$31.44	$67.50	$97.07
Owens-Illinois	$28.25	0.52	0.74	0.53	$46.96	$12.94	$18.42
Procter & Gamble	**$118.25**	**2.14**	**2.86**	**1.07**	**$55.50**	**$127.08**	**$169.84**
Sears	**$30.13**	**1.09**	**1.65**	**1.28**	**$27.60**	**$38.51**	**$58.29**
Standard Oil (Cal.)	$32.00	0.75	1.20	0.83	$41.23	$25.67	$41.07
Texaco	$31.13	0.63	0.93	0.63	$56.86	$22.57	$33.31
U.S. Steel	$21.00	0.32	0.49	NMF	$43.67	$0.00	$0.00
Union Carbide	$52.88	0.69	1.01	0.33	$69.60	$15.85	$23.20
United Technologies	$56.63	0.82	1.34	1.11	$54.42	$49.53	$80.94
Westinghouse	$38.88	0.62	1.07	1.17	$38.96	$28.26	$48.77
Woolworth	$25.88	0.45	0.74	1.18	$32.00	$16.99	$27.94
DJIA	1046.54	1.12	1.65	0.88	43.98	965.29	1416.27

TABLE 6.14

Benchmark Investing's 1984 Dow Jones Industrial Monitor

DJIA Stocks	12/31/83 Price	Historical Market/Book Low	Historical Market/Book High	ROE Ratio	1984 Book	Downside Target	Upside Target
Allied Corp	$55.75	0.71	1.14	1.33	$49.23	$46.49	$74.64
Alcoa	$44.88	0.67	1.05	0.74	$40.39	$20.03	$31.38
American Brands	$59.25	0.95	1.31	1.08	$39.25	$40.27	$55.53
American Can	$46.88	0.64	0.86	1.13	$43.62	$31.55	$42.39
American Express	$32.63	1.32	2.16	0.76	$20.20	$20.26	$33.16
AT&T	$61.50	0.83	1.01	1.09	$67.40	$60.98	$74.20
Bethlehem Steel	$28.50	0.38	0.57	NMF	$20.02	$0.00	$0.00
DuPont	$52.00	0.97	1.46	0.98	$50.06	$47.59	$71.63
Eastman Kodak	$76.13	1.74	2.79	0.79	$30.59	$42.05	$67.42
Exxon	**$37.38**	**0.92**	**1.24**	**1.15**	**$36.85**	**$38.99**	**$52.55**
General Electric	$58.63	1.50	1.97	1.02	$27.64	$42.29	$55.54
General Foods	$51.38	0.93	1.31	1.00	$42.15	$39.20	$55.22
General Motors	**$74.38**	**0.82**	**1.23**	**1.41**	**$75.49**	**$87.28**	**$130.92**
Goodyear Tire	$30.38	0.55	0.83	1.34	$29.78	$21.95	$33.12
IBM	$122.00	2.18	3.10	1.21	$43.23	$114.03	$162.16
Inco	$14.63	0.84	1.40	NMF	$9.32	$0.00	$0.00
International Harvester	$11.50	0.47	0.69	NMF	$(19.31)	$0.00	$0.00
International Paper	$59.00	0.76	1.16	0.48	$66.04	$24.09	$36.77
Merck	**$90.38**	**2.88**	**4.02**	**0.88**	**$35.40**	**$89.72**	**$125.23**
MMM	$82.50	2.10	3.00	1.03	$32.80	$70.95	$101.35
Owens-Illinois	$37.38	0.52	0.73	1.05	$47.67	$26.03	$36.54
Procter & Gamble	$56.88	1.98	2.62	0.97	$30.42	$58.42	$77.31
Sears	$37.13	0.97	1.48	1.24	$29.48	$35.46	$54.10
Standard Oil (Cal.)	$34.63	0.74	1.16	0.77	$43.15	$24.59	$38.54
Texaco	$35.88	0.60	0.85	0.61	$55.15	$20.18	$28.60
U.S. Steel	$30.38	0.32	0.49	0.62	$45.36	$9.00	$13.78
Union Carbide	$62.75	0.68	0.99	0.60	$69.90	$28.52	$41.52
United Technologies	$72.50	0.81	1.27	1.14	$60.08	$55.48	$86.98
Westinghouse	$54.75	0.63	1.04	1.21	$42.80	$32.63	$53.86
Woolworth	$35.13	0.46	0.76	1.36	$32.80	$20.52	$33.90
DJIA	1258.64	1.06	1.55	0.99	44.15	1002.46	1653.50

TABLE 6.15

Benchmark Investing's 1985 Dow Jones Industrial Monitor

DJIA Stocks	12/31/84 Price	Historical Market/ Book Low	High	ROE Ratio	1985 Book	Downside Target	Upside Target
Allied Corp.	$34.50	0.73	1.11	0.64	$33.17	$15.50	$23.56
Alcoa	$37.00	0.69	1.06	0.30	$39.84	$8.25	$12.67
American Brands	$64.25	1.01	1.35	1.10	$43.00	$47.77	$63.86
American Can	$50.50	0.67	0.90	1.06	$47.57	$33.78	$45.38
American Express	$37.63	1.30	2.05	0.89	$22.82	$26.40	$41.64
AT&T	$19.50	1.22	1.57	1.00	$13.68	$16.69	$21.48
Bethlehem Steel	$17.50	0.38	0.56	NMF	$15.13	$0.00	$0.00
Chevron	$31.25	0.75	1.14	0.64	$45.47	$21.83	$33.17
DuPont	$49.50	0.94	1.34	0.82	$51.62	$39.79	$56.72
Eastman Kodak	$71.88	1.63	2.48	0.32	$43.59	$22.74	$34.59
Exxon	$45.00	0.93	1.23	1.12	$39.80	$41.46	$54.83
General Electric	$56.63	1.54	1.93	0.94	$30.49	$44.14	$55.31
General Foods	$55.88	0.95	1.33	1.00	$46.85	$44.51	$62.31
General Motors	$78.38	0.83	1.20	1.06	$91.98	$80.92	$117.00
Goodyear Tire	$26.00	0.58	0.87	0.90	$32.44	$16.93	$25.40
IBM	$123.13	2.19	3.05	0.97	$51.98	$110.42	$153.78
Inco	$12.38	0.84	1.40	0.47	$4.10	$1.62	$2.70
International Harvester	$8.13	0.45	0.67	NMF*	$(22.03)	$0.00	$0.00
International Paper	$53.88	0.74	1.09	0.27	$66.60	$13.31	$19.60
Merck	**$93.25**	**2.71**	**3.65**	**0.96**	**$37.50**	**$97.56**	**$131.40**
MMM	$78.63	2.04	2.80	0.91	$34.98	$64.94	$89.13
Owens-Illinois	$40.25	0.53	0.76	1.16	$51.30	$31.54	$45.23
Procter & Gamble	$57.00	1.86	2.42	0.69	$31.49	$40.41	$52.58
Sears	$31.75	0.96	1.38	1.00	$31.79	$30.52	$43.87
Texaco	$34.13	0.60	0.85	0.71	$57.04	$24.30	$34.42
U.S. Steel	$26.13	0.43	0.68	0.76	$43.80	$14.31	$22.64
Union Carbide	$36.75	0.65	0.97	0.18	$59.40	$6.95	$10.37
United Technologies	$36.25	0.85	1.32	1.12	$31.58	$30.06	$46.69
Westinghouse	$26.13	0.69	1.07	1.43	$21.03	$20.75	$32.18
Woolworth	$37.00	0.52	0.80	1.38	$37.60	$26.98	$41.51
DJIA	1211.57	1.05	1.49	0.85	40.80	926.65	1370.74

TABLE 6.16

Benchmark Investing's 1986 Dow Jones Industrial Monitor

DJIA Stocks	12/31/85 Price	Historical Market/ Book Low	High	ROE Ratio	1986 Book	Downside Target	Upside Target
AlliedSignal	$46.75	0.75	1.15	1.49	$21.04	$23.51	$36.05
Alcoa	$38.50	0.69	1.02	0.31	$41.99	$8.98	$13.28
American Can	$60.00	0.70	0.88	1.26	$48.00	$42.34	$53.22
American Express	$53.00	1.25	2.01	1.06	$25.20	$33.39	$53.69
AT&T	$25.00	1.28	1.67	1.31	$12.64	$21.19	$27.65
Bethlehem Steel	$15.63	0.33	0.48	NMF	$11.98	$0.00	$0.00
Chevron	$38.13	0.74	1.14	0.40	$45.29	$13.41	$20.65
DuPont	$67.88	0.86	1.24	0.96	$54.74	$45.19	$65.16
Eastman Kodak	$50.00	1.37	1.99	0.41	$28.29	$15.89	$23.08
Exxon	$55.13	0.92	1.24	0.87	$44.60	$35.70	$48.11
General Electric	$72.75	1.54	1.83	0.91	$33.14	$46.44	$55.19
General Motors	$70.38	0.77	1.07	0.73	$83.09	$46.70	$64.90
Goodyear Tire	$31.25	0.59	0.85	0.94	$30.93	$17.15	$24.71
IBM	$155.50	2.13	3.00	0.64	$56.67	$77.25	$108.81
Inco	$13.25	0.75	1.25	NMF	$9.30	$0.00	$0.00
International Harvester	$8.50	0.45	0.67	NMF	$(4.25)	$0.00	$0.00
International Paper	$50.75	0.64	0.88	0.71	$70.00	$31.81	$43.74
McDonald's	$80.88	1.74	2.56	0.97	$29.02	$48.98	$72.06
Merck	$137.00	2.44	3.32	1.29	$37.68	$118.60	$161.38
MMM	$89.75	1.92	2.59	0.90	$39.04	$67.46	$91.00
Owens-Illinois	$52.75	0.45	0.63	1.21	$55.65	$30.30	$42.42
Philip Morris	**$87.63**	**1.62**	**2.23**	**1.19**	**$47.54**	**$91.65**	**$126.16**
Procter & Gamble	$69.75	1.63	2.18	0.70	$33.90	$38.68	$51.73
Sears	$39.00	0.82	1.20	0.95	$33.98	$26.47	$38.74
Texaco	$30.00	0.55	0.82	0.37	$56.71	$11.54	$17.21
U.S. Steel	$26.63	0.50	0.75	NMF	$23.25	$0.00	$0.00
Union Carbide	$70.88	0.57	0.88	1.46	$23.61	$19.65	$30.33
United Technologies	$43.75	0.91	1.37	0.69	$29.14	$18.30	$27.55
Westinghouse	$44.50	0.81	1.31	1.50	$21.13	$25.67	$41.52
Woolworth	$60.00	0.60	0.93	1.28	$44.98	$34.54	$53.54
DJIA	1546.67	1.09	1.53	0.94	40.31	1173.19	1646.77

TABLE 6.17

Benchmark Investing's 1987 Dow Jones Industrial Monitor

DJIA Stocks	12/31/86 Price	Historical Market/ Book Low	High	ROE Ratio	1987 Book	Downside Target	Upside Target
Allied Signal	$40.13	0.81	1.25	1.16	$20.87	$19.61	$30.26
Alcoa	$33.88	0.70	1.03	0.94	$43.62	$28.70	$42.23
American Can	$84.13	0.70	0.88	1.37	$53.25	$51.07	$64.20
American Express	$57.50	1.38	2.15	0.51	$20.22	$14.23	$22.17
AT&T	$25.00	1.37	1.80	1.30	$13.46	$23.97	$31.50
Bethlehem Steel	$6.25	0.33	0.48	0.51	$14.74	$2.48	$3.61
Chevron	$45.38	0.74	1.13	0.34	$46.13	$11.61	$17.72
DuPont	$84.00	0.89	1.30	0.99	$58.65	$51.68	$75.48
Eastman Kodak	$68.59	1.40	2.05	1.45	$27.83	$56.49	$82.72
Exxon	$70.13	0.95	1.30	0.81	$48.76	$37.52	$51.34
General Electric	$86.00	1.62	1.90	0.99	$36.50	$58.54	$68.66
General Motors	$66.00	0.77	1.07	0.88	$89.09	$60.37	$83.89
Goodyear Tire	**$41.88**	**0.63**	**0.94**	**2.15**	**$32.19**	**$43.60**	**$65.06**
IBM	$120.00	2.12	2.98	0.66	$64.06	$89.63	$125.99
Inco	$11.75	0.82	1.41	0.55	$9.40	$4.24	$7.29
International Paper	$75.13	0.64	0.91	1.00	$72.62	$46.48	$66.08
McDonald's	$60.75	1.88	2.81	0.96	$15.44	$27.87	$41.65
Merck	$124.00	2.60	3.83	2.03	$16.11	$85.03	$125.25
MMM	$116.63	2.11	2.82	0.94	$44.48	$88.22	$117.91
Navistar	$4.75	0.45	0.67	NMF	$(0.50)	$0.00	$0.00
Owens-Illinois	$53.00	0.45	0.63	1.21	$55.65	$30.30	$42.42
Philip Morris	$72.00	1.68	2.44	1.22	$28.83	$59.09	$85.82
Procter & Gamble	$76.38	1.67	2.22	0.78	$35.44	$46.16	$61.37
Sears	$39.75	0.85	1.24	1.11	$35.89	$33.86	$49.40
Texaco	$35.88	0.54	0.80	0.41	$37.36	$8.27	$12.25
Union Carbide	$22.50	0.65	1.02	2.47	$9.43	$15.14	$23.76
United Technologies	$46.00	0.96	1.44	1.04	$32.90	$32.85	$49.27
USX	$21.50	0.50	0.75	0.70	$23.00	$8.05	$12.08
Westinghouse	$55.75	1.00	1.58	1.29	$24.92	$32.15	$50.79
Woolworth	$38.63	0.69	1.09	1.26	$26.54	$23.07	$36.45
DJIA	1895.95	1.06	1.52	1.07	35.75	1370.12	1964.71

TABLE 6.18

Benchmark Investing's 1988 Dow Jones Industrial Monitor

DJIA Stocks	12/31/87 Price	Historical Market/ Book Low	High	ROE Ratio	1988 Book	Downside Target	Upside Target
AlliedSignal	$28.25	0.96	1.49	1.39	$22.35	$29.82	$46.29
Alcoa	$46.75	0.69	0.96	1.35	$51.80	$48.25	$67.13
American Express	$22.38	1.46	2.36	1.30	$12.10	$22.97	$37.12
AT&T	$27.00	1.45	2.06	1.27	$14.40	$26.52	$37.67
Bethlehem Steel	$16.75	0.42	0.74	3.42	$21.80	$31.31	$55.17
Boeing	$37.00	1.08	1.74	0.60	$38.65	$25.05	$40.35
Chevron	$39.63	0.74	1.17	0.87	$42.95	$27.65	$43.72
Coca-Cola	$38.13	2.32	3.58	1.33	$9.30	$28.70	$44.28
DuPont	$87.46	0.94	1.54	1.13	$64.60	$68.62	$112.42
Eastman Kodak	$49.00	1.49	2.23	1.42	$20.95	$44.33	$66.34
Exxon	$38.13	0.88	1.24	0.98	$24.45	$21.09	$29.71
General Electric	$44.13	1.70	2.41	1.00	$20.50	$34.85	$49.41
General Motors	$61.38	0.73	1.08	0.62	$95.00	$43.00	$63.61
Goodyear Tire	$60.00	0.68	1.09	1.92	$41.15	$53.73	$86.12
IBM	$115.50	2.04	2.93	0.72	$68.75	$100.98	$145.04
International Paper	$42.25	0.65	0.99	1.66	$41.25	$44.51	$67.79
McDonald's	$44.00	1.91	3.02	0.95	$18.20	$33.02	$52.22
Merck	$158.63	3.13	4.90	1.81	$20.85	$118.12	$184.92
Minnesota Mining	$64.38	1.97	2.81	1.02	$24.50	$49.23	$70.22
Navistar	$4.25	1.41	2.94	1.00	$2.40	$3.38	$7.06
Philip Morris	$85.63	1.82	2.78	1.29	$34.00	$79.83	$121.93
Primerica	$24.13	0.95	1.55	0.90	$26.70	$22.83	$37.25
Procter & Gamble	$85.38	1.67	2.31	0.96	$37.10	$59.48	$82.27
Sears	$33.50	0.84	1.51	1.01	$38.50	$32.66	$58.72
Texaco	$37.25	0.57	0.87	0.88	$39.30	$19.71	$30.09
USX	$29.75	0.50	0.75	0.70	$23.00	$8.05	$12.08
Union Carbide	$21.75	0.70	1.14	3.10	$14.35	$31.14	$50.71
United Technologies	$33.88	0.95	1.45	1.02	$36.15	$35.03	$53.47
Westinghouse	$49.75	1.05	1.73	1.23	$28.80	$37.20	$61.28
Woolworth	$34.50	0.74	1.24	1.30	$29.00	$27.90	$46.75
DJIA	1938.83	1.18	1.84	1.27	$32.35	1931.38	3000.50

TABLE 6.19

Benchmark Investing's 1989 Dow Jones Industrial Monitor

DJIA Stocks	12/31/88 Price	Historical Market/ Book Low	High	ROE Ratio	1989 Book	Downside Target	Upside Target
AlliedSignal	$32.50	0.84	1.33	1.36	$23.65	$27.02	$42.78
Alcoa	$56.00	0.70	1.07	1.26	$57.75	$50.94	$77.86
American Express	**$26.63**	**1.52**	**2.39**	**1.30**	**$13.85**	**$27.37**	**$43.03**
AT&T	**$28.75**	**1.45**	**2.06**	**1.30**	**$15.60**	**$29.41**	**$41.78**
Bethlehem Steel	$23.25	0.43	0.74	2.30	$27.00	$26.70	$45.95
Boeing	$60.63	1.08	1.74	0.86	$43.20	$40.12	$64.64
Chevron	$45.75	0.75	1.17	0.80	$45.60	$27.36	$42.68
Coca-Cola	$44.62	2.49	3.73	1.39	$10.60	$36.69	$54.96
DuPont	$88.33	0.94	1.42	1.03	$69.40	$67.19	$101.50
Eastman Kodak	$45.13	1.54	2.26	1.36	$23.75	$49.74	$73.00
Exxon	$44.00	0.94	1.31	0.87	$26.40	$21.59	$30.09
General Electric	$44.75	1.70	2.41	1.00	$23.10	$39.27	$55.67
General Motors	$83.50	0.72	1.06	0.96	$102.30	$70.71	$104.10
Goodyear Tire	**$51.13**	**0.74**	**1.16**	**1.62**	**$43.90**	**$52.63**	**$82.50**
IBM	$121.88	2.04	2.94	0.74	$74.35	$112.24	$161.76
International Paper	**$46.38**	**0.65**	**0.99**	**1.56**	**$47.05**	**$47.71**	**$72.66**
McDonald's	$48.13	1.96	2.98	0.95	$21.50	$40.03	$60.87
Merck	$57.88	3.13	4.91	1.74	$9.30	$50.65	$79.45
Minnesota Mining	$62.00	2.01	2.81	1.09	$26.15	$57.29	$80.09
Navistar	$5.38	1.41	2.94	0.14	$2.85	$0.56	$1.17
Philip Morris	$101.88	1.93	2.80	1.19	$39.80	$91.41	$132.61
Primerica	$10.38	0.71	0.89	0.90	$15.70	$10.03	$12.58
Procter & Gamble	$87.00	1.71	2.33	0.99	$41.00	$69.41	$94.57
Sears	$40.88	0.84	1.28	1.00	$39.70	$33.35	$50.82
Texaco	$51.13	0.57	0.87	0.83	$40.40	$19.11	$29.17
USX	$29.25	0.64	0.93	1.30	$22.40	$18.64	$27.08
Union Carbide	**$25.63**	**0.74**	**1.21**	**2.57**	**$17.85**	**$33.95**	**$55.51**
United Technologies	$41.13	0.95	1.45	0.98	$39.55	$36.82	$56.20
Westinghouse	$52.63	1.05	1.73	1.14	$32.90	$39.38	$64.89
Woolworth	$51.75	0.76	1.35	1.31	$32.65	$32.51	$57.74
DJIA	2168.57	1.20	1.83	1.15	$33.52	1999.63	3042.64

TABLE 6.20

Benchmark Investing's 1990 Dow Jones Industrial Monitor

DJIA Stocks	12/31/89 Price	Historical Market/ Book Low	High	ROE Ratio	1990 Book	Downside Target	Upside Target
AlliedSignal	$34.88	0.90	1.38	1.23	$25.50	$28.23	$43.28
Alcoa	$75.00	0.72	1.10	1.69	$67.25	$81.83	$125.02
American Express	$34.88	1.62	2.56	1.19	$15.40	$29.69	$46.91
AT&T	$45.50	1.71	2.47	1.55	$13.40	$35.52	$51.30
Bethlehem Steel	$18.50	0.36	0.58	0.96	$24.50	$8.47	$13.64
Boeing	$59.34	1.13	1.83	1.19	$31.25	$42.02	$68.05
Chevron	$67.75	0.79	1.25	0.90	$46.45	$33.03	$52.26
Coca-Cola	$77.25	2.76	4.30	1.59	$10.75	$47.18	$73.50
DuPont	$123.13	1.00	1.48	1.43	$73.50	$105.11	$155.56
Eastman Kodak	**$41.13**	**1.60**	**2.31**	**1.28**	**$23.30**	**$47.72**	**$68.89**
Exxon	$50.00	1.15	1.59	0.87	$27.25	$27.26	$37.69
General Electric	$64.50	1.78	2.48	1.06	$26.00	$49.06	$68.35
General Motors	$42.25	0.57	0.94	0.96	$70.10	$38.36	$63.26
Goodyear Tire	$43.50	0.84	1.32	0.74	$41.00	$25.49	$40.05
IBM	**$94.13**	**1.97**	**2.79**	**0.69**	**$75.85**	**$103.10**	**$146.02**
International Paper	$56.50	0.65	1.05	1.29	$52.60	$44.11	$71.25
McDonald's	$34.50	2.00	3.06	0.94	$12.25	$23.03	$35.24
Merck	$77.50	4.07	6.06	1.46	$11.80	$70.12	$104.40
Minnesota Mining	$79.63	2.08	2.88	1.17	$30.90	$75.20	$104.12
Navistar	$3.88	1.41	2.94	0.14	$2.85	$0.56	$1.17
Philip Morris	$41.63	1.93	2.83	1.23	$11.05	$26.23	$38.46
Primerica	$28.50	0.95	1.55	0.90	$26.70	$22.83	$37.25
Procter & Gamble	$70.25	1.78	2.53	1.27	$18.15	$41.03	$58.32
Sears	$38.13	0.85	1.30	1.02	$42.40	$36.76	$56.22
Texaco	$58.88	0.64	0.96	1.31	$32.30	$27.08	$40.62
USX	$35.75	0.64	0.93	1.30	$22.40	$18.64	$27.08
Union Carbide	$23.25	0.73	1.20	1.28	$19.15	$17.89	$29.41
United Technologies	$54.25	0.95	1.45	1.00	$44.85	$42.61	$65.03
Westinghouse	$74.00	1.30	2.01	1.18	$34.25	$52.54	$81.23
Woolworth	$63.88	0.96	1.61	1.35	$35.40	$45.88	$76.94
DJIA	2753.20	1.30	1.98	1.10	$31.44	2295.15	3498.72

TABLE 6.21

Benchmark Investing's 1991 Dow Jones Industrial Monitor

DJIA Stocks	12/31/90 Price	Historical Market/ Book Low	High	ROE Ratio	1991 Book	Downside Target	Upside Target
AlliedSignal	$27.00	0.97	1.47	1.08	$26.05	$27.29	$41.36
Alcoa	$57.63	0.86	1.33	1.10	$66.35	$62.77	$97.07
American Express	**$20.63**	**1.65**	**2.67**	**1.07**	**$15.15**	**$26.75**	**$43.28**
AT&T	**$30.13**	**1.79**	**2.62**	**1.26**	**$14.80**	**$33.38**	**$48.86**
Bethlehem Steel	$14.75	0.47	0.89	0.42	$23.00	$4.54	$8.60
Boeing	**$45.38**	**1.23**	**2.00**	**1.56**	**$25.00**	**$47.97**	**$78.00**
Chevron	$72.63	0.86	1.27	1.22	$44.20	$46.37	$68.48
Coca-Cola	$46.50	3.30	5.19	1.38	$6.68	$30.42	$47.84
DuPont	$36.75	1.05	1.53	1.20	$26.20	$33.01	$48.10
Eastman Kodak	$41.63	1.65	2.33	1.44	$21.65	$51.44	$72.64
Exxon	$51.75	1.25	1.67	0.93	$28.00	$32.55	$43.49
General Electric	$57.38	1.86	2.66	1.11	$27.20	$56.16	$80.31
General Motors	$34.38	0.63	0.94	0.47	$62.95	$18.64	$27.81
Goodyear Tire	$18.88	0.84	1.40	0.27	$34.10	$7.73	$12.89
IBM	$113.00	1.75	2.46	0.81	$76.35	$108.23	$152.14
International Paper	$53.50	0.74	1.19	1.05	$56.55	$43.94	$70.66
McDonald's	$29.13	2.12	3.25	1.00	$12.90	$27.35	$41.93
Merck	$89.96	4.62	6.76	1.38	$13.25	$84.48	$123.61
Minnesota Mining	$85.75	2.19	2.98	1.11	$30.30	$73.66	$100.23
Navistar	$2.25	1.24	2.77	N/A	$1.33	$0.00	$0.00
Philip Morris	$51.75	2.25	3.42	1.25	$14.90	$41.91	$63.70
Primerica	$8.50	0.96	1.51	0.25	$22.50	$5.40	$8.49
Procter & Gamble	$86.63	1.98	2.85	1.32	$22.05	$57.63	$82.95
Sears	**$25.38**	**0.83**	**1.31**	**0.80**	**$42.15**	**$27.99**	**$44.17**
Texaco	$60.50	0.72	1.03	1.46	$33.60	$35.32	$50.53
USX	$30.50	0.65	0.95	0.99	$32.67	$21.02	$30.73
Union Carbide	$16.38	0.86	1.45	0.55	$18.50	$8.75	$14.75
United Technologies	$47.88	1.00	1.52	1.03	$41.55	$42.80	$65.05
Westinghouse	$28.50	1.36	2.12	1.17	$18.35	$29.20	$45.52
Woolworth	$30.25	1.06	1.76	1.20	$19.95	$25.38	$42.13
DJIA	2633.66	1.49	2.27	1.03	$30.37	2563.03	3904.76

TABLE 6.22

Benchmark Investing's 1992 Dow Jones Industrial Monitor

DJIA Stocks	12/31/91 Price	Historical Market/ Book		ROE Ratio	1992 Book	Downside Target	Upside Target
		Low	High				
AlliedSignal	$43.88	1.02	1.55	1.17	$24.30	$29.00	$44.07
Alcoa	$64.38	0.81	1.19	0.63	$59.40	$30.31	$44.53
American Express	$20.50	1.49	2.39	0.76	$16.65	$18.85	$30.24
AT&T	**$39.13**	**1.89**	**2.68**	**1.66**	**$14.95**	**$46.90**	**$66.51**
Bethlehem Steel	$14.00	0.44	0.80	NMF	$3.50	$0.00	$0.00
Boeing	$47.75	1.35	2.04	1.23	$27.50	$45.66	$69.00
Caterpillar	**$43.88**	**1.08**	**1.63**	**1.43**	**$40.75**	**$62.93**	**$94.98**
Chevron	$69.00	0.94	1.38	0.83	$43.15	$33.67	$49.42
Coca-Cola	$80.25	3.95	6.52	1.36	$7.85	$42.17	$69.61
Disney	$114.50	2.69	4.40	1.10	$35.20	$104.16	$170.37
Dupont	$46.63	1.13	1.62	0.87	$25.50	$25.07	$35.94
Eastman Kodak	**$48.25**	**1.64**	**2.31**	**1.48**	**$20.90**	**$50.73**	**$71.45**
Exxon	$60.88	1.33	1.73	0.84	$28.35	$31.67	$41.20
General Electric	$76.50	1.92	2.64	1.11	$27.95	$59.57	$81.90
General Motors	$28.88	0.66	0.98	NMF	$39.40	$0.00	$0.00
Goodyear Tire	$53.50	0.78	1.33	0.86	$41.70	$27.97	$47.70
IBM	$89.00	1.69	2.42	0.57	$75.80	$73.02	$104.56
International Paper	$70.75	0.81	1.15	0.81	$55.10	$36.15	$51.33
McDonald's	$38.00	2.16	3.16	0.94	$14.70	$29.85	$43.66
Merck	$166.66	5.29	7.87	1.39	$16.50	$121.33	$180.50
Minnesota Mining	$95.25	2.36	2.94	0.94	$30.90	$68.55	$85.40
Philip Morris	$80.25	2.73	3.96	1.33	$16.15	$58.64	$85.06
J. P. Morgan	$68.63	1.10	1.72	1.21	$32.65	$43.46	$67.95
Procter & Gamble	$93.88	2.40	3.27	1.19	$20.20	$57.69	$78.60
Sears	$37.88	0.80	1.24	1.11	$40.85	$36.27	$56.23
Texaco	$61.25	0.81	1.13	1.01	$34.75	$28.43	$39.66
Union Carbide	$20.25	0.80	1.32	0.92	$18.40	$13.54	$22.34
United Technologies	$54.25	1.07	1.56	1.04	$28.60	$31.83	$46.40
Westinghouse	$18.00	1.34	2.10	0.96	$10.85	$13.96	$21.87
Woolworth	$26.50	1.09	1.76	1.23	$17.25	$23.13	$37.34
DJIA	3168.83	1.62	2.41	1.03	$28.66	2562.24	3811.73

TABLE 6.23

Benchmark Investing's 1993 Dow Jones Industrial Monitor

DJIA Stocks	12/31/92 Price	Historical Market/ Book Low	High	ROE Ratio	1993 Book	Downside Target	Upside Target
AlliedSignal	$60.50	1.17	1.76	1.18	$28.60	$39.49	$59.40
Alcoa	$71.63	0.85	1.27	0.96	$61.05	$49.82	$74.43
American Express	**$24.88**	**1.63**	**2.57**	**0.98**	**$15.90**	**$25.40**	**$40.05**
AT&T	$51.00	1.96	2.79	1.48	$15.25	$44.24	$62.97
Bethlehem Steel	$16.00	0.66	1.31	0.73	$4.20	$2.02	$4.02
Boeing	$40.13	1.36	2.10	1.35	$28.50	$52.33	$80.80
Caterpillar	**$53.63**	**1.10**	**1.66**	**1.27**	**$41.00**	**$57.28**	**$86.44**
Chevron	$69.50	0.99	1.39	1.13	$43.40	$48.55	$68.17
Coca-Cola	$41.88	5.07	7.84	1.46	$4.00	$29.61	$45.79
Disney	$43.00	2.82	4.58	1.04	$10.35	$30.35	$49.30
DuPont	$47.13	1.21	1.72	1.13	$27.50	$37.60	$53.45
Eastman Kodak	**$40.50**	**1.74**	**2.42**	**1.67**	**$21.90**	**$63.64**	**$88.51**
Exxon	$61.13	1.45	1.88	0.87	$29.65	$37.40	$48.50
General Electric	$85.50	2.06	2.81	1.08	$30.90	$68.75	$93.78
General Motors	$32.25	0.59	0.85	0.72	$34.60	$14.70	$21.18
Goodyear Tire	$68.38	0.97	1.57	1.15	$47.90	$53.43	$86.48
IBM	**$50.38**	**1.65**	**2.34**	**0.63**	**$63.45**	**$65.96**	**$93.54**
International Paper	$66.63	0.85	1.23	0.77	$55.55	$36.36	$52.61
McDonald's	$48.75	2.25	3.33	0.89	$17.75	$35.54	$52.61
Merck	$43.38	5.67	8.79	1.07	$6.95	$42.16	$65.37
Minnesota Mining	$100.63	2.40	3.16	0.94	$34.70	$78.28	$103.07
Philip Morris	$77.13	3.05	4.51	1.40	$16.80	$71.74	$106.08
J. P. Morgan	$65.75	1.12	1.73	1.13	$38.25	$48.41	$74.77
Procter & Gamble	$53.63	2.59	3.52	1.20	$12.00	$37.30	$50.69
Sears	$45.50	0.87	1.33	1.19	$37.40	$38.72	$59.19
Texaco	$59.75	0.92	1.25	1.21	$35.70	$39.74	$54.00
Union Carbide	$16.63	1.07	1.94	0.61	$15.20	$9.92	$17.99
United Technologies	$48.13	1.14	1.65	1.05	$31.15	$37.29	$53.97
Westinghouse	$13.38	1.46	2.38	0.74	$11.45	$12.37	$20.17
Woolworth	$31.63	1.27	2.01	0.95	$17.70	$21.36	$33.80
DJIA	3301.11	1.69	2.53	1.03	$27.01	3165.65	4734.45

TABLE 6.24

Benchmark Investing's 1994 Dow Jones Industrial Monitor

DJIA Stocks	12/31/93 Price	Historical Market/ Book Low	High	ROE Ratio	1994 Book	Downside Target	Upside Target
AlliedSignal	$79.00	1.43	2.11	1.65	$20.80	$49.08	$72.42
Alcoa	$69.38	0.95	1.38	0.29	$38.95	$10.73	$15.59
American Express	$30.88	1.60	2.51	1.30	$13.55	$28.18	$44.21
AT&T	$52.50	2.19	3.07	1.75	$12.20	$46.76	$65.54
Bethlehem Steel	$20.38	0.82	1.57	1.24	$5.50	$5.59	$10.71
Boeing	$43.25	1.38	2.10	0.49	$28.00	$18.93	$28.81
Caterpillar	$89.00	1.22	1.89	2.13	$28.25	$73.41	$113.73
Chevron	$87.13	0.98	1.39	1.46	$45.25	$64.74	$91.83
Coca-Cola	$44.63	5.94	8.73	1.45	$4.40	$37.90	$55.70
Disney	$42.63	3.07	4.77	1.01	$11.15	$34.57	$53.72
DuPont	$48.25	1.42	1.97	1.50	$17.60	$37.49	$52.01
Eastman Kodak	$56.25	1.89	2.67	1.75	$12.10	$40.02	$56.54
Exxon	$63.13	1.57	2.02	0.82	$28.30	$36.43	$46.88
General Electric	$104.88	2.15	2.94	1.10	$32.90	$77.81	$106.40
General Motors	$54.88	0.82	1.22	2.95	$7.30	$17.66	$26.27
Goodyear Tire	$45.75	1.14	1.84	1.96	$18.30	$40.89	$66.00
IBM	$56.50	1.58	2.30	0.67	$33.80	$35.78	$52.09
International Paper	$67.75	0.90	1.28	0.60	$51.75	$27.95	$39.74
McDonald's	$57.00	2.37	3.44	0.85	$19.15	$38.58	$55.99
Merck	**$34.38**	**5.20**	**8.09**	**0.72**	**$9.35**	**$35.01**	**$54.46**
MMM	$108.75	2.52	3.29	1.04	$31.40	$82.29	$107.44
Philip Morris	**$55.63**	**3.09**	**4.70**	**1.20**	**$15.05**	**$55.81**	**$84.88**
J. P. Morgan	$69.38	1.15	1.76	1.01	$53.40	$62.02	$94.92
Procter & Gamble	$55.63	2.93	3.97	1.39	$9.95	$40.52	$54.91
Sears	$57.00	0.93	1.40	1.11	$31.05	$32.05	$48.25
Texaco	$64.75	1.04	1.40	1.13	$34.70	$40.78	$54.90
Union Carbide	$22.38	1.23	2.24	1.03	$9.20	$11.66	$21.23
United Technologies	$62.00	1.23	1.80	1.16	$26.35	$37.60	$55.02
Westinghouse	$14.13	1.71	2.77	1.01	$0.95	$1.64	$2.66
Woolworth	$25.38	1.31	2.09	0.76	$10.05	$10.01	$15.96
DJIA	3754.09	1.86	2.76	1.22	$22.02	3500.65	5192.58

TABLE 6.25

Benchmark Investing's 1995 Dow Jones Industrial Monitor

DJIA Stocks	12/31/94 Price	Historical Market/ Book Low	High	ROE Ratio	1995 Book	Downside Target	Upside Target
AlliedSignal	$34.00	1.68	2.42	1.45	$12.85	$31.30	$45.09
Alcoa	$86.63	1.02	1.46	0.70	$43.65	$31.17	$44.61
American Express	**$29.50**	**1.65**	**2.54**	**1.31**	**$15.30**	**$33.07**	**$50.91**
AT&T	$50.25	2.52	3.43	1.57	$12.75	$50.44	$68.66
Bethlehem Steel	$18.00	0.98	1.77	2.06	$8.00	$16.15	$29.17
Boeing	$47.00	1.42	2.09	0.51	$29.20	$21.15	$31.12
Caterpillar	**$55.13**	**1.41**	**2.13**	**2.05**	**$19.70**	**$56.94**	**$86.02**
Chevron	$44.63	1.19	1.64	1.32	$23.85	$37.46	$51.63
Coca-Cola	$51.50	6.73	9.69	1.26	$5.50	$46.64	$67.15
Disney	$46.00	3.19	4.80	0.96	$13.30	$40.73	$61.29
DuPont	**$56.13**	**1.58**	**2.18**	**1.73**	**$20.70**	**$56.58**	**$78.07**
Eastman Kodak	**$47.75**	**2.06**	**2.91**	**1.78**	**$13.95**	**$51.15**	**$72.26**
Exxon	$60.75	1.66	2.12	0.99	$29.10	$47.82	$61.08
General Electric	$51.00	2.25	3.07	1.08	$18.05	$43.86	$59.85
General Motors	$42.13	0.93	1.45	2.00	$14.05	$26.13	$40.75
Goodyear Tire	**$33.63**	**1.25**	**2.03**	**1.73**	**$21.40**	**$46.28**	**$75.15**
IBM	**$73.50**	**1.52**	**2.23**	**1.35**	**$39.50**	**$81.05**	**$118.91**
International Paper	$75.38	0.95	1.34	0.93	$55.20	$48.77	$68.79
McDonald's	$29.25	2.48	3.50	0.94	$10.30	$24.01	$33.89
Merck	$38.13	4.54	7.05	0.70	$10.65	$33.85	$52.56
MMM	$53.38	2.60	3.37	1.09	$16.90	$47.89	$62.08
Philip Morris	**$57.50**	**3.15**	**4.73**	**1.19**	**$16.70**	**$62.60**	**$94.00**
J. P. Morgan	$56.13	1.17	1.74	0.91	$56.85	$60.53	$90.02
Procter & Gamble	$62.00	3.30	4.40	1.33	$12.35	$54.20	$72.27
Sears	**$46.00**	**0.96**	**1.44**	**1.44**	**$34.75**	**$48.04**	**$72.06**
Texaco	$59.88	1.17	1.53	1.07	$34.15	$42.75	$55.91
Union Carbide	$29.38	1.49	2.66	1.25	$11.25	$20.95	$37.41
United Technologies	$62.88	1.34	1.92	1.23	$30.60	$50.43	$72.26
Westinghouse	$12.25	1.90	3.08	1.00	$3.55	$6.75	$10.93
Woolworth	$15.00	1.33	2.19	0.75	$11.20	$11.17	$18.40
DJIA	3834.44	1.98	2.90	1.26	$21.51	4426.23	6473.98

TABLE 6.26

Benchmark Investing's 1996 Dow Jones Industrial Monitor

DJIA Stocks	12/31/95 Price	Historical Market/ Book Low	High	ROE Ratio	1996 Book	Downside Target	Upside Target
AlliedSignal	$47.50	1.32	1.96	1.45	$14.95	$28.61	$42.49
Alcoa	**$52.88**	**0.97**	**1.45**	**2.15**	**$28.95**	**$60.38**	**$90.25**
American Express	$41.38	1.55	2.43	1.27	$16.95	$33.37	$52.31
AT&T	$64.75	2.40	3.33	1.82	$13.00	$56.78	$78.79
Bethlehem Steel	$13.88	0.70	1.19	1.89	$7.10	$9.39	$15.97
Boeing	$78.38	1.35	2.04	0.68	$30.30	$27.82	$42.03
Caterpillar	$58.75	1.71	2.33	1.92	$21.25	$69.77	$95.06
Chevron	$52.38	1.11	1.56	1.15	$23.20	$29.61	$41.62
Coca-Cola	$74.25	6.23	9.08	1.62	$2.50	$25.23	$36.77
Disney	$58.88	3.10	4.65	1.15	$15.30	$54.54	$81.82
DuPont	$69.88	1.48	2.06	2.32	$19.30	$66.27	$92.24
Eastman Kodak	$67.00	1.87	2.68	1.68	$15.95	$50.11	$71.81
Exxon	$81.13	1.51	1.97	1.00	$34.30	$51.79	$67.57
General Electric	$72.00	2.21	2.89	1.25	$19.00	$52.49	$68.64
General Motors	$52.88	0.83	1.27	2.45	$20.35	$41.38	$63.32
Goodyear Tire	$45.38	0.99	1.60	1.40	$25.00	$34.65	$56.00
IBM	**$91.38**	**1.66**	**2.44**	**1.56**	**$46.60**	**$120.68**	**$177.38**
International Paper	$37.88	0.89	1.31	1.48	$27.30	$35.96	$52.93
McDonald's	$45.13	2.40	3.48	0.96	$11.15	$25.69	$37.25
Merck	$65.63	4.51	6.95	0.92	$9.95	$41.28	$63.62
MMM	$66.38	2.46	3.21	1.00	$17.50	$43.05	$56.18
Philip Morris	$90.25	2.93	4.42	1.56	$17.95	$82.05	$123.77
J. P. Morgan	$80.25	1.11	1.65	0.88	$56.60	$55.29	$82.18
Procter & Gamble	$83.00	2.96	3.96	1.33	$15.30	$60.23	$80.58
Sears	$39.00	0.92	1.43	2.10	$12.40	$23.96	$37.24
Texaco	$78.50	0.94	1.28	1.11	$34.55	$36.05	$49.09
Union Carbide	$37.50	0.93	1.56	1.87	$23.25	$40.43	$67.82
United Technologies	$94.88	1.24	1.81	1.21	$32.65	$48.99	$71.51
Westinghouse	$16.38	1.53	2.45	0.79	$2.95	$3.57	$5.71
Woolworth	$13.00	1.19	1.91	0.59	$9.85	$6.92	$11.10
DJIA	5117.12	1.83	2.68	1.42	$20.85	4701.31	6868.19

TABLE 6.27

Benchmark Investing's 1973 Purchases

1973 Purchases	12/31/72 Price	12/31/73 Price	1973 Dividend	1973 Total Return
Allied Chemical	$29.00	$49.00	$1.29	73.41%
American Can	$31.63	$26.25	$2.20	−10.05%
American Telephone	$52.75	$50.13	$2.87	0.47%
Bethlehem Steel	$29.38	$33.00	$1.65	17.94%
DuPont	$177.50	$159.00	$5.76	−7.18%
General Motors	$81.13	$46.13	$5.25	−36.67%
International Harvester	$38.38	$25.75	$1.50	−29.00%
International Nickel	$31.88	$35.25	$1.20	14.34%
International Paper	$41.88	$52.00	$1.75	28.34%
Johns-Manville	$31.25	$16.50	$1.20	−43.36%
Texaco	$37.50	$29.38	$1.73	−17.04%
Union Carbide	$50.00	$34.13	$2.08	−27.58%
U.S. Steel	$30.50	$37.63	$1.61	28.66%
Woolworth	$31.25	$18.38	$1.20	−37.34%
Benchmark picks				−3.22%
DJIA	1020.01	850.86		−13.12%

TABLE 6.28

Benchmark Investing's 1974 Purchases

1974 Purchases	12/31/73 Price	12/31/74 Price	1974 Dividend	1974 Total Return
Allied Chemical	$49.00	$28.38	$1.53	−38.96%
Alcoa*	$32.33	$29.88	$1.34	−3.43%
American Can	$26.25	$29.00	$2.40	19.62%
Bethlehem Steel	$33.00	$24.88	$2.30	−17.64%
Exxon	$94.13	$64.63	$5.00	−26.03%
International Nickel	$35.25	$21.50	$1.60	−34.47%
International Paper	$52.00	$35.75	$1.75	−27.88%
Owens-Illinois	$30.88	$33.75	$1.58	14.41%
Standard Oil (Cal.)	$35.00	$22.25	$1.93	−30.91%
Swift	$24.88	$27.88	$0.75	15.07%

Continued

TABLE 6.28

Concluded

1974 Purchases	12/31/73 Price	12/31/74 Price	1974 Dividend	1974 Total Return
Texaco	$29.38	$20.88	$2.10	−21.78%
Union Carbide	$34.13	$41.38	$2.18	27.63%
United Aircraft	$23.75	$32.63	$1.96	45.64%
U.S. Steel	$37.63	$38.00	$2.21	6.86%
Benchmark picks				−5.13%
DJIA	850.86	616.24		−23.14%

*Split 3–2.

TABLE 6.29

Benchmark Investing's 1975 Purchases

1975 Purchases	12/31/74 Price	12/31/75 Price	1975 Dividend	1975 Total Return
Esmark	$27.88	$31.63	$1.22	17.83%
General Foods	$17.88	$27.63	$1.43	62.53%
General Motors	$30.75	$57.63	$2.40	95.22%
Westinghouse	$10.00	$13.38	$0.97	43.50%
Woolworth	$9.38	$22.00	$1.20	147.33%
Benchmark picks				73.28%
DJIA	616.24	852.41		44.40%

TABLE 6.30

Benchmark Investing's 1976 Purchases

1976 Purchases	12/31/75 Price	12/31/76 Price	1976 Dividend	1976 Total Return
Allied Chemical	$33.25	$40.00	$1.80	25.71%
Alcoa	$38.63	$57.25	$1.39	51.80%
American Can	$31.38	$39.00	$2.30	31.61%
American Telephone	$50.88	$63.50	$3.80	32.27%
Chrysler	$10.13	$20.38	$0.30	104.15%
DuPont	$126.50	$135.13	$5.25	10.97%
General Electric	$46.13	$55.38	$1.70	23.74%
General Foods	$27.63	$30.25	$1.54	15.06%
General Motors	$57.63	$78.50	$5.55	45.84%
International Harvester	$22.38	$33.00	$1.70	55.05%
International Paper	$57.75	$68.88	$2.00	22.74%
Johns-Manville	$23.25	$33.50	$1.35	49.89%
Owens-Illinois	$51.88	$56.25	$0.94	10.24%
Procter & Gamble	$89.00	$93.63	$2.05	7.51%
Sears	$64.50	$69.00	$1.60	9.46%
Standard Oil (Cal.)	$29.38	$41.00	$2.15	46.87%
Union Carbide	$61.13	$61.88	$2.50	5.32%
United Technologies	$23.19	$38.88	$2.40	78.01%
Westinghouse	$13.38	$17.63	$0.97	39.01%
Benchmark picks				35.01%
DJIA	852.41	1004.65		22.72%

TABLE 6.31

Benchmark Investing's 1977 Purchases

1977 Purchases	12/31/76 Price	12/31/77 Price	1977 Dividend	1977 Total Return
Allied Chemical	$40.00	$44.25	$1.85	15.25%
American Can	$39.00	$38.34	$2.50	4.72%
American Telephone	$63.50	$60.50	$4.20	1.89%
DuPont	$135.13	$120.38	$5.76	−6.65%
General Electric	$55.38	$49.88	$2.40	−5.60%
General Motors	$78.50	$62.88	$6.80	−11.24%

Continued

TABLE 6.31

Concluded

1977 Purchases	12/31/76 Price	12/31/77 Price	1977 Dividend	1977 Total Return
Goodyear Tire	$23.75	$17.25	$1.20	−22.32%
International Harvester	$33.00	$30.75	$1.85	−1.21%
Johns-Manville	$33.50	$32.50	$1.55	1.64%
MMM	$56.63	$48.50	$1.70	−11.35%
Procter & Gamble	$93.63	$85.88	$2.40	−5.71%
Sears*	$34.50	$28.00	$2.16	−12.58%
Standard Oil (Cal.)	$41.00	$38.88	$2.35	0.56%
Westinghouse	$17.63	$18.13	$0.97	8.34%
Benchmark picks				−3.16%
DJIA	1004.65	831.17		−12.71%

*Split 2–1.

TABLE 6.32

Benchmark Investing's 1978 Purchases

1978 Purchases	12/31/77 Price	12/31/78 Price	1978 Dividend	1978 Total Return
Alcoa	$46.63	$47.75	$1.80	6.26%
American Brands	$43.00	$50.38	$3.83	26.07%
American Telephone	$60.50	$60.50	$4.60	7.60%
Bethlehem Steel	$21.13	$19.63	$1.00	−2.37%
DuPont	$120.38	$126.00	$7.26	10.70%
Eastman Kodak	$51.13	$58.63	$2.23	19.03%
Exxon	$48.13	$49.13	$3.30	8.93%
General Electric	$49.88	$47.13	$2.50	−0.50%
General Foods	$31.50	$32.13	$1.68	7.33%
Johns-Manville	$32.50	$22.63	$1.80	−24.83%
MMM	$48.50	$63.13	$2.00	34.29%
Owens-Illinois	$23.88	$17.88	$1.11	−20.48%
Procter & Gamble	$85.88	$88.88	$2.70	6.64%
United Technologies	$35.88	$38.88	$2.00	13.94%
Westinghouse	$18.13	$16.63	$0.97	−2.92%

Continued

TABLE 6.32

Concluded

1978 Purchases	12/31/77 Price	12/31/78 Price	1978 Dividend	1978 Total Return
Woolworth	$18.88	$19.38	$1.40	10.06%
Benchmark picks				6.24%
DJIA	831.17	805.01		2.69%

TABLE 6.33

Benchmark Investing's 1979 Purchases

1979 Purchases	12/31/78 Price	12/31/79 Price	1979 Dividend	1979 Total Return
Alcoa	$47.75	$54.88	$2.60	20.38%
American Brands	$50.38	$67.88	$4.63	43.93%
Bethlehem Steel	$19.63	$21.13	$1.50	15.28%
DuPont*	$42.00	$40.38	$2.75	2.69%
Eastman Kodak	$58.63	$48.13	$2.90	−12.96%
Esmark	$24.00	$28.63	$1.84	26.96%
Exxon	$49.13	$55.13	$3.90	20.15%
General Electric	$47.13	$50.63	$2.75	13.26%
General Foods	$32.13	$33.38	$1.95	9.96%
Inco	$15.75	$23.75	$0.50	53.97%
International Harvester	$36.25	$39.13	$2.35	14.43%
International Paper	$36.50	$37.00	$2.20	7.40%
MMM	$63.13	$50.25	$2.40	−16.60%
Owens-Illinois	$17.88	$20.25	$1.26	20.30%
Procter & Gamble	$88.88	$74.25	$3.10	−12.97%
Standard Oil (Cal.)	$46.88	$56.38	$2.90	26.45%
Texaco	$23.88	$28.88	$2.12	29.82%
Union Carbide	$34.00	$42.00	$2.90	32.06%
United Technologies	$38.88	$43.00	$2.20	16.26%
Woolworth	$19.38	$25.13	$1.60	37.93%
Benchmark picks				17.43%
DJIA	805.01	838.74		10.52%

*Split 3–1.

TABLE 6.34

Benchmark Investing's 1980 Purchases

1980 Purchases	12/31/79 Price	12/31/80 Price	1980 Dividend	1980 Total Return
Allied Chemical	$49.13	$53.50	$2.15	13.27%
American Brands	$67.88	$77.50	$5.88	22.83%
Eastman Kodak	$48.13	$69.75	$3.20	51.57%
Exxon	$55.13	$80.63	$5.40	56.05%
Goodyear Tire	$12.88	$16.00	$1.30	34.32%
IBM	$64.38	$67.88	$3.44	10.78%
Inco	$23.75	$20.38	$0.69	−11.28%
Merck	$72.25	$84.75	$2.28	20.46%
Procter & Gamble	$74.25	$68.88	$3.40	−02.65%
Standard Oil (Cal.)	$56.38	$99.50	$3.60	82.87%
Texaco	$28.88	$48.00	$2.45	74.69%
Union Carbide	$42.00	$50.25	$3.10	27.02%
United Technologies	$43.00	$61.00	$2.20	46.98%
U.S. Steel	$17.50	$24.75	$1.60	50.57%
Westinghouse	$20.13	$29.63	$1.40	54.15%
Benchmark picks				35.44%
DJIA	838.74	963.99		21.41%

TABLE 6.35

Benchmark Investing's 1981 Purchases

1981 Purchases	12/31/80 Price	12/31/81 Price	1981 Dividend	1981 Total Return
Allied Chemical	$53.50	$43.88	$2.34	−13.61%
DuPont	$42.00	$37.25	$2.75	−4.76%
Eastman Kodak	$69.75	$71.13	$3.51	7.01%
General Foods	$30.25	$31.75	$2.20	12.23%
Goodyear Tire	$16.00	$19.00	$1.30	26.87%
Sears	$15.25	$16.13	$1.36	14.69%
Union Carbide	$50.25	$51.38	$3.30	8.82%
U.S. Steel	$24.75	$29.88	$1.60	27.19%
Westinghouse	$29.63	$25.50	$1.80	−7.86%
Benchmark picks				7.84%
DJIA	963.99	875.00		−3.40%

TABLE 6.36

Benchmark Investing's 1982 Purchases

1982 Purchases	12/31/81 Price	12/31/82 Price	1982 Dividend	1982 Total Return
General Electric	$57.38	$94.88	$3.36	71.21%
General Foods	$31.75	$39.63	$2.30	32.06%
IBM	$56.88	$96.25	$3.44	75.26%
Procter & Gamble	$80.38	$118.25	$4.10	52.21%
Sears	$16.13	$30.13	$1.36	95.23%
Benchmark picks				65.20%
DJIA	875.00	1046.54		25.79%

TABLE 6.37

Benchmark Investing's 1983 Purchases

1983 Purchases	12/31/82 Price	12/31/83 Price	1983 Dividend	1983 Total Return
Allied Corp.	$32.38	$55.75	$2.40	79.59%
DuPont	$35.88	$52.00	$2.49	51.87%
Exxon	$29.75	$37.38	$3.12	36.13%
General Motors	$62.38	$74.38	$2.80	23.73%
IBM	$96.25	$122.00	$3.71	30.61%
Procter & Gamble*	$59.13	$56.88	$2.25	0.00%
Sears	$30.13	$37.13	$1.36	27.75%
Benchmark picks				35.67%
DJIA	1046.54	1258.64		25.65%

*Split 2–1.

TABLE 6.38

Benchmark Investing's 1984 Purchases

1984 Purchases	12/31/83 Price	12/31/84 Price	1984 Dividend	1984 Total Return
Exxon	$37.38	$45.00	$3.36	29.37%
General Motors	$74.38	$78.38	$4.75	11.76%
Merck	$89.66	$93.25	$3.00	7.35%
Benchmark picks				16.16%
DJIA	1258.64	1211.57		1.08%

TABLE 6.39

Benchmark Investing's 1985 Purchases

1985 Purchases	12/31/84 Price	12/31/85 Price	1985 Dividend	1985 Total Return
Merck	$93.25	$137.00	$3.18	50.33%
Benchmark picks				50.33%
DJIA	1211.57	1546.67		32.78%

TABLE 6.40

Benchmark Investing's 1986 Purchases

1986 Purchases	12/31/85 Price	12/31/86 Price	1986 Dividend	1986 Total Return
Philip Morris*	$44.19	$71.88	$2.48	68.27%
Benchmark picks				68.27%
DJIA	1546.67	1895.95		26.92%

*Split 2–1.

TABLE 6.41

Benchmark Investing's 1987 Purchases

1987 Purchases	12/31/86 Price	12/31/87 Price	1987 Dividend	1987 Total Return
Goodyear Tire	$41.88	$60.00	$1.60	47.09%
Benchmark picks				47.09%
DJIA	1895.95	1938.83		6.02%

TABLE 6.42

Benchmark Investing's 1988 Purchases

1988 Purchases	12/31/87 Price	12/31/88 Price	1988 Dividend	1988 Total Return
AlliedSignal	$28.25	$32.50	$1.80	21.42%
Alcoa	$46.75	$56.00	$1.30	22.57%
American Express	$22.88	$26.63	$0.76	19.71%
Bethlehem Steel	$16.75	$23.25	$0.00	38.81%
International Paper	$42.25	$46.38	$1.20	12.62%
Union Carbide	$21.75	$25.63	$1.15	23.13%
Benchmark picks				23.05%
DJIA	1938.83	2168.57		15.95%

TABLE 6.43

Benchmark Investing's 1989 Purchases

1989 Purchases	12/31/88 Price	12/31/89 Price	1989 Dividend	1989 Total Return
American Express	$26.63	$34.88	$0.86	34.21%
AT&T	$28.75	$45.50	$1.20	62.43%
Goodyear Tire	$51.13	$43.50	$1.90	−11.21%
International Paper	$46.38	$56.50	$1.53	25.12%

Continued

TABLE 6.43

Concluded

1989 Purchases	12/31/88 Price	12/31/89 Price	1989 Dividend	1989 Total Return
Union Carbide	$25.63	$23.25	$1.00	−5.38%
Benchmark picks				21.03%
DJIA	2168.57	2753.20		31.71%

TABLE 6.44

Benchmark Investing's 1990 Purchases

1990 Purchases	12/31/89 Price	12/31/90 Price	1990 Dividend	1990 Total Return
Eastman Kodak	$41.13	$41.63	$2.00	6.08%
IBM	$94.13	$113.00	$4.84	25.19%
Benchmark picks				15.63%
DJIA	2753.2	2633.66		−0.57%

TABLE 6.45

Benchmark Investing's 1991 Purchases

1991 Purchases	12/31/90 Price	12/31/91 Price	1991 Dividend	1991 Total Return
American Express	$20.63	$20.50	$0.94	3.93%
AT&T	$30.13	$39.13	$1.32	34.25%
Boeing	$45.38	$47.75	$1.00	7.43%
Sears	$25.38	$37.88	$2.00	57.13%
Benchmark picks				25.69%
DJIA	2633.66	3168.83		23.93%

TABLE 6.46

Benchmark Investing's 1992 Purchases

1992 Purchases	12/31/91 Price	12/31/92 Price	1992 Dividend	1992 Total Return
AT&T	$39.13	$51.00	$1.32	33.71%
Caterpillar	$43.88	$53.63	$0.60	23.59%
Eastman Kodak	$48.25	$40.50	$1.70	−12.54%
Benchmark picks				14.92%
DJIA	3168.83	3301.11		7.34%

TABLE 6.47

Benchmark Investing's 1993 Purchases

1993 Purchases	12/31/92 Price	12/31/93 Price	1993 Dividend	1993 Total Return
American Express	$24.88	$30.88	$1.00	28.14%
Caterpillar	$53.63	$89.00	$0.60	67.07%
Eastman Kodak	$40.50	$56.25	$2.00	43.83%
IBM	$50.38	$56.50	$0.50	13.14%
Benchmark picks				38.04%
DJIA	3301.11	3754.09		16.72%

TABLE 6.48

Benchmark Investing's 1994 Purchases

1994 Purchases	12/31/93 Price	12/31/94 Price	1994 Dividend	1994 Total Return
Merck	$34.38	$38.13	$1.14	14.22%
Philip Morris	$55.63	$57.50	$2.86	8.50%
Benchmark picks				11.36%
DJIA	3754.09	3834.44		4.95%

TABLE 6.49

Benchmark Investing's 1995 Purchases

1995 Purchases	12/31/94 Price	12/31/95 Price	1995 Dividend	1995 Total Return
American Express	$29.50	$41.38	$0.90	43.32%
Caterpillar	$55.13	$58.75	$1.20	8.74%
DuPont	$56.13	$69.88	$1.60	27.35%
Eastman Kodak	$47.75	$67.00	$1.60	43.66%
Goodyear Tire	$33.63	$45.38	$0.95	37.76%
IBM	$73.50	$91.38	$0.50	25.01%
Philip Morris	$57.50	$90.25	$3.48	63.01%
Sears*	$46.00	$39.00	$31.67	53.63%
Benchmark picks				37.81%
DJIA	3834.44	5117.12		36.48%

*Spun off Allstate, distributing .927035 shares of Allstate Corp.

TABLE 6.50

Benchmark Investing's 1996 Purchases

1996 Purchases	12/31/95 Price	12/31/96 Price	1996 Dividend	1996 Total Return
Alcoa	$52.88	$63.75	$1.33	23.07%
IBM	$91.38	$151.50	$1.30	67.21%
Benchmark picks				45.14%
DJIA	5117.12	6448.27		28.57%

CHAPTER 7

When to Sell Stocks

The key to making money in stocks is not to get scared out of them.

Peter Lynch
Beating the Street*

We've all been taught to take profits when we can and not to be greedy. Everyone's heard the adage that bulls and bears make money on Wall Street, but pigs get slaughtered. In the Roaring Twenties, Wall Street tycoon Bernard Baruch boasted that his fortune came from selling stocks too soon. Conventional Wall Street wisdom dictates that we should be prepared to sell our winners.

Using a disciplined strategy for selling a stock is just as important to successful investing as having a disciplined buying strategy. Most professional investors will tell you that deciding when to sell is more difficult than deciding when to buy. There are a number of reasons to sell a stock. The most obvious one is that the stock reaches a price target that reflects limited appreciation potential for the future. This is especially true for mature companies found in the Dow Industrials. It is best to sell them when they reach their target prices. On the other hand, as Peter Lynch pointed out, the key to making large sums of money in the stock market is to stay with winning stocks as long as possible. "When you've found the right stock and bought it, all the evidence tells you it's going higher, and

*New York: Simon & Schuster, 1993, p. 36.

everything is working in your direction, then it's a shame if you sell," Lynch wrote.[1]

Suppose benchmark investing's formula had a one-year price range of $30 on the downside and $44 on the upside for a particular stock. Would it be smart to buy the shares at $30 then sell after they rose to $44? After all, that would be a healthy 47 percent profit in one year. In spite of the temptation to realize the gain, the best thing to do in most situations is to hold onto the stock and let the profits continue to grow year after year. In fact, it would be a mistake to sell the stock simply because benchmark investing's formula had an upside target price of $44 for that year.

What investors should do in this case is to consider the longer-term price targets to see if the stock has superior appreciation potential. If so, it would be astute to hold onto the stock.

But which price target should an investor use? It depends on your investment time frame. For example, in mid-1996, Coca-Cola was overvalued at $53 for anyone with a one-year time horizon or less (see Figure 7.1). According to the benchmark investing formula, Coca-Cola would not climb significantly higher than $53 before mid-1997 so long as it continued to trade within its historical ranges. (Coke traded as high as $62.50 in February 1997 before falling back to $53.75 in April 1997.) However, anyone with a time frame exceeding one year should have held onto Coke shares for longer-term gains.

"Most of the money I make is in the third or fourth year that I've owned something," Lynch noted.[2]

Benchmark investing's preference is to hold onto a stock so long as it has potential for above-average gains. Let's look at a brief example using benchmark investing's actual recommendations from 1991 to 1996 (see Table 7.1). For this illustration, we'll assume that an investor is making buys and sells in a taxable account. What's more, we'll assume that the investor made $1000 investments (with no commissions factored in) and sold at the end of each year.

As Table 7.1 shows, the investor would have averaged after-tax annual returns of 20.75 percent while netting $4925.57 in profits on an original investment of $23,000. However, had that same investor focused on the longer term and held onto each of the stocks *without*

---

1   Peter Lynch, *One Up on Wall Street* (New York: Simon and Schuster, 1989), p. 253.

2   Ibid., p. 272.

FIGURE 7.1

Coca-Cola, 7/5/96–1/2/98

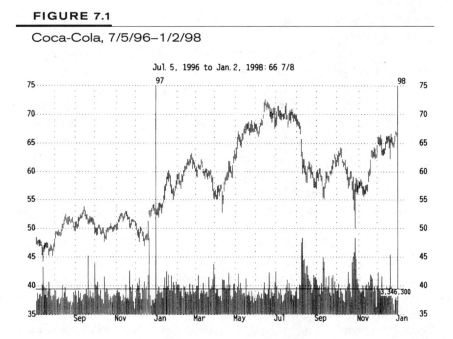

selling and paying capital gains taxes, the net profits would have been far more impressive (see Table 7.2). In fact, the $23,000 initial investment would have climbed to $52,906 by the end of 1996, giving the investor unrealized gains of nearly $30,000 rather than realized gains of $4925.57.

So which style of trading makes more sense? Would you prefer to focus on the longer term and pay much less money in commissions and capital gains taxes while growing your nest egg at an accelerated rate? Or would you rather trade more often and pay your broker and the IRS more in commissions and taxes while seeing your profits reduced significantly by costly transactions? I don't know about you, but it seems like the clear choice is to focus on the long term and net higher gains.

Let's get back to Coca-Cola. Benchmark investors had a huge gain in an overvalued stock after paying a split-adjusted $20.88 in the summer of 1994. Those investors with a shorter time horizon would have been wise to sell their Coke shares. But those with a longer-term perspective should have held onto their shares because Coke's long-term potential for growth was still impressive. Everyone has seen what holding onto high-quality stocks like Coke has

TABLE 7.1

What a $1000 Original Investment Would Have Become
If Sold Each Year

Year	Purchases	1991 Gain	After-Tax % Net Gain	After-Tax Net Gain
1991	American Express	3.93%	2.83%	$28.30
	AT&T	34.25%	24.66%	$246.66
	Boeing	7.43%	5.35%	$53.50
	Sears	57.13%	41.13%	$411.30
1992	AT&T	33.71%	24.27%	$242.27
	Caterpillar	23.59%	16.98%	$169.80
	Eastman Kodak	−12.54%	−12.54%	−$125.40
1993	American Express	28.14%	20.26%	$202.60
	Caterpillar	67.07%	48.29%	$482.90
	Eastman Kodak	43.83%	31.55%	$315.50
	IBM	13.14%	9.46%	$94.60
1994	Merck	14.22%	10.24%	$102.38
	Philip Morris	8.50%	6.12%	$61.20
1995	American Express	43.32%	31.19%	$311.9
	Caterpillar	8.74%	6.29%	$62.90
	DuPont	27.35%	19.69%	$196.92
	Eastman Kodak	43.66%	31.44%	$314.35
	Goodyear Tire	37.76%	27.19%	$271.87
	IBM	25.01%	18.01%	$180.07
	Philip Morris	63.01%	45.36%	$435.60
	Sears	53.63%	38.61%	$386.14
1996	Alcoa	23.07%	16.61%	$166.10
	IBM	67.21%	48.39%	$483.91

TABLE 7.2

What a $1000 Original Investment Would Have Become
without Selling

Year	Purchases	Value as of 12/31/96
1991	American Express	$3291
	Boeing	$2915
	AT&T	$2319
	Sears	$3922
1992	AT&T	$1709
	Caterpillar	$3643
	Eastman Kodak	$1954
1993	American Express	$2512
	Caterpillar	$2964
	Eastman Kodak	$2218
	IBM	$3194
1994	Merck	$2475
	Philip Morris	$2300
1995	American Express	$1987
	Caterpillar	$1420
	DuPont	$1766
	Eastman Kodak	$1754
	Goodyear Tire	$1589
	IBM	$2100
	Philip Morris	$2120
	Sears	$1847
1996	Alcoa	$1231
	IBM	$1672

done for Warren Buffett. Here's a way investors can emulate the great one from Omaha.

TO SELL OR NOT TO SELL?

In stocks, it is the gut and not the head that determines whether you hold on for the long term. By 1994, AlliedSignal's shares had averaged 37 percent gains during the previous three years. Although Allied was trading at $79.00 at the beginning of the year, benchmark investing's formula predicted that the stock would trade between $77.34 and $111.14 over the next three to five years. Consequently, I faced the possibility of a loss on the low side and just 8 percent average returns on the upside over the longer term. Because of its limited long-term potential, I decided to sell Allied. At first, it looked like selling Allied was the correct call, since the stock lost 12.28 percent in 1994. However, Allied rebounded sharply, gaining 44 percent in 1995 and 42.95 percent in 1996. Obviously, I would have made more money by remaining invested in Allied for the long term. With perfect hindsight, I should have stuck with Allied.

The benchmark investor who invested $10,000 in Allied at the beginning of 1991 and held on until the end of 1996 would have seen that investment climb to $56,816. The investor who sold at the beginning of 1994 at $79 a share, would have realized a long-term gain of $19,444. After paying 28 percent capital gains taxes, the benchmark investor would have a net gain of $14,000. Had the investor reinvested the $24,000 in benchmark's other recommendations in 1994, he or she would have had a total of $47,221 by the end of 1996.

If you've invested in stocks long enough, you have probably had the experience of selling too soon. Eventually, it happens to everyone. Even the most thoughtful investor is susceptible to the gnawing fear of losing unrealized gains. In 1977, Peter Lynch had just started managing Fidelity Magellan when he invested a sizable 3 percent of the fund in Warner Communications at $26. Six months later, Warner had climbed to $32 and he began to worry because a technical analyst had told him the stock was "extremely extended" at $26. Lynch ignored his fears, but when the stock hit $38 he sold "for no conscious reason." What happened next?

"Of course after I sold, the stock continued its ascent to $50, $60, $70, and over $180," Lynch wryly recalled.[3]

Each investor must determine what course of action to follow when it comes to taking profits. In the AlliedSignal example, investors were presented with an overvalued stock that had below-average profit potential for the next market cycle. True, they would have been faced with paying large capital gains taxes, but there were other Dow stocks that the investors could have shifted their net profits into in 1994.

---

3   Ibid., p. 252.

It would be wonderful if all our answers about whether to sell were black and white. Ultimately, however, only the investor can answer whether selling a short-term overvalued stock, paying the resulting capital gains taxes, then reinvesting the net proceeds into high-quality, undervalued Dow stocks makes sense. The only time it is easy to know when to sell is when a stock is trading above its long-term price projection. That means the stock should not rise at all over the next three to five years. In this case, even the most devoted fan of a company must decide to sell.

In considering whether to sell an investment, investors should ignore the price paid and judge the future potential of the company. The original cost basis should play no part in the decision. Nevertheless, human nature has a way of taking over the decision-making process. That being the case, it is easier for most investors to sell a profitable investment standing above the price paid than to sell a losing position.

Why should investors be so willing to sell their best stocks while leaving their losers intact? Behavioral finance researchers have discovered that losses have a greater psychic impact than do gains. In general, people cannot bring themselves to sell stocks at a loss because they tend to be risk-averse. This helps explain the propensity of people to widely diversify their investment portfolios. According to leading British investor George Ross Goobey, it is a sort of human vanity which cannot admit that the original purchase was wrong. And since people feel the pain of loss more than they do the pleasure of an equivalent gain, as long as they don't sell a losing stock position they need not acknowledge a loss and experience the distress. They continue to take odd comfort in the fact that they are experiencing only a paper loss rather than a realized one.

Every investor will make mistakes from time to time. It is the nature of investing that losses will occur. The key is to recognize mistakes early and pare them from your portfolio. Your ultimate goal should be to allow your winners to run as long as possible—5, 10, 20, 30 years and more is the ideal investment. Do not let human nature prevent you from doing what's best in the long run. This striking difference in attitude will benefit you immensely. Therefore, admit your mistakes early and sell, and keep your winners in a benchmark investing portfolio where they belong.

CHAPTER 8

They Never Ring a Bell at the Top

Investment results largely depend on how one behaves near the top and near the bottom.

*John Maynard Keynes**

The stock market is perhaps one of the greatest tests of a person's patience and will. For those lucky investors who can sit back and take an objective view of the factors influencing the Dow, the potential for profits is great. However, for those who lose sight of their goals and let emotions rule their actions, the potential for disaster is very real. Wouldn't it be amazing, therefore, to know exactly when the stock market is getting ready to peak? Better still, how remarkable would it be to know exactly when to make a plunge into stocks at the market's absolute low?

Even though benchmark investing wasn't developed to be used as a market forecasting tool, it is a highly accurate indicator of just where the market is in terms of value. Benchmark investing was created to uncover the true value of individual companies. A meaningful side effect of benchmark investing is that it does for the Dow index exactly what it does for each individual Dow stock. It accurately forecasts whether the Dow Jones Industrial Average is at its peak or its bottom. Although many investors would consider this

---

* Milo Keynes, *Essays on John Maynard Keynes* (London: Cambridge University Press, 1975), p. 228.

knowledge to be extremely important, others might argue that they're not buying the market—they're simply buying undervalued stocks that will widely outperform the market over the long term.

The main benefit of knowing whether the Dow is too high or too low is peace of mind. During July 1996, the Dow dropped to 5350 after reaching 5760 earlier in the year. According to benchmark's formula, the Dow should have traded between 4788 and 6883 in mid-1996. Therefore, the benchmark investor could rest assured in the knowledge that the market could expect no worse than an 11 percent drop from those levels as long as the market traded within its historical levels of valuation. Benchmark investors armed with this information could ignore Wall Street analysts, who had again worked themselves into a lather over expectations of inflation and were calling for another major market correction. In fact, one of Wall Street's most visible and heavily marketed "gurus" warned her subscribers to get out of the stock market in July, and later again in August, so sure was she of the market's pending weakness. Contrary to her forecast, the market climbed nearly 3000 points higher over the next 13 months. That's another example of why independent investors need benchmark investing.

With the analytical power of the benchmark formula behind them, independent investors can ignore Wall Street analysts and the investment media and enjoy that rare commodity of conviction and peace of mind regarding the Dow. Indeed, how many investors would have benefited from knowing that the Dow was extremely overvalued on August 27, 1987? Had benchmark's formula been created at that time, it would have projected a trading range of 1648 to 2450. According to benchmark investing's forecast, the Dow was treading on dangerously high ground at 2700 and faced a potential downside of 41 percent. Had benchmark's formula been available in 1987, the benchmark investor would have known that there was a very good possibility of the market suffering a huge collapse in order to correct its excess valuation.

Herein lies the dilemma for the benchmark investor. Let's suppose that an independent investor holds a Dow stock that has appreciated sharply. To sell would mean paying enormous capital gains taxes. Also assume that while overvalued now, the stock holds superior appreciation potential for the longer term. This is a highly likely possibility for benchmark investors. In fact, it happens all the time. Now, let's throw in a highly overvalued stock market like that in 1987. What should the long-term benchmark investor do?

Clearly, the first possibility is for the benchmark investor to remain fully invested and weather the nastiness of the bear market. For those who did so in 1987, their recovery time was minimal compared with the average bear market. However, there have been extended periods when the Dow failed to advance. For example, the Dow stood at 874 in 1964 (see Table 8.1). It took nearly 17 years for the index to finally clear that level for good. Who wants to wait a decade or more for the market to advance? No one, of course. And that's where LEAPS can be of benefit.

LONG-TERM EQUITY ANTICIPATION SECURITIES (LEAPS)

There is another alternative for benchmark investors who are holding stocks that have already made huge gains but still have fantastic long-term appreciation potential. And that is to make use of long-term equity anticipation securities, otherwise known as LEAPS. As the name implies, LEAPS are longer-term options. Their longer shelf life makes them behave much differently from their first cousin, the shorter-term option.

Options grant the buyer the right, but not the obligation, to buy—in the case of calls—or sell—in the case of puts—a specified amount of an underlying stock at a predetermined price on or before a given date. For example, an investor who thinks IBM could rise above $170 within the next two months could buy a July $170 call option for $700. In this case, the investor is betting $700 ($7 times 100 shares) that IBM will rise before the option's expiration date on the third Saturday in July. If IBM rises to $177, the investor will break even. However, if IBM stays at $170 or drops lower, *the investor will lose his or her entire investment.* IBM would have to rise above $177 for the investor to realize a profit on expiration day.

LEAPS, on the other hand, grant the holder the right to buy or sell shares of a stock at a predetermined price on or before a given date *up to two years in the future.* This longer-term characteristic of LEAPS acts as an important benefit to the investor, because the erosion-of-time premium takes place at a much slower pace than for shorter-term options.

TABLE 8.1

Year-End Dow Jones Industrial Average Closing Prices

Year	Closing Price	Percentage Change
1961	731.14	18.71
1962	652.10	−10.81
1963	762.95	17.00
1964	874.13	14.57
1965	969.26	10.88
1966	785.69	−18.94
1967	905.11	15.20
1968	943.75	4.27
1969	800.36	−15.19
1970	838.92	4.82
1971	890.20	6.11
1972	1020.01	14.58
1973	850.86	−16.58
1974	616.24	−27.52
1975	852.41	38.32
1976	1004.65	17.86
1977	831.17	−17.27
1978	805.01	−3.15
1979	838.74	4.19
1980	963.99	14.93
1981	875.00	−9.23
1982	1046.54	19.60
1983	1258.64	20.27
1984	1211.57	−3.74
1985	1546.67	27.66
1986	1895.95	22.58
1987	1938.83	2.26
1988	2168.57	11.85
1989	2753.20	26.96
1990	2633.66	−4.34
1991	3168.83	20.32
1992	3301.11	4.17
1993	3754.09	13.72
1994	3834.44	2.14
1995	5117.12	33.45
1996	6448.27	26.01
1997	7908.25	22.64

The Chicago Board Options Exchange introduced LEAPS in October 1990. Equity LEAPS trade on more than 270 stocks in units known as contracts, each of which generally represents 100 shares of underlying stock. Therefore, an investor who purchased five LEAPS calls owns long-term options representing 500 shares of underlying stock. As of late 1997, open interest in LEAPS exceeded 5.1 million contracts—the equivalent of 510 million shares of stock.

One reason for the immense popularity of LEAPS is that investors can use them to diversify their portfolios. LEAPS offer investors an alternative to stock ownership at a fraction of the price of the underlying shares. That way, they risk less capital than is required to purchase stock. Should a stock appreciate to a level above the exercise price of the LEAPS, the call holder may exercise the option and purchase shares at a price below the current market price. That same investor, as is most usually the case, may otherwise sell the call in the open market for a profit.

LEAPS puts provide investors with a means to hedge current stock holdings. Investors should consider purchasing LEAPS puts if they are concerned with the downside risk of a particular stock that they own but do not wish to sell. Purchase of a LEAPS put gives the investor the right to sell the underlying stock at the strike price up until the cutoff time for the submission of exercises notices prior to the option's expiration.

As with any option position, the investor's risk is limited to the premium paid for the position. Risk varies, of course, depending on the strategy followed. A common stock can be held indefinitely in the hopes that its value will increase, whereas every option has an expiration date. If an option is not closed out or exercised prior to its expiration date, it ceases to exist as a financial instrument. For this reason, an option is considered a wasting asset.

At the beginning of 1996, Texaco was trading at $78.25. Its in-the-money 1997 65 LEAPS call was trading for $15 (using in-the-money calls is a conservative strategy for bullish investors). By November 1996, Texaco's common had risen 27 percent to $100 a share, but the LEAPS calls had risen a whopping 133 percent to $35 per contract.

I do not mean to imply that all LEAPS trades will be anywhere near as profitable, but this illustrates the fantastic leverage that LEAPS offer investors.

Although most investors think of speculation when they consider options, LEAPS can also be used to protect portfolios. Let's consider a hypothetical situation in which you have a large unrealized gain in a Dow stock. You strongly believe that the stock holds significant upside potential for the next several years, but the overall market is dangerously overvalued, as it was in August 1987. Of course, you could simply weather a bear market with the knowledge that your stock over the long term will appreciate to your target levels. In the short run, however, your portfolio will suffer.

Suppose, however, that you now buy LEAPS puts to protect your portfolio during an anticipated market downturn. For simplicity's sake, let's follow one example through several scenarios to see the pluses and minuses of buying LEAPS.

Example (set on Monday, January 3, in the future)

Stock	Price	LEAPS Put	Strike	Put Cost
IBM	200	January (2 years out)	200	18.50
IBM	224	April	200	13.88
IBM	141	July	200	75.88

In this example, you own 100 shares of IBM that you bought years earlier at $66 a share, for a $13,400 unrealized gain. Even though you believe the Dow is way overvalued, you don't want to sell because you think IBM could rise as high as $400 a share over the next three to five years. Still, you realize that IBM and the Dow aren't trading at bargain levels now, so you buy a two-year LEAPS put with a strike price of $200 for $1850.

Three months later, your IBM stock has climbed to $224 a share. That's the good news. The not-so-bad news is that your two-year LEAPS put has fallen to $1388. But after another three months, the expected market crash occurs, sending IBM plummeting from $224 to $141, down 37 percent. In the meantime, your LEAPS put has galloped to $7588—a $5738 gain, which helps offset your $5900 "loss" from the $200 level. In other words, you would have a real gain you could exercise versus an unrealized loss from the $200 level. So let's assume you think IBM is as low as it will go and sell your put outright to realize a $5738 profit.

You could theoretically purchase more shares of IBM at $141 with the profits from your LEAPS. Then, when IBM climbs to $400 four years later in this storybook example, you would have 140 shares instead of 100 shares. And your total gain would be $43,662 versus $33,400—a 31 percent improvement over buying and holding. In the meantime, you enjoyed the added advantage of not having to suffer any emotional strains from seeing your shares plummet in the bear market. Plus, in the long run, you added another $10,000 to your net worth.

So how does benchmark investing's formula predict price ranges for the Dow? Benchmark investors need only do the same math for all 30 stocks combined as they do for each individual Dow stock. Again, the benchmark strategy was developed to be used with individual stocks. But over the years, it has accurately forecasted levels of valuation for the Dow—a side benefit that, at the very least, has calmed benchmark investors (see Table 8.2).

THE DOW INDUSTRIALS CALCULATED

When Charles Dow invented the Dow Jones Industrial Average on May 26, 1896, calculating the self-named index was fairly simple. He added the prices of 12 stocks and divided by 12. It was a straightforward method that worked well before the invention of calculators and computer spreadsheets. Today, the Dow is a financial icon. That is, when people ask how the market is doing, they're generally referring to the Dow. Ironically, the Dow isn't a very accurate measure of the overall stock market. For one thing, it's based only

TABLE 8.2

Benchmark Investing's Market Forecasts: 1991–1997

Year	Forecasted Benchmark		Actual Dow Closing	
	Low	High	Low	High
1991	2563	3904	2470	3168
1992	2562	3811	3136	3413
1993	3165	4734	3251	3754
1994	3500	5192	3635	3945
1995	4426	6473	3867	5181
1996	5131	7526	5032	6547
1997	6056	8851	6391	8259

on huge, blue-chip stocks. There are no small stocks, and no foreign stocks either.

The principles of the calculation are the same as they were 100 years ago, but a few things have changed. First, there are 30 Dow stocks as compared with the original 12. The Dow expanded to 30 companies in 1928. And the divisor has undergone a series of adjustments that has serious implications for the Dow. Some of the adjustments reflect the changing stocks that compose the average. Suppose that Dow Jones & Company decided to remove IBM from the index and substitute Oracle. IBM was trading at $133 a share at the time of this writing, and Oracle at $45.50. Without a compensating adjustment, the switch would make the Dow drop by roughly 262 points, because the Dow is a simple price-weighted index that was conceived in a pencil-and-paper era.

Other adjustments are made in the divisor whenever a company splits its stock. In a 2-for-1 split, each shareholder gets one additional share for every share held. This split also has the effect of reducing the Dow divisor, which stood at 0.25089315 at the end of 1997. In effect, it has become a multiplier, since a one-point move in any Dow stock moves the average up or down about four points.

The Dow is unique in that it is price-weighted. A 5 percent move in IBM affects the Dow much more than a 5 percent move in Sears (see Table 8.3). Critics argue that the Dow is a crude index because it gives the higher-priced Dow stocks a greater impact than their lower-priced cousins. Woolworth had the greatest percentage gain in the Dow in 1996, but its effect on the index was slight because of its relatively low share price.

Moreover, General Electric and United Technologies had similar gains of 26 percent in the same period, but United Technologies had a bigger impact on the Dow because its point rise was greater. By contrast, GE had 10 times the effect of United Technologies in the capitalization-weighted Standard & Poor's 500, because GE had 10 times the market value. Each company is weighted by its stock market value in the S&P 500. GE, with $175 billion in stock market value, counted 125 times as much as Bethlehem Steel.

GE, Coca-Cola, and Intel—the three most highly capitalized companies in the S&P 500—accounted for 25 percent of the advance in the 500-stock average in the first nine months of 1996.

To many people, the Dow seems like a financial rock of ages. But even from its earliest months, the Dow has been anything but

TABLE 8.3

The Effects of Higher-Priced Stocks on the Dow

Company	Share Price 9/30/96	YTD Percentage Change	Contribution to Dow's Rise in Points	Contribution to Dow's Rise in Percent
IBM	124.50	36.25	98.03	12.8
UTX	120.38	26.88	75.47	9.9
GE	91.00	26.39	56.23	7.3
ALD	65.88	38.68	54.38	7.1
DD	88.13	26.13	54.01	7.1
CAT	75.38	28.30	49.20	6.4
BA	94.50	20.57	47.72	6.2
PG	97.50	17.47	42.91	5.6
KO	50.88	37.04	40.69	5.3
TX	92.00	17.20	39.95	5.2
EK	78.50	17.16	34.03	4.4
CHV	62.63	19.57	30.33	4.0
JPM	88.88	10.75	25.53	3.3
UK	45.63	21.67	24.05	3.1
Z	20.63	58.65	22.57	2.9
AA	59.00	11.58	18.13	2.4
S	44.75	14.74	17.02	2.2
AXP	46.25	11.78	14.48	1.9
MRK	70.38	7.24	14.06	1.8
IP	42.50	12.21	13.69	1.8
DIS	63.25	7.43	12.95	1.7
MMM	69.75	5.08	9.99	1.3
MCD	47.38	4.99	6.66	0.9
WX	18.63	13.74	6.66	0.9
XON	83.25	2.62	6.29	0.8
GT	46.13	1.65	2.22	0.3
MO	89.75	−0.55	−1.48	−0.2
BS	10.00	−27.93	−11.47	−1.5
GM	48.00	−9.22	−14.43	−1.9
T	52.25	−9.31	−36.99	−4.8

Source: *Barron's.*

immutable. After only three months, Charles Dow replaced North American Company, a streetcar and power business, with U.S. Cordage, a rope maker. And before 1896 was out, U.S. Cordage ran into financial problems and had most of its operations—and place in the index—taken over by Standard Rope & Twine.

Over the years, more than 60 stocks have come and gone in the Dow. Some came in when the average was expanded to 20 stocks in 1916 and to 30 in 1928. Others changed as a result of mergers and acquisitions. The most recent changes were made in March 1997 (see Table 8.2), when Johnson & Johnson, Wal-Mart, Hewlett-Packard, and Travelers joined the ranks replacing Bethlehem Steel, Texaco, Woolworth, and Westinghouse. The changes were the most extensive since 1959. Prior to the 1997 changes, Disney, Caterpillar, and J.P. Morgan replaced Primerica, USX, and Navistar on May 3, 1991.

Table 8.4 summarizes changes in the DJIA since 1928. To track changes, begin in the 1928 column and work across. For example, General Foods replaced Postum in 1929 and was included in the Dow until 1985, when Philip Morris replaced it in the index. Some stocks have been in and out of the Dow. General Electric was a charter Dow stock that was dropped in 1898 for a few months and for six years in 1901–1907. IBM was in from 1932 to 1939, and came back in 1979. Some names of Dow stocks that evoke memories of yesteryear are Victor Talking Machine, Nash Motors, Radio Corp., and Central Leather.

THE DOW'S 1000-POINT DATES

The first Dow Jones Industrial Average was published on May 26, 1886, at a level of 40.94. It took more than 86 years for the DJIA to get to 1000. Below are the Dow's 1000-point dates.

Level	Date Reached	Percentage Move	Months to Get There
1000	11/14/72	2340	1037
2000	1/8/87	100	170
3000	4/17/91	50	51
4000	2/23/95	33	46
5000	11/21/95	25	9
6000	10/14/96	20	11
7000	2/13/97	17	4
8000	7/16/97	14	5

TABLE 8.4

Changes in the Dow Jones Industrial Average since 1928

1928	1930s	1950s	1970s	1980s	1990s
Allied Chemical & Die			Allied Corp.*	Allied-Signal* (93)	AlliedSignal* (93)
Wright Aeornautical	Hudson Motor (30)	Aluminum Co. of			Alcoa
Curtiss-Wright(29)	Cola-Cola (32)	America (50)			
	National Steel (35)				
North American	Johns-Manville (30)			Amer. Express (82)	American Express
Victor Talking Machine	IBM (32)				AT&T
Nat'l Cash Register (29)	AT&T (39)				
International Nickel			Inco Ltd.* (75)	Boeing (87)	Boeing
International Harvester				?????? (88)	Caterpillar (91)
Goodrich	Standard Oil (Cal.) (30)			Chevron (87)	Chevron
Texas Gulf Sulfur	Int. Shoe (32)	Owens-Illinois (59)		Coca-Cola (87)	Coca-Cola
	United Aircraft (33)				
	Natl. Distillers (34)				
U.S. Steel				USX* (86)	Walt Disney (91)
American Sugar	Borden (30)				DuPont
	Du Pont (30)				
American Tobacco	Eastman Kodak (30)				Eastman Kodak
Standard Oil (NJ)			Exxon* (72)		Exxon
General Electric					General Electric
General Motors					General Motors

Continued

TABLE 8.4
(Concluded)

1928	1930s	1950s	1970s	1980s	1990s
Atlantic Refining					Goodyear Tire
Bethlehem Steel					Hewlett-Packard (97)
Chrysler			IBM (79)		IBM
Paramount Public	Loew's (32)	Intl. Paper (56)			International Paper
Texas Corp.		Texaco * (59)			Johnson & Johnson (97)
General Railway Signal	Liggett & Myers (30)			McDonald's (85)	McDonald's
	Amer. Tobacco (32)				
Mack Trucks	Drug Inc. (32)	Swift & Co. (59)	Esmark* (73)		Merck
	Corn Products (33)		Merck (79)		
American Smelting		Anaconda (59)	MMM (76)		MMM
American Can	General Foods (29)			Primerica* (87)	J. P. Morgan (91)
Postum Inc.				Philip Morris (88)	Philip Morris
Nash Motors	United Trans. (30)				Proctor & Gamble
	Proctor & Gamble (32)				
Sears Roebuck					Sears Roebuck
Westinghouse					Travelers (97)
Union Carbide					Union Carbide
Radio Corp.	Nash Motors (32)		United Tech* (75)		United Technologies
	United Aircraft (39)				
Woolworth					Wal-Mart (97)

* Denotes company name change.

CHAPTER 9

Minimizing Your Risk

The Wall Street game should only be played by those who can afford to lose.

Barron's, 1921

Wall Street has long been symbolized by the bull and the bear. The bull signifies a rising stock market while the bear represents a downward-moving market. It's ironic that these two creatures are chosen to symbolize Wall Street behavior, since animal-like demeanor rules the market at most times.

Consider the bull. This large, powerful creature represents wild enthusiasm, rushing headlong into danger that most beasts would avoid. Bullish, fearless behavior is also known as greed. Meanwhile, the bear stands for fearful, defensive sentiment. The bear will charge only when terrified, just as panic-stricken investors will attack stocks with a vengeance and hungrily maul the stock market. Bearish behavior typifies a growing fear bordering on mass hysteria.

This is the scenario that awaits people when they must decide whether to invest money in the stock market. Whether we like it or not, the truth is that we have to take risks just to stop losing money to inflation. As best-selling financial author Peter L. Bernstein points out, "All of life is a search for rewards we cannot win without taking risk: risk management begins from the moment we awaken and continues until we retire at night."[1]

---

1 Peter L. Bernstein, "From Superstition to Supercomputer," Peter L. Bernstein, Inc. *Newsletter*, September 15, 1995.

This stock market risk can't be avoided if we wish to maintain our buying power in the future. In real inflation-adjusted terms, an investment made during 1925 in risk-free Treasury bills would be worth only about the same amount today. By the same token, an investment in the Dow would have yielded gains of nearly 100 times that of Treasury bills and 80 times inflation.

To own stocks—even undervalued Dow stocks—benchmark investors must be willing to accept risk. To help minimize the dangers, you could follow the principles of diversification that market professionals have embraced over the years. The bromide "don't place all your eggs in one basket" sums up the approach. However, another adage also applies: it's possible to fall off a log two ways. If you diversify too widely, you run the risk of putting excessive amounts in bad companies and not enough money in spectacular investments.

RISK DEFINED

Although investors desire high returns in the stock market, they realize that investing involves a trade-off between risk and expected return. If there were no risks, stocks would never be cheap. However, most investors own portfolios containing more risk than they realize for a particular return. In fact, most of us don't even have a clue as to how much risk our portfolios hold. But how do we measure risk?

First, let's define risk. In decision theory and statistics, risk means uncertainty for which the probability distribution is identified—otherwise known as standard deviation. For the average investor, however, risk simply means the possibility of losing value. The science of risk management thrives on Wall Street because it allows individuals and professionals to take more risk than they otherwise would by quantifying danger through the concept of probability. Without such acceptance of risk, the first skyscraper would not have been built and no one would have ever flown in a NASA spacecraft.

What makes investing so challenging is that it is characterized by the acceptance of risk. Good investors must be able to understand and tolerate this potential danger. They must accept the reality that without risk there would be no superior returns. Risk and return are related. It is a fact that benchmark investors must adopt, not spurn.

Remember: risk is omnipresent in the stock market, and the rules of the game can never be overthrown. Risk is a given when it comes to finance.

THE PROFESSIONAL INVESTOR AND RISK

Throughout the second half of this century, many of the brightest minds in finance have struggled to construct a practical theory of risk management. Among the professional investment crowd, investment risk is generally defined as the probable capriciousness of future returns. For example, the U.S. Treasury bill is generally considered to have the least amount of risk; investors have a very high degree of assurance of receiving that amount of interest from the government. Common stocks possess higher risks than Treasury bills. That's because no one can guarantee that any gain will occur, or that losses of principal won't be the result. Astute investors realize that such riskier investments could lead to significant losses.

Modern portfolio theory (MPT) holds that widespread diversification—purchasing stocks with low correlation to each other—can significantly reduce portfolio risk. The biggest risk to an investor isn't losses, according to MPT, but the variable nature of returns and volatility. But contrary to this accepted wisdom, there are opportunities for independent investors to buy undervalued stocks. According to money manager and best-selling financial author Michael O'Higgins, "Large institutional investors, who dominate market volume and cause sharp volatility through program trading, have created more opportunities than disadvantages for personal investors."[2]

There are several types of risk that professional investors must consider. The first is price risk. Money can be lost if too high a price is paid for a stock. Another is interest rate risk. If inflation pushes rates higher than expected, stocks will suffer. The third risk is associated with an individual company and the risk that it may blunder or suffer from poor management. In extreme situations, companies can go bankrupt, in which case investors lose their entire investment to this business risk. The fourth risk is market risk, which simply cannot be avoided. Still, investors are rewarded for taking this last risk.

---

2   Michael O'Higgins, *Beating the Dow* (New York: HarperCollins Publishing, 1991), p. 4.

Other risks that professionals encounter are political, liquidity, reinvestment, credit, regulatory, currency, liability, contract, volatility, funding, and yield curve risks.

Ever since the emergence of MPT in the 1950s, professional investors have attempted to reduce risk by diversifying it away—or indexing it away. The mantra of the professional is that diversification is crucial to efficient portfolio management. In fact, the mutual fund industry relies heavily on this premise of wide diversification for added safety, which explains why the average stock mutual fund held 131 companies at the end of 1997.[3]

One of the few rules of investing that's worth heeding is that it pays to be claustrophobic. Whenever you find yourself going along with the crowd, it's time to alter your course. What prompts this bold assertion is that professionals are concerned more with the risk of buying individual stocks than with outperforming the stock market. All this has not gone unnoticed. The 2494 general stock mutual funds that Lipper Analytical Services tracked from January 1 through December 26, 1996, averaged 42 *percent lower returns* than the Dow Jones Industrial Average. The funds collectively averaged a meager 19.63 percent compared with the Dow's impressive 27.94 gain—even though funds, unlike the Dow, have the advantage of adding dividends to their showing.

Many managers are willing to accept these mediocre results because they believe that in an efficient market no reward can be earned over the market rate of return by taking more individual stock risk or more group stock risk. They'd rather own a broad array of stocks that mimic the market than a group of undervalued companies. Contemporary managers attempt to balance the dollar amount of their individual stocks. They're fastidious about how much money they have invested in various industries. Often, all this diversification leads to subpar performances.

ADVANTAGES OF THE INDEPENDENT INVESTOR

Fortunately, unlike professional money managers, independent benchmark investors don't have to worry about achieving balance with indexes. Nor do they have to fear losing their jobs if they don't maintain a diversified portfolio. Benchmark investors enjoy the

---

3   Roger Lowenstein, "Intrinsic Value," *The Wall Street Journal*, November 20, 1997, p. C1.

luxury of being able to concentrate on outstanding companies selling at attractive levels. In doing so, they have an opportunity to duplicate the market conduct of the all-time master of investing, Warren Buffett, who believes that diversification is "something people do to protect themselves from their own stupidity."[4]

The October 1987 market crash caused prices to fall momentarily to attractive levels, but Buffett still kept a trim portfolio. He owned a total of three companies at year's end: Capital Cities/ABC, GEICO, and the Washington Post. Imagine, having over $2 billion invested in only three companies! That certainly defied traditional Wall Street behavior.

By May 1989, Buffett had acquired 93.4 million shares of Coca-Cola for Berkshire-Hathaway, the textile company he bought in 1965. The $1.023 billion investment represented 35 percent of Berkshire's stock portfolio. It was another bold move—one that few, if any, traditional financial analysts would have recommended. But Buffett's Coke purchase rose nearly twelvefold to well over $11.6 billion by late 1997.

Buffett, in fact, disagrees with Benjamin Graham's tenet of owning lots of stocks for diversification. Instead, Buffet believes that too many stocks *increase* the riskiness of a portfolio. In Buffett's opinion, investors are better served if they concentrate on locating a few spectacular investments rather than jumping from one mediocre idea to another. He contends that success can be traced to a few investments.

"An investor should act as though he had a lifetime decision card with just 20 punches on it," Buffett proclaims. "With every investment decision his card is punched, and he has one fewer available for the rest of his life."[5]

That's why Buffett buys boldly when he comes across a business for sale at an attractive price. In Berkshire's 1991 annual report, Buffett quoted from a letter written by economist John Maynard Keynes:

> As time goes on, I get more and more convinced that the right method in investments is to put fairly large sums into enterprises which one thinks one knows something about and in management of which one thoroughly believes. It is a mistake

---

4   Mary Buffett, *Buffettology* (New York: Simon & Schuster, 1997), p. 173.

5   Warren Buffett, comments at Berkshire-Hathaway annual meeting, Omaha, 1992.

to think that one limits one's risk by spreading too much between enterprises about which one knows little and has no special reason for special confidence. . . . One's knowledge and experience is definitely limited and there are seldom more than two or three enterprises at any given time [in] which I personally feel myself entitled to put full confidence.[6]

In 1971, when professional money managers were selling bonds to purchase stocks, Buffett could find no compelling stocks to add to Berkshire's common stock portfolio, which then totaled $11.7 million. Three years later, during the latter stages of a savage bear market that eliminated nearly half the value of the Dow, Buffett finally began buying attractively priced stocks. By 1975, Berkshire's portfolio was worth $39 million. And at the end of 1978, Berkshire had a market value of $220 million, with an unrealized gain of $87 million. All this occurred while the Dow Jones Industrial Average declined from 890 to 805.

How did Buffett manage to prosper while most seasoned professionals on Wall Street floundered? He succeeded by buying a handful of companies at bargain prices. In fact, in 1978 Berkshire's portfolio consisted of just a few stocks in only two industry groups: finance and consumer cyclicals. Buffett simply followed the legendary investor and author Philip Fisher's advice against diversification to reduce risk, and commented, "A lot of great fortunes in the world have been made by owning a single wonderful business. If you understand the business, you don't need to own very many of them."[7]

Of course, Buffett had the potential to look either intelligent or incredibly foolish, depending on the vagaries of the stock market. Benchmark investors must realize, however, that the market will at some point recognize the true value of their investments and the price of the stocks will most likely move higher—*although there are never any guarantees that this will occur.*

The clear conclusion here is that benchmark investors should attempt to diversify their portfolios to mitigate risk. More specifically, however, they should avoid mimicking the Wall Street professionals

---

6   Robert Hagstrom, *The Warren Buffett Way* (New York: John Wiley & Sons, 1994), pp. 67–68.

7   Warren Buffett, addressing the New York Society of Security Analysts, December 6, 1996.

who attempt to show broad market diversification in their portfolios. Rather, they should attempt to copy Buffett's style of investing in a few outstanding (and undervalued) businesses. Benchmark investors should also be as fearless as fund manager Michael Price, of Mutual Shares fame, who admits that he attempts to stay fully invested at all times regardless of short-term market conditions.

"Let's find cheap stocks is my goal when I come to work every morning," Price proclaims. "I'm looking for that margin of safety that cushions risk. I don't say we'll keep 20 percent in cash because the market's too high. We stay fully invested."[8]

It is clearly better to own a handful of undervalued stocks at attractive prices than run the risk of owning a broad market representation. As the renowned Sir John Templeton told John Train in *The Money Masters*, "A paradox of collecting for profit—whether stocks, works of art, real estate, or anything else—is that the best buy can never be what the dealer or gallery is pushing at the time."[9] Templeton became one of the wealthiest and most respected men in the world by insisting on buying a handful of stocks that were "being thrown away" by other investors. There's no question that benchmark investors should attempt to do the same.

RELATIVE RISK-ADJUSTED RETURNS

How can I be so certain that it is better to own a handful of undervalued stocks rather than owning a broadly diversified indexlike portfolio? Of course, I can point to benchmark investing's superior absolute returns since 1973 as one argument. But calculation of absolute performance is generally only one part of the story. Although everyone is interested in absolute returns, most investors should also be interested in *relative performance*. In other words, how much risk are you taking to achieve your returns?

Although it is often quite difficult to define risk, most practitioners agree that the return of a portfolio must be related to risk in order to provide a full picture of the manager's performance. In fact, this problem of defining risk has consumed financial theorists for nearly four decades. The consensus definition of risk among professionals involves the standard deviation of portfolio returns, using

8   Michael Price, comments at sales presentation in San Mateo, California, 1996.

9   John Train, *The Money Masters* (New York: Harper & Row Publishers, 1980), p. 173.

Standard Deviation Explained

Harry Markowitz won the 1990 Nobel prize in economic sciences for being the first to measure portfolio risk in 1952. Markowitz used standard deviation to measure the range around the average value in which returns are likely to fall approximately two-thirds of the time.

For example, annual returns for large company stocks over long periods have averaged nearly 11 percent with a standard deviation of about 20 percent. Therefore, in two years out of three, large company stock returns should range from a negative 9 percent to a positive 31 percent. A two-standard-deviation range encompasses 95 percent of all yearly returns. Thus, in 19 out of 20 years, the return for large company stocks would be expected to range from –29 percent to +51 percent.

quarterly returns. These risk-adjusted returns take the volatility of a portfolio, or standard deviation of returns, into account when considering absolute returns. Portfolios with high standard deviations are considered to be *riskier* than those with low standard deviations.

But how do you quantify relative returns once you know a portfolio's return? For example, how can you determine if a 15 percent return with 22 percent volatility (standard deviation) is superior to a 16 percent gain with 28 percent volatility? Various methods have been developed for measuring trade-offs between risk and return, but the Sharpe ratio, devised in the 1960s, has become the most widely accepted measure to determine relative returns.

The Sharpe Ratio: A Screening Device

The Sharpe ratio is a screening tool that clearly shows the added value of a particular manager or style. Developed in 1966 by William F. Sharpe for the purpose of studying portfolio performance on a risk-adjusted basis, the simplest definition of the term is *an expression of the added value realized by a portfolio for each unit of risk accepted.* Naturally, any risk-averse investor would like this valuation to be as high as possible.

$$\text{Sharpe ratio formula} = \frac{\text{Return} - \text{risk-free rate of return}}{\text{Standard deviation of portfolio}}$$

The Sharpe ratio looks at returns earned in excess of T-bill rates per unit of total risk assumed. To arrive at the ratio, take the average return from a portfolio or index, subtract the risk-free rate of interest from T-bills, and then divide that number by the standard deviation of return. *The higher the Sharpe ratio, the better: the more return that is realized at each given level of risk.* Once you have this ratio, you can compare risk-adjusted portfolios. And you can quantify whether it's better to own a piece of every Dow company or a handful of undervalued Dow stocks.

Table 9.1 shows some examples for large cap portfolios. Surprisingly, the portfolio with the least amount of risk (Portfolio A) had the lowest Sharpe ratio. Meanwhile, Portfolios B and C added more value than the Dow Jones Industrial Average in spite of their higher volatility. In other words, you would have been rewarded for taking incrementally higher risk than the index in this case. With both portfolios, you would have realized over 1.60 units of return for each unit of risk. Portfolio C has a higher return, but also incurred a higher degree of risk, as expressed by the standard deviation. Therefore, Portfolio B earned the highest return relative to the risk it took.

TABLE 9.1

Sharpe Ratios for Different Portfolios with Large Cap Investment Styles

	(1) Return	(2) T-bills	(3) Standard Deviation	(1)–(2) (3) Sharpe Ratio
Portfolio A	12.54%	3.99%	9.70%	0.88
Portfolio B	21.95%	3.99%	9.99%	1.80
Portfolio C	22.96%	3.99%	11.75%	1.61
Dow Industrials	16.97%	3.99%	9.66%	1.34

Sharpe ratios are a great way to screen for the added value that a specific manager or style has offered in the past. It is a far better method than simply relying upon absolute returns. And its offers a measure of performance consistency that you can use in any screening process. By using the Sharpe ratio, you can find a method with the highest reward-to-volatility ratio. As you can see from Table 9.2, benchmark investing would have provided investors with better risk-adjusted returns than simply investing in all 30 Dow stocks during the 10-year period from 1987 through 1996. Not only would you have enjoyed greater returns with benchmark investing, you also would have realized less risk in order to beat the Dow. So you see, investors can outperform the market by sticking with this superior strategy of immunizing their emotions and forcing themselves to buy industrial stocks when they are under distress and are undervalued. Benchmark investing is logical and consistent, and can stand the strain of scrutiny.

TABLE 9.2

Determining Risk-Adjusted Returns of the Dow and Benchmark Investing

Year	DJIA	T-Bills	Benchmark Investing
1987	6.02%	5.47%	47.07%
1988	15.95%	6.35%	23.05%
1989	31.71%	8.37%	21.03%
1990	−0.57%	7.81%	15.63%
1991	23.93%	5.60%	25.69%
1992	7.34%	3.51%	14.92%
1993	16.72%	2.90%	38.04%
1994	4.95%	3.90%	11.36%
1995	36.48%	5.60%	37.81%
1996	28.57%	5.15%	45.14%
Average	17.11%	5.47%	27.98%
Standard deviation	7.65%		9.47%

Risk-adjusted Dow return = 11.64%/7.65% = 1.52
Risk-adjusted benchmark return = 22.51% /9.47% = 2.38

Of course, diversification has become an article of faith on Wall Street, with fund managers typically stuffing their portfolios with hundreds of stocks. Warren Buffett labeled this kind of asset allocation the Noah School of Investing, and suggested that these managers would be better off piloting arks. But a few nondiversified funds have popped up on the investment screen recently. Since the beginning of 1996, according to *Research* magazine, 16 "concentrated" mutual funds have hit the market.[10] James Gipson, manager of the nondiversified Clipper Fund, says the reason for running a concentrated fund is simple. "If you are intellectually honest with yourself, you realize you have only a limited number of really good ideas."[11] The fund had just 19 stocks and more than $700 million in assets in the fourth quarter of 1997.

According to Morningstar Inc. president Don Phillips, nondiversified investing can be a powerful tool that increases the odds of beating market averages. He pointed to Gipson's Clipper Fund and the long-closed Sequoia Fund as funds that have delivered superior results over time with concentrated portfolios. "The vast majority of funds are grossly overdiversified," Phillips complained to *The Wall Street Journal*.[12]

Indeed, many highly regarded fund professionals invest their personal money à la Buffett and Fisher. Robert Rodriquez, manager of FPA Capital Fund, which topped all but three other stock funds between 1987 and 1996, has no reservations about putting as much as 50 percent of his net worth at risk. And Ron Baron, of Baron Asset Fund, admits he has never owned more than 10 stocks in his personal portfolio.

There is no law of investing that requires you to lower risk by owning every industry group within your portfolio. You do not have to include 20, 30, or 40 stocks in your portfolio to achieve adequate diversification. And as the legendary Philip Fisher advised, you can reduce your workload by reducing the number of companies you own. Fisher, one of Buffett's mentors who warned against stressing diversification, would rather own a few outstanding companies than a large number of average businesses. His portfolio usually included

---

10 Rebecca McReynolds, "Conviction Investing," *Research*, December 1997, p. 48.

11 Karen Damato, "Big Bets: Some Fund Managers Up Ante," *The Wall Street Journal*, March 3, 1997, p. C1.

12 Ibid.

fewer than 10 companies, and often three or four companies represented 75 percent of his stock portfolio.

THE PERFECT PITCH

It is my sincere belief that benchmark investors will be far better
served by owning a handful of Dow stocks bought at bargain-base-
ment levels. But such a strategy calls for patience in overvalued
markets and incredible fortitude in bear markets. Understandably,
it is difficult to wait in the wings with idle cash during a roaring bull
market, especially when you read about the latest technology stock
that has doubled in the last two weeks. You will be sorely tempted
to throw your dollars at such succulent, mouthwatering targets. But
I advise benchmark investors not to get caught up in savory short-
term inducements.

Instead, you should ask yourself which you would rather do:
(1) earn 50 percent in six months and end up having to pay taxes, or
(2) earn 20 percent a year for the next 10 years in an undervalued
Dow stock? If you agree with me that the latter choice is far more
attractive, you'll have to wait patiently for what Warren Buffett calls
the perfect pitch. Baseball players know it as the hitter's pitch, or the
old fastball down the middle, which you can knock right out of the
park. Of course, there won't be many perfect pitches in bullish
markets. At the beginning of 1985, 1986, and 1987, there was only
one undervalued stock to buy in the Dow. And at the beginning of
1996 and 1997, there was only a total of three stocks combined to buy.
Believe me, when markets are soaring ahead as they were in those
years, investors want action, not inaction! But the best times to invest
over the last 25 years have been when people fearfully pulled away
from stocks—that is, after the market was bombed. The bottom line
is that in order to become a successful investor, you will have to
consciously wait for such times to swing for the fence and never
waver from this strategy. That would be as ridiculous as giving Babe
Ruth or Hank Aaron a signal to square up for a bunt instead of going
for a homer.

So be patient and wait for that pitch right down the middle. It
will come.

It always does.

CHAPTER 10

Investment Mistakes to Avoid

Lack of knowledge tends to make investors too cautious during bear markets and too confident in bull markets—sometimes at considerable cost.*

Charles Ellis,
Investment Policy

Steve Martin is one of the funniest people in the world. My favorite Steve Martin story happened while he and his wife, Anne, and their four kids were vacationing in Florida. Steve's first mistake was buying a really expensive set of new golf clubs without first discussing the purchase with Anne. I suppose that's why they say men are from Mars. Anyway, Steve was so anxious to try out his new clubs that he got up at dawn without waking Anne or the kids to play 18 holes at the Cocoa Beach Country Club.

Steve was paired up with a married couple in their seventies who went to great lengths to warn him about the alligators all around the course. But Steve was thinking more along the line of birdies than alligators during the first nine holes as he played the best golf of his life with those new titanium clubs. He'd never driven as far or as straight before. His Tiger Woods-like drives left him in great shape to hit lofted iron shots onto the greens in regulation. For the first time in his life, Steve Martin was playing great golf. And there was

*Homewood, Ill.: Dow Jones-Irwin, 1985, p. 26.

nothing that was going to stand in the way of a record round for him that day. Nothing!

But as he and his partners were making the turn at the tenth hole, they could see a storm approaching from the Atlantic Ocean. What's a little rain on a day like this, Steve thought as the threesome pressed on, knowing they would probably get caught in drenching rain. Steve's good fortune continued on the back nine until they approached the seventeenth hole, a par three surrounded by a lake.

That's when the rain began to fall. Steve grabbed his new seven iron and wiped off the grip as best he could before settling over his tee shot with the quiet determination of an Arnold Palmer. As he began his backswing, Steve could feel the club slip out of his grasp. He said he felt like he was in a dream, because he knew what was happening but could do nothing to stop his swing. As the club approached impact with his ball it went flying from Steve's hands, sailing 20 yards away into the swampy lake.

Somewhat miraculously, the new club was barely sticking up out of the dark waters as the rain continued to pelt down. Steve had already fought one battle over buying the club. He didn't want to try to explain to Anne how he lost one on the first day he had it, so he headed for the lake as his playing partners began to remind him of the alligators in the waters. Reasoning, incorrectly, that the creatures couldn't stay underwater for long periods, he thought he would be forewarned by bubbles on the surface if any danger lurked.

In dark green water up to his waist, he slowly approached his new club while keeping a sharp lookout for air bubbles. Suddenly, from out of nowhere, he felt something hit his back. Before he knew it, something was splashing from behind. Panic-stricken, Steve immediately dove underwater to make a desperate plunge for the club. He somehow managed to reach it and emerged from the water to splash his way toward shore as fast as he could, club in hand. By the time he dragged himself out of the bay, Steve saw the elderly couple literally doubled over in laughter, with tears streaming from their eyes. You see, it hadn't been an alligator behind him, only hundreds of harmless tiny fish that also swam in the bay. Steve had panicked needlessly over an imagined fear.

Sadly, many of us do the same thing when it comes to investing. We focus on fear instead of reality. As a result, investing myths and mistakes abound. A few days before the most devastating period in stock market history, the *Ladies' Home Journal* published an interview with General Motors senior executive John J. Raskob. In that interview, with the presumptuous title "Everybody Ought to Be Rich," Raskob recommended that the average American citizen put $15 a month into stocks. The article appeared a few days before the Dow Jones Industrial Average peaked on September 3, 1929, at 381.17. Nearly three years later, on July 8, 1932, the Dow stood at 41.22, a sickening decline of 89 percent. Raskob and his advice were held in ridicule for years to come. In fact, one U.S. senator from Indiana went so far as to blame him for the stock market crash because he had recommended that ordinary people buy stocks at the market's peak.

If there were any doubts that Raskob was either a fool or a rascal, the April 27, 1992, issue of *Forbes* magazine called Raskob the "worst offender" of those who viewed stocks as a guaranteed path to riches.

In any event, Raskob's "foolhardy" recommendation turned out to be good advice, even allowing for the horrendous crash. If investors had followed his counsel by investing $15 a month into stocks for the next 20 years, they would have accumulated almost $9000. After 30 years, investors would have had more than $60,000. The moral? *You must have long-range investment goals to keep you from being frustrated by short-term failures. Short-term, nervous trading will lead only to despair, whereas long-term investing will reap rewards.* Stocks have always outperformed all other assets for the patient investor.

As benchmark investors prepare to achieve their most important long-range goals, they should also be aware of common investment mistakes which, once avoided, will make their journey easier.

TRYING TO TIME THE STOCK MARKET

In investing, history lessons are inevitably painful for those who fail to pay attention to the past. Consider vice-presidential candidate Jack Kemp's record in 1995. Kemp traded $2 million worth of stocks that year, resulting in losses totaling $77,000, according to *The Wall Street Journal*'s September 12, 1996, issue. A typical trade in 1995 saw Kemp buy Mercury Finance in May and sell it in July. Another had him buying Telefonos de Mexico in January and selling out less than two weeks later. He bought Aetna Life & Casualty in February and held it for a total of five days.

In 1995, Kemp made a remarkable 189 trades, often buying and selling in the blink of an eye. Instead of calling the former NFL

TABLE 10.1

Market Time versus Timing the Market: August 6, 1982, to December 29, 1995

Investment Period	Annualized Return
Full Period	14.1%
Less 10 biggest up days	10.0%
Less 20 biggest up days	7.5%
Less 30 biggest up days	5.4%
Less 40 biggest up days	3.5%
Less 50 biggest up days	1.7%
Less 60 biggest up days	0.1%

Source: Smith Barney research.

quarterback Mr. Touchdown, he could have been called Mr. Whirl-wind.

Market timing is risky business (see Table 10.1). One of the big risks investors take in their effort to time the market is being out of stocks when the market has a big upward move. For example, had you been in cash instead of stocks during only the five best days in the market out of 3500 trading days from May 26, 1970, to April 29, 1994, you would have doubled your investment (see Figure 10-1). However, had you not tried to time the market by being in cash those five days and remained in stocks the whole time, you would have *tripled* your investment. As the renowned Peter Bernstein says, market timing is indeed a risky strategy! "For true long-term investors—that small group of people like Warren Buffett who can shut their eyes to short-term fluctuations and who have no doubt that what goes down will come back up—volatility represents opportunity rather than risk, at least to the extent that volatile securities tend to provide richer returns than more placid securities."[1]

Warren Buffett, the foremost investor of our age, never tries to time the market. Besides, timing costs a fortune in commissions, and studies have shown that even if you bought at all the worst possible times (see Chapter 2), you'd still do quite well in the long run. Steer

---

1   Peter L. Bernstein, *Against the Gods* (New York: John Wiley & Sons, 1996), p. 261.

FIGURE 10.1

Risks of Market Timing: Compound Returns 1982 through 1995

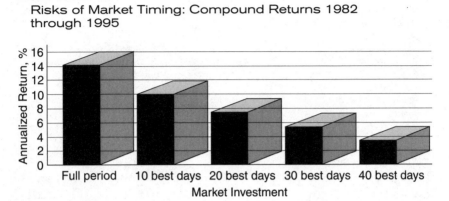

clear of this get-rich-quick scheme, which has its foundation in fear (see Figure 10.1).

RELYING ON ADVISERS

Is there a discipline more frothy and faddish nowadays than mutual fund management? It's hard to think of one that also has such broad influence in America today. Attractive new mutual funds with sexy performance results testify to Wall Street's love of hot managers, who rake in money by the fistful so long as their hot streaks burn bright. Tens of thousands of investors attest to their immediate attraction. They shoveled billions last year into the pockets of hot managers. Into this overheated environment comes a warning. These icons of 1990s investing exemplify what can go wrong. Plenty.

In its November 3, 1996, edition, *The New York Times* set out to determine if any of the 20 largest mutual funds in several categories were badly underperforming their peers. With the aid of fund researcher Morningstar Inc., the *Times* found that nine huge funds had sunk to the bottom 5 percent of their peer groups during the 12 months ending September 30, 1996 (see Table 10.2). In a period when the Dow rose more than 25 percent, these nine funds averaged just 4.22 percent.

Despite the temptation to cast these nine mutual funds as merely wasting investors' money, the fact is that most of the funds enjoyed five-year average returns near their peer group averages though still below the market's return. The point is that *even the best*

TABLE 10.2

Selected Large Mutual Fund Performances: October 1, 1995,
to September 30, 1996

Fund	Total 1-Year Returns	Peer Fund Average	Assets in Millions
Prudential Equity Income B	9.99%	16.64%	$931
Aim Value A	5.26%	16.32%	$4,633
Fidelity Magellan	3.00%	16.32%	$51,683
20th Century Growth	2.28%	16.32%	$4,740
Crabbe Huson Special	−3.79%	15.98%	$571
Neuberger & Berman Guardian	7.15%	17.84%	$4,901
USAA Income	3.26%	11.17%	$1,720
Fidelity Balanced	5.61%	10.87%	$4,011
Fidelity Advanced Income & Growth	5.21%	10.87%	$2,947

Source: Morningstar Inc.

mutual funds can hit rough spots. That's why it is far better for indus-
trious investors to embrace the benchmark approach as a high-
quality, low-cost method of investing. Let others who don't want to
think or achieve superior results stick with the highly advertised
fund managers and their hot records.

*Ambitious investors who wish to succeed should think for themselves,
not outsource the job to high-priced advisers.*

What is so bad about a stock market that keeps going up? A few
things. For one, investors become frustrated by not keeping up with
market gains. Convinced that they need to make up for lost time,
and money, they turn to Wall Street for advice. In the mistaken belief
that only an MBA from Harvard knows how to invest wisely, they
pay hefty fees to the hottest fund managers, who rarely if ever match
market gains. *Achieving above-average market results requires discipline
and patience, not a business degree from an Ivy League school.*

In this era of mutual funds, investors reward sizzling new funds
with piles of "hot" cash. In 1996, many of the hottest new mutual
funds sprinted out of the gate only to stumble badly after their
winning streaks attracted lots of money. Consider the Artisan Small
Cap Fund, which broke out of the starting blocks with a scintillating

30 percent return in its first nine months in 1995. But Artisan's 1996 return trailed the return of a Lipper index of small stock funds in the same period by 68 percent.

Artisan was hardly an exception. Fidelity Investments fired, demoted, or shuffled 24 stock mutual fund managers in March 1996 in the most sweeping stock fund shake-up in the firm's 50-year history. The action saw an incredible 30 percent of its stock managers being moved. Months later, Jeffery Vinik left Fidelity's Magellan Fund after posting inferior returns compared with the market. According to the December 8, 1996, edition of *The New York Times*, more than half of the $225 billion invested in Fidelity's stock funds had been put under new managers in 1996.

Of course, mutual fund managers aren't the only professionals who tumble on those slippery banana peels that litter Wall Street. Four top financial newsletter writers recommended their favorite U.S. stocks in *Worth* magazine in late August 1996. Notably, none of the stocks recommended had inched higher over the next two months and one had dropped an appalling 46 percent. During that same period, the Dow rose 6.8 percent and the Nasdaq 6.1 percent. So much for relying on the pros.

The best investment ideas will come from your own homework. As a result, you should not be intimidated. And you should certainly not depend on others who make a living taking irrational actions. Consider that hedge fund operator Victor Niederhoffer went bust by losing over $500 million of his clients' money when he sold out-of-the-money S&P 500 index options in a huge gamble that the market would turn around on "Gray Monday," October 27, 1997. Instead, to Niederhoffer's horror, the Dow lost 554.26 points, its biggest one-day point loss ever.

According to Yale behavioral finance economist Robert J. Shiller, half the investors he surveyed in 1997 "admitted that they weren't good at picking stocks, but for some reason most thought they were good at picking people who were good at picking stock."[2] It's doutful, however, if many of Niederhoffer's former clients feel so good about their ability to pick people to invest their money for them now.

---

2   Peter Coy, "Headed for Bubble Trouble?" *Business Week,* November 17, 1997, p. 57.

OVERCONFIDENCE

Modern investors are more sophisticated today, but still are subject to the same vagaries of the human psyche. In fact, as *Wall Street Journal* columnist and author Roger Lowenstein claims, "people repeatedly make errors in judgment, not randomly, but in a way that can be predicted and catergorized."[3] The astonishing collapse of the stock market in October 1987, unrelated to any news or specific catalyst, is a perfect example. Fundamental analysis and value investing as begun by Ben Graham certainly recognize the fallible nature of human psychology and attempt to systematically profit from this knowledge. Contrarian strategies are built around the core belief that investors make the wrong decisions most of the time and that the road to success is best assured by doing the opposite of what everyone else is doing in the market.

One of the best pitfalls to avoid is overconfidence when it comes to investing in stocks. Pride goeth before a fall. This indisputable truism is nowhere more regularly lived out than on Wall Street, and the regularity has something to do with bull market cycles. Admonition of excessive pride could hardly be more timely, since we're treading the waters of an all-time Dow high tide. Pride in past accomplishments can, and often does, lead to dangerous self-infatuation, a progressive loss of the ability to see beyond yesterday and the trouble that lies ahead. Triumph undermines judgment because it instills overconfidence, which is more dangerous than despair on Wall Street. Investors are never closer to destruction than at this time. They presume much too much about the workings of the market, which does not provide unlimited gains. It never has, nor will it ever.

Investors also underestimate the capacity of bear markets to wipe away gains and demoralize even the heartiest apostles of value investing. Just remember, no one is invincible. As an investor, you must never assume you're going to win. You should always remain humble but courageous. That way, you will be able to adhere to the most important tenet of buying only at the lowest level of valuation. You must also have the discipline to accept responsibility and to stand firm, even in the worst of times.

---

3   Roger Lowenstein, "Intrinsic Value," *The Wall Street Journal*, June 6, 1996, p. C1.

One of the most striking findings of behavioral scientists is that investors acquire too much confidence and think that they are right far more frequently than they really are. This is diametrically opposed to the widely held belief that people are able to process information rationally and in an unbiased manner. Numerous examples abound to support this phenomenon. For instance, 90 percent of drivers consider themselves above average. Of course, that is statistically impossible. Also, nearly all people consider themselves above average in the ability to get along with others. Another statistical no-no.

Behavioral finance has found that people tend to be too optimistic and overconfident of their chances of success in the stock market. People often see order where it doesn't exist and interpret accidental success to be the result of skill. Therefore, they think they know more than they really do and systematically make incorrect decisions as a result. A measure of caution in making and relying on Wall Street forecasts might be a key to protecting investors from unhappy results. Much like Buffett's margin of safety.

The irony of behavioral finance is that most investors see their own choices as rational but other people's decisions as the result of their disposition. If we were all rational investors, recent successes would not cause overconfidence, nor would recent losses result in overcautiousness.

THE MISTAKE OF GREED

Although it's true that we've been warned since childhood of the dangers of greed, the attraction of a quick buck is almost impossible to resist. Remember Brian McGuire, the anesthesiologist from Billings, Montana, who thought he had found the perfect investment? McGuire invested $100,000 in a fund that appeared both conservative and safe. It was neither. Audited by a large and famous accounting firm and affiliated with a Swiss bank, the fund traded currencies on the Isle of Jersey, an offshore financial tax haven promoted as one of the world's most reputable. Even if things went wrong, the most an investor supposedly could lose was 10 percent.

But McGuire lost more than 10 percent. He and 81 other investors lost 95 percent as $27 million vanished into thin air. The trader who misappropriated the $27 million was arrested as he was about to leave town. It turns out that the fund manager had inflated the returns that were supposedly audited by a partner of Touche Ross & Company, now Deloitte & Touche.

The point is, greed gets more investors into trouble than any other factor. Whenever an investment sounds too good to be true, it probably is. In this case, returns of 20 percent and higher were projected along with the risk factor of losing a maximum of only 10 percent.

UNCLEAR INVESTMENT OBJECTIVES

The first step before beginning any investment program is to define your goals. Believe it or not, that's what Warren Buffett does. What are you trying to achieve with your money? Are you seeking to build wealth over time? Do you need to preserve capital and use it to generate a current income stream? What are your tax concerns? It is clear that goals need to be clarified and developed in keeping with your tolerance for risk.

Once your goals have been established, the next step is to have a full understanding of all the investments you're considering for your portfolio. The very best managed companies frequently trade at substantial discounts from what they are worth for one irrational, temporary reason or another. There's no question, however, that as an investor you must understand completely what you are investing in. Once you have done your homework and are confident that you know more about the company than the stock market does, invest! Be sure to ask questions until the answers make sense. Buying stock without understanding the company's operating functions can be disastrous. Also find out how the investment fits into your overall portfolio. How does it compare with other investments with a similar rate of return or potential for growth? What are the risks involved? Finally, ask yourself if the stock is trading at a significant discount to its value.

"Investment must be rational; if you can't understand it, don't do it," warns Warren Buffett.[4]

For benchmark investors, an appropriate goal should be to outperform the Dow by investing in only the most undervalued

---

4   "Warren Edward Buffett," *Forbes 400* (October 21, 1991), p. 151.

stocks in the index. To place an absolute figure on that "overperformance" is inappropriate: 15 or 20 percent may be far too high during bear cycles, whereas it may be way too low during bull phases of the market. Too many investors expect to get rich quick and are disappointed when their expectations go unrealized. In the world of investments, building wealth takes patience, discipline, and a basic understanding of the principles of investing. Setting goals and developing a sound financial plan are part of that process.

IGNORING THE CONSEQUENCES OF TAXES

Many investors are unaware of how taxes can severely erode their investments. As a result, they ignore the tax consequence, which can devour huge chunks of gains from a portfolio. According to Chicago mutual fund researcher Morningstar Inc., diversified U.S. stock funds gained an average of 91.9 percent in the five years ending in 1996. However, after taxes, this dwindled to just 71.5 percent. If that weren't bad enough, mutual funds can also generate yearly taxes when the fund itself trades, when you sell, and when you reinvest interest and dividends in the fund. Unknown to many mutual fund investors is the fact that a fund can sell a position with a very large capital gain that the fund has held for years. The gain from selling the old stock with a winning position will get paid out as a capital gains distribution unless the fund has an offsetting loss.

Capital gains distributions, required by law to permit funds to avoid paying taxes themselves, leave their recipients (shareholders) with an income tax obligation even if they reinvest their money right back into additional shares of the fund. Therefore, it's possible for an investor to buy a mutual fund, actually have an unrealized loss when the fund drops in value, but still have to pay taxes on "capital gains" realized from the sale of the stock by the fund.

To continue this hypothetical but very realistic example, let's say you invested $20,000 in a stock fund before a capital gain distribution was made and that you take the payout in cash. We'll assume that the $100 million stock fund has $50 million in unrealized gains that it suddenly realizes in order to buy other, more attractive stocks or simply to raise cash. The fund manager has $50 million of capital gains to account for, but you would have 50 percent gains to report to the IRS on a phantom "profit" paid out to you. Obviously, one strategy would be to avoid all stock funds with large unrealized gains, but that could eliminate some excellent funds from consideration.

That might sound prohibitive until you consider that the American Heritage Growth Fund reported 1996 capital gains of $1.42 a share, almost 90 percent of its net asset value. Meanwhile, the Kemper Growth Fund posted a distribution of $4.35 a share in capital gains, nearly 25 percent of its value. Admittedly, these are extreme examples, but the fact remains that lots of funds make big payouts to investors. For example, Parkstone's Small Capital fund had 55 percent of its portfolio made up of unrealized gains at the beginning of 1997. More alarming is the fact that its average turnover rate at that time was 67 percent, meaning that an investor could expect a huge "capital gain" by owning the fund. Ironically, Parkstone's Small Capital "A" shares posted a 6.92 percent *loss* in 1997 but still paid $1.29 in *long-term capital gains.*

You can check where a fund's portfolio status stands in the *Value Line Mutual Fund Survey,* which reports potential capital gains exposure under the heading "unrealized appreciation." *Morningstar* also reports this information.

Even so, you can think you have a tax-efficient fund and still be rudely surprised. Consider the surprisingly large year-end distribution of capital gains that stunned holders of the Berger 100 Fund, which made a whopping distribution equal to over one-third of its total asset value at the end of 1997 following a change of managers. Before that, the Denver fund had earned a reputation as being tax-friendly to investors by consistently paying only modest or no distributions in most years.

Ideally, the best choice for investors is to buy and hold a handful of stocks. That way, taxes are not a problem. Warren Buffett has held stocks for decades, and his net worth continues to grow. The advantage of holding stocks is astronomical. According to SEI's expected long-term returns, the percentage lost to taxes by holding varying classes of stocks and bonds ranges from the minimum of 28.85 percent (small cap growth stocks) to the high of 38.15 percent (taxable bonds).

Buy and hold may not be very sexy, or the in-thing to do. But it certainly is the most profitable in the long run. Clearly, tax-efficient investing is not an easy strategy to live by. One strategy anyone can use is to match capital gains with capital losses. Although I don't advocate this approach, if you absolutely must sell an overvalued stock with a sizable gain, you can choose to realize the loss in a favored stock that has fallen, then buy it back 31 days later in order to avoid the IRS "wash sale" rule. Then apply the loss to offset an equivalent capital gain. In your IRA or 401(k), you can ignore taxes and simply seek the best returns. But in your taxable portfolio, you must never fail to consider the devastating impact of taxes.

MAGAZINE AND MEDIA INVESTMENT "ADVICE"

On "Gray Monday," October 27, 1997, the Dow crashed 554.26 points—the twelfth worst percentage loss in Wall Street history. What was so amazing was how much attention the media focused on the market slide. In fact, for the first time ever, the national television networks alarmed daytime soap opera watchers with stock market updates warning them about the huge losses. Who knows how much fear the national media created with their unusual tactics?

One of my favorite examples of why we shouldn't become too alarmed when the media does, was the headline that ran above the April 9, 1996, *Associated Press* story about the previous day's market: "Stocks Plunge After Worrisome Weekend." The cut line beneath a picture of traders on the floor of the New York Stock Exchange that accompanied the story said that stocks "plunged" in response to unexpectedly strong employment data. However, had readers taken the time to review the text of the story, they would have discovered that the Dow had "plunged" a grand total of 88.51 points to finish at 5594.37—a whopping 1.56 percent loss. So much for the credibility of our national financial media.

As for the nation's most popular financial magazine, you'd be better served by canceling your subscription than heeding its "investment advice." According to a Smith Barney Consulting Group study, its six-year record of performance woefully trailed that of the market (see Table 10.3). The magazine's cumulative return was 21.4 percent, whereas the market gained 108.8 percent during the same period.

Of course, competition for advertising dollars and national subscribers is fierce. That's why you see plenty of headlines like "Best Performing Money Managers" and "How to Make a Lot of Money!" and "Retire with All the Money You Will Ever Need!" Perhaps it would be best for investors to avoid stories with exclamation points anywhere in the headline.

TABLE 10.3

Buy-Sell Recommendations, Six-Year Performance Review:
1990–1995

	Annualized Return	Cumulative Return
Buys	3.3%	21.4%
Stock Market	13.1%	108.8%

Princeton University conducted a study of how the stock mutual funds fared that were selected for the *Forbes* honor roll. Table 10.4 highlights the fact that in three-, five-, and eight-year periods, the honor roll recipients widely underperformed the market. And in Table 10.5 you will see how a majority of *Morningstar*'s five-star funds performed below the market from 1990 to 1994.

According to a Columbia University survey, in seeking investment advice, investors rely most heavily on published performance ratings, followed by commissioned financial advisers. The same survey also indicated that investors select their investments on the basis of performance track records, followed by the fees charged in doing business.

Clearly, there are many outstanding, solid, academic-based financial publications that can be a wonderful source of information. Publications such as *The Wall Street Journal, Investor's Business Daily, Barron's, Forbes, Fortune, Business Week, Value Line, Worth, Smart Money,* and *Bloomberg* are excellent choices. They will richly reward any investor with a wealth of information. But don't rely on past performance, fees, or frightening headlines to make up your mind for you. Instead, remember that strategies such as benchmark investing produce superior returns because investors dump stocks that have languished for a long time. When the stock finally perks up, investors, including editors, reporters, and publishers, are too slow to accept the clear and visible evidence of the change.

Therefore, dare to be a long-term, independent, rational investor all on your own. Dare to ignore the national media when they tout a good company as if it were a good investment. You'll find that

TABLE 10.4

$100,000 Investment in <u>Forbes</u> Honor Roll Mutual Funds versus the Market: 1983–1990

	Forbes Honor Roll	Stock Market	Percent Trailing the Stock Market
At end of year 3	$127,190	$165,864	23%
At end of year 5	$149,508	$203,241	26%
At end of year 8	$221,686	$337,799	34%

Source: Princeton University Study.

TABLE 10.5

Morningstar's Five-Star Stock Funds: 1990–1994

Year	Percent below Average in Following Year
1990	52.6%
1991	71.1%
1992	56.0%
1993	63.6%

Source: Lipper Analytical Services.

you make far more money by investing in a "bad" Dow company than a good one, much to the surprise of the media. And you'll avoid most of the common investment mistakes awaiting you along the way. That has been a guiding principle of Warren Buffett over the past 40 years, and he's not even a behavioral scientist.

CHAPTER 11

May the Northwest Quadrant Be with You

The best of seers is he who guesses well.

Euripides

The ancient Greek storyteller Euripides had no idea what the term *northwest quadrant* meant. Nor do many investors today realize that such a place exists. Actually, the term is a Wall Street creation that didn't exist until recent times.

No, it's not an area of land in Oregon. Nor is it a *Star Wars* term for a far-off sector of the galaxy. But it is very real and a very desirable destination for the scientists of Wall Street. In fact, this is what Wall Street is about. That's because the northwest quadrant is the pot of gold at the end of the rainbow. It's that precious upper-left-hand quarter plotted on a chart that represents higher annual returns with less risk than a comparable index such as the Dow (see Figure 11.1).

Only those managers who've enjoyed the Midas touch with their portfolios while realizing less risk than their comparable index ever reach this destination. In a sense, it's very much like combining the speed of a Ferrari with the power of a tank in one awesome vehicle. Incredible wealth springs from the northwest quadrant for those fortunate few with vision who are richly rewarded with huge influxes of new capital to invest.

Of course, you too are capable of achieving success in the northwest quadrant, thanks to benchmark investing. Just because

FIGURE 11.1

Risk-Return Analysis

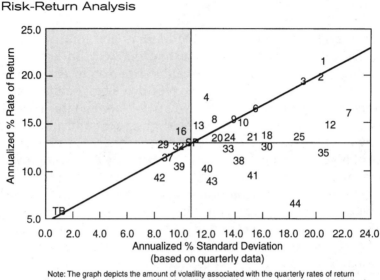

Note: The graph depicts the amount of volatility associated with the quarterly rates of return
generated by the investment adviser. Annualized rates of return are depicted on the vertical axis
and volatility on the horizontal axis.

Warren Buffett is the wealthiest investor in America doesn't mean
that he has any more intelligence, creativity, or special gifts than you
do. We tend to think that people who have accomplished extraordinary things are somehow so very different from the rest of us. Yet
the more we examine them, the more we see that they achieved their
greatness because they had extraordinary discipline. These rare
people refused to be denied, and they never allowed short-term
failures to stop their later long-term success. They were relentless in
pursuit of their goals and dreams, just as you can learn to be.

As strange as it may sound, you are as gifted as Buffet or any
of the other amazing investors mentioned throughout this book.
And the great news is that you can emulate their methods and good
habits to copy their success. This means that it's possible for you to
end up in the northwest quadrant if you focus on the long-term
future and adopt some of the important qualities about to be mentioned in the remainder of this chapter. You'll have to go against the
prevailing wisdom peddled by Wall Street. But that's OK. That's the
path to wealth.

It is important to note that simply copying Michael Jordan's methods and work habits won't enable you to defy gravity and win the next NBA slam dunk contest. Nor will duplicating Tiger Woods' putting style allow you to win the Masters golf tournament next year. Therefore, it is unlikely that just by following Buffett's style of investing you will become the wealthiest person in America. The important point is that if you take on Buffett's best habits, you will become a better investor. Maybe you won't become the wealthiest person in America or run the largest or most successful mutual fund, but by applying those most important characteristics to your own style of investing you can become an extremely successful investor whom many will admire and wish to emulate.

Who are the best mentors to mimic? Although the following list of investors is hardly exhaustive, it is a great place for you to begin investigating. Those outstanding investors who have been left out have the consolation that they are in good company. In addition to the following group of investors, you may know of others in your own community or may read about worthy candidates in the invest-ment media who warrant following.

The common denominator among all the great investors is their passion for investing, a passion that borders on obsession. It's not genius or brilliance that made them successful, although John Tem-pleton was a Rhodes scholar and the others certainly are brilliant if by that you mean focused so intently as to be fixated with achieving their goal. All are utterly dedicated to their style of investing; they're disciplined, focused, and patient in the face of adversity; and they can stand alone in that adversity. *The other common trait among these investors is that they insist upon buying dollar bills for 60 cents or less.*

FAYEZ SAROFIM

Barton Biggs once told a writer from *Barron's* that money manager Fayez Sarofim is a pension consultant's nightmare. That's because the manager of over $40 billion doesn't believe in the efficient market theory (EMT). Nor does he believe in diversification as EMT's solu-tion to risk in the market.

Sarofim's style is simple. He invests heavily in a relatively small number of well-known companies with household names like Philip Morris, Merck, and Procter & Gamble. One of the most amazing things about Sarofim is just how few people seek to imitate his style of investing. Of the more than 3000 mutual funds that concentrate on U.S. stocks, Sarofim's Dreyfus Appreciation Fund is one of only a handful with concentrated positions in blue-chip growth companies.

It's a strategy that anyone can duplicate. Sarofim's goal is to invest in great companies with a clear path ahead of them. Yet most mutual fund pros assume the Cokes and Procter & Gambles are so well followed by Wall Street that they can't get an edge by owning them. Sarofim concludes that most investors tend to sell their winners and hang onto their losers, thinking their losers will have a better day in the future. Yet it's the opposite strategy of holding onto winners that actually pays off.

His firm's top 10 stocks represent about 50 percent of his assets under management. For example, he's held Philip Morris for 30 years. He claims he doesn't need to diversify widely, since large companies like Coke are already diversified into countries around the world. And he hates to pay taxes. He points out that a dollar compounded at 15 percent annually grows to $16.37 over 20 years. But that same dollar grows to just $5 if the investor has to pay a 44 percent tax rate on a 15 percent annual gain.

ROBERT TORRAY

Torray began managing pension funds in 1972. Today, he manages about $2.5 billion in institutional pension assets. But when several friends asked him to open a mutual fund, he obliged them in 1990. A $10,000 investment in his self-named Torray Fund would have grown to $38,690 from the fund's inception in December 1990 until the end of 1997. Not only did Torray beat the pants off the market, but he did so with less risk. Yes, he's another northwest quadrant investor.

A strict buy-and-hold investor, Torray had 43 investments in his fund in 1997. His goal for the year was to have zero turnover in his portfolio. He considers himself a contrarian investor who likes the very big, financially strong companies that have good competitive positions. His favorite time to buy is when the Wall Street consensus is wrong and things turn sour. He buys only after analyzing a business and after the stock has dropped drastically in price. He doesn't study the stock market, economic trends, or the Federal

Reserve's raising or lowering of rates. His central idea is to buy the best businesses possible for a fair price.

Torray's greatest asset for benchmark investors to mimic: he ignores what everyone else is earning and focuses on his portfolio alone.

ROBERT SANBORN

Considered the best large cap growth fund manager in America, Robert Sanborn thinks in terms of 20 to 30 years when he's evaluating potential investments. He will buy a stock only when he'd like to own the whole company. And he buys only when a company is selling at 60 percent or less of what Sanborn reckons as the price a rational buyer would pay for it as a whole.

"We approach every stock we invest in by asking, 'How can we lose money on this thing?'" Sanborn told *The Wall Street Journal* (January 8, 1998).

His largest holdings at the end of 1997 were First USA, Philip Morris, Mellon Bank, Black & Decker, and Polaroid. You'll notice that these companies are all very high-quality franchises, with high barriers to entry and dominant market positions and phenomenal international opportunities. Sanborn picks his investments one at a time, using a bottom-up approach that focuses on the business rather than the economy. Historically, his Oakmark Fund has had an average 18 percent rate of turnover.

He and his staff of seven analysts grill company managements on their long-term strategic plans in their quest to find bargains that are trading well below their private market values. A $10,000 investment in Sanborn's $6 billion fund in August 1991 would have grown to $49,865 by the end of 1997, more than twice the rise in the S&P 500 during that same period. And, you guessed it, Sanborn doubled the market with less risk, which makes him another northwest quadrant resident.

WILLIAM J. RUANE

Bill Ruane and Warren Buffett met in 1951 in Ben Graham's investment class at Columbia University. Twenty years later, when Buffett wound up his Buffett Partnership, he asked Ruane to set up a fund to handle all his partners. The Sequoia Fund was the result of that request. Today, the fund manages $3.3 billion, yet holds over 90 percent of its assets in just seven stocks: Federal Home Loan Mortgage (27.7), Progressive Corp. of Ohio (25.6), Harley Davidson (9.4), Johnson & Johnson (9.3), Wells Fargo (7.1), Walt Disney (6.8), and Household International (4.3).

Not surprisingly, Ruane thinks a lot like Buffett. All the stocks he and comanager Richard T. Cunniff buy in his Sequoia Fund must be easily understood, must enjoy sound financial and franchise values, and must be trading below their intrinsic value. Ruane consistently keeps his top-rated fund heavily concentrated in just a handful of stocks, and often in just one industry. For example, at the end of 1997 Sequoia had 84 percent of its portfolio invested in financial companies.

Since 1972, Ruane's fund has averaged 18.27 percent a year, handily beating the S&P 500's 8.33 percent return. Had you invested $10,000 in Sequoia at that time, you would have seen it grow to $655,421 by the end of 1997. Only four other mutual funds turned in better returns than Sequoia after 1970. But none of the four other funds had the same manager, as did Sequoia during that entire period.

MICHAEL PRICE

Whenever a money manager hits on an investment style that is wildly successful, the clones come out of the woodwork. Oddly enough, that hasn't been the case with Michael Price, whose style has been labeled "vulture investing." Throughout a career that began in 1975, Price has been willing to invest in dismal failures, undervalued companies that are takeover candidates and out-of-favor restructuring candidates. He buys companies like Chase Manhattan, General Motors, and Philip Morris when they're down and out. A hypothetical $10,000 invested evenly between his three funds in 1980 would have grown to $148,540 by the end of 1997 with far less volatility than the S&P 500.

Price comes to work every day looking for the best bargains to buy. He doesn't try to time the market, although large piles of cash accumulate in his multi-billion dollar funds from time to time as he searches for more bargains.

Price's greatest asset for benchmark investors to mimic: his willingness to go wherever he has to in his intensive quest for bargains.

JOHN NEFF

It is sometimes good to know that even the best investors in the history of investing have had bad years. That was the case in 1989 when the venerable Neff experienced his roughest year in a long and glorious run that began at the Vanguard Windsor Fund in 1964. A disciplined, patient investor, the then 58-year-old manager was going through uncharacteristic adversity by trailing the stock market by 17 percent. Neff is a great example to would-be northwest quadrant inhabitants, because he was willing to stick with his disciplined strategy even when he'd had his worst year in a quarter of a century.

Neff found value where others saw only problems, so he often bought when the crowd was fleeing the scene. Although he was still up 15 percent in 1989, the S&P 500 turned in a 31.6 percent total return, far outdistancing his Vanguard Windsor Fund. And 1990 didn't see any significant improvement in Neff's portfolio, yet he averaged a 13.8 percent compound annual return for Windsor's investors from June 30, 1964, through December 31, 1995, when he retired.

Neff's trademark in running the multi-billion dollar stock fund was concentrating bets on large companies trading at below-market multiples. For instance, when a certain sector of the market was out of favor, Neff would buy, then hold on unyieldingly. According to the value manager, right eventually wins out. But, as Neff says, "You have to show a little patience in this business."

Under Neff's guidance, the fund's top 10 holdings usually accounted for more than one-third of the portfolio. A hypothetical $10,000 invested in Windsor at the beginning of 1973 would have grown to $294,350 by the end of 1995. In contrast, that same amount invested in the S&P 500 would have grown to just $66,060 during the same period.

John Neff's greatest asset for benchmark investors to mimic is patience.

WARREN BUFFETT

F. Scott Fitzgerald wrote that the very rich are different from you and me. He was right. Warren Buffett is different because he was willing to have $2 billion invested in just three stocks at the end of 1987. Most investors would have that kind of loose change scattered in hundreds, if not thousands, of investments in a widely diversified portfolio of bonds, money funds, and stocks. Of course, Buffett's fortunes have swelled considerably since 1987. At the end of 1997, his estimated net worth was in the $23 billion range.

Warren Buffett is the wealthiest investor in America and perhaps the most respected stock investor since the fabled Benjamin Graham. Actually, Buffett became a disciple of Graham after reading *The Intelligent Investor* in 1949 while attending the University of Nebraska. The following year, Buffett attended Columbia University to study under Graham.

After graduation Buffett offered to work for Graham for nothing, but when Graham declined, Buffett went back to Omaha to work for his father's brokerage firm. Still, Buffett kept in touch with Graham, who finally hired him to work for the Graham-Newman Corporation, where he spent two years learning from the master. After the apprenticeship Buffett returned to Omaha, where he began his own investment company, starting with a $100,000 family partnership.

As the partnership increased in value and his reputation spread, more money poured in. His investors were more than well compensated for their trust in the young Nebraskan. For every $1000 invested in 1956, each investor ended up with $39,000 by the time Buffett folded up the partnership in 1969, declaring that he couldn't find any more bargains in the market. Buffett's profit participation in the $100 million partnership had made him worth nearly $25 million. After the partnership was terminated, Buffett was able to invest in his favorite stocks at giveaway prices following the 1973–1974 bear market.

Warren Buffett's greatest asset for benchmark investors to mimic is his daring to ignore the conventional Wall Street banter. He doesn't care which direction the Dow takes, and he certainly has no interest in all the prophets and their predictions.

AND HONORABLE MENTION TO . . .

There remains a long and distinguished list of great investment professionals who also deserve mention. For example, Sir John Templeton was an amazing value investor who sought bargains throughout the world. That's why his name is synonymous with global investing. He was the founder of the family of some three dozen mutual funds that bear his name. Well known for his spiritual convictions, Templeton believed that one of the results of a spiritual attitude is that you want to work hard, to be wiser, and to make fewer mistakes. In his view, the good that comes to such a person, in whatever form that good may appear, is not the purpose of spirituality but its consequence. The Rhodes scholar's style was to uncover undervalued stocks worldwide that everyone else was throwing away. He then held onto the stocks for an average of four years, which usually gave his bargain stocks enough time to be recognized.

John Templeton's greatest asset for benchmark investors to mimic was his vision to buy what everyone else on Wall Street was trashing.

Peter Lynch is the legendary former manager of the Fidelity Magellan mutual fund and best-selling author of *One Up on Wall Street* and *Beating the Street.* Perhaps as respected for his humility as for his outstanding performance in the market, Lynch had an especially keen awareness for true value. He and his staff—which number not one economist among them—were the hardest-working and best-performing group on Wall Street for more than 13 years. Like Babe Ruth, he has a record of consistency and excellence that will stand for a long time.

Peter Lynch's greatest asset for benchmark investors to mimic is his self-effacing humor and keen eye for value. Lynch had a laserlike focus on beating the stock market. He neither cared nor bothered about which direction the economy was headed. The only thing he cared about was which direction his beloved stocks were headed.

Mario Gabelli is another money manager who can be called one of the truly great stock pickers of our time. The chief investment officer of Gamco Investors, the New York money management firm, Gabelli also heads up a broker-dealer, several mutual funds, and other ventures when he's not busy jetting across the country marketing his funds and his stocks. The likable former *Value Line* analyst looks at a company's real earnings—before interest, taxes, and depreciation cloud the picture. His goal is to make 10 percent after taxes.

Mario Gabelli's greatest asset for benchmark investors to mimic is adhering to the discipline of buying only undervalued companies.

David Dreman is the contrarian's contrarian. He literally wrote the book on contrarian investing in *The New Contrarian Investment Strategy*. His other writings include *Psychology and the Stock Market* and *Contrarian Investment Strategy* as well as articles for *Forbes, Barron's, Financial Analysts Journal, The New York Times, The Christian Science Monitor, Money,* and numerous other newspapers and periodicals. Dreman is known for his numerous studies, which conclude that stocks with the lowest price-earnings (P/E) multiples offer investors greater long-term potential than any other group of stocks. All stocks in which Dreman invests are followed on an intensive, ongoing basis, with the most important criteria being low P/E multiples and low price-to-book-value relationships. He favors stocks that are falling out of favor with Wall Street's points of view. Dreman invests in 25 large or medium-size companies divided among 15 to 20 industries. And he has patience, so much so that his average yearly portfolio turnover is a paltry 25 to 30 percent, quite low by industry standards, but quite profitable for his investors.

This next investment great might surprise you because he made his name as a retailer rather than in investing, but Sam Walton created as much wealth on Wall Street as anyone in his time. The native of Kingfisher, Oklahoma, who founded Wal-Mart brought a down-home country spirit to retailing. His innovative style saw his single store in 1962 grow to a 2300-store empire that posted revenues of $67 billion by the time of his death in 1993. Although not usually considered along with other mentors in the investment field, Walton did as much as anyone to bring the true meaning of shareholder relations to America.

Other great investors you might take the time to investigate are Benjamin Graham and Philip Fisher, Buffett's early mentors; Martin Whitman; Walter Schloss; Charles Munger, Buffett's long-time partner; Rick Guerin of Pacific Partners L.P.; Stan Perlmeter; Franklin Balance Sheet manager William Lippman; Cornerstone Growth fund manager James O'Shaughnessy; and Thomas Marsico.

What you'll find is great investors of intellect, character, and good temperament who know how to identify bargain companies selling at considerably less than their private "intrinsic" value. That's how they became successful and wealthy. They didn't worry about any so-called January effect, whether the Fed was going to raise rates, where the economy was headed, or who was going to get elected to the White House. They simply cared about buying a business worth a dollar that they could temporarily buy for 60 cents or less. And they did it over and over again. It is extraordinary to me that more investors don't do likewise. But the great news is that you can begin to do so today. So I encourage you to have the courage to go ahead and buy more for your money than you're paying and focus on the long-term results, not on what happens in the weeks and months ahead.

When you successfully exploit this difference between price and value often and long enough, you will enjoy similar results as the mentors mentioned in this book. If you compound $1.00 at 15 percent for 20 years, it will grow to $16.37. And if you let it compound for 25 years, it will become $32.92. What are you waiting for?

CHAPTER 12

Benchmark's Self-Test

I hear and I forget. I see and I remember. I do and I understand.

Chinese proverb

Here is where you will find out if you're ready to begin investing real money with the benchmark investing method. Included in the following self-test are all the data necessary to calculate valuation levels for the 30 stocks in the exercise. It's all that any benchmark investor needs to make valuation judgments.

The test has been stacked with more winners than losers, but not all are big winners. Some of the stocks included in the test barely eked out gains. There are 17 winners and 13 losers among the 30 stocks. Of the 17 winners, the 10 best gainers averaged returns of 53.30 percent. It's possible that you could score even higher—but it's not likely, since one of the stocks that you should identify as undervalued actually lost 18 percent. This "loser" was added to give the test more of a real-world flavor, since there will be losses even when you've done everything right. Unfortunately, that's life.

Again, you have all the tools you need in order to calculate valuation levels and make all-important investment decisions. To "pass," you should select at least 7 of the top 10 gainers before deciding that you're ready to invest real money in the market (see Table 12.1). If you select Merck, which lost 18 percent in 1993, you made the "correct" choice according to the benchmark formula. This

TABLE 12.1

Top Gainers in Self-Test

Year	Stock	Return
1995	Merck	75.37%
1989	Philip Morris	74.60%
1991	AlliedSignal	68.44%
1993	Caterpillar	67.07%
1995	Philip Morris	63.00%
1989	McDonald's	49.80%
1995	American Express	43.32%
1992	AT&T	33.71%
1995	AT&T	31.48%
1992	American Express	26.24%

is simply a good example to prove that not all undervalued benchmark choices make money in the real world all the time.

Let's review the necessary steps to evaluate a stock's valuation levels using benchmark's formula.

1. Find the average return on equity for the previous 10 years.

2. Divide the current year's return on equity by its 10-year average return on equity to find the adjusted ROE ratio.

3. Find the average book value for the previous 10 years. Also find the average low and high stock prices for the same period.

4. Calculate the stock's average yearly low price.

5. Find the average low *and* high market-to-book values for the previous 10 years. To do so, divide the average low and high prices by the average book value from step 3.

6. Find the downside target by first multiplying the stock's low market-to-book average multiple by the adjusted ROE ratio. Then multiply that number by its current book value.

7. Find the upside target by first multiplying the stock's high market-to-book average multiple by the adjusted

ROE ratio. Then multiply that number by its current book value.

Again, let's look at IBM stock as an example:

10-year average return on equity	16.52%
Current return on equity (ROE)	24.50%
Adjusted ROE ratio	1.48
10-year average book value	$47.25
10-year average low stock price	$78.44
Average low market-to-book ratio	1.66
10-year average high stock price	$116.24
Average high market-to-book ratio	2.46
Current book value (BV)	$46.30

Downside target price = 1.66 (low market/book) × 1.48 (ROE ratio) × $46.30 (BV) = $113.74

Upside target price = 2.46 (high market/book) × 1.48 (ROE ratio) × $46.30 (BV) = $168.56

Benchmark Imnvesting's Self-Test

Stock 1

	1991	1990	1989	1988	1987	1986	1985	1984	1983	1982	1981
Return on equity	13.50	13.70	14.80	14.20	12.30	15.00	6.90	14.40	13.10	6.60	14.00
Average ROE											
Book value	$26.05	$25.10	$23.53	$22.09	$20.87	$21.04	$33.17	$32.82	$29.78	$37.45	$36.87
Average book value											
Low price		$24.90	$31.80	$28.00	$26.00	$36.80	$33.80	$28.30	$21.40	$19.20	$26.00
Average low market/book											
High price		$37.90	$40.40	$36.90	$49.30	$54.50	$48.10	$37.50	$38.80	$30.30	$39.90
Average high market/book											
Current ROE ratio											
Downside target price											
Average target price											
Upside target price											
Current price	$26.00										

Stock 2

	1992	1991	1990	1989	1988	1987	1986	1985	1984	1983	1982
Return on equity	12	14.50	14.60	20.30	20.60	8.60	17.90	15.10	13.20	12.70	19.00
Average ROE											
Book value	$16.65	$13.95	$13.21	$12.90	$11.39	$10.11	$12.60	$11.41	$10.10	$9.47	$7.96
Average book value											
Low price		$18.00	$17.50	$26.40	$22.90	$20.80	$25.30	$17.90	$12.50	$14.00	$8.80
Average low market/book											
High price		$30.40	$35.30	$39.40	$30.40	$40.60	$35.10	$27.50	$19.50	$24.80	$17.70
Average high market/book											
Current ROE ratio											
Downside target price											
Average target price											
Upside target price											
Current price	$20.50										

Stock 3

	1992	1991	1990	1989	1988	1987	1986	1985	1984	1983
Return on equity	20	3.20	19.40	21.20	19.80	13.90	13.00	9.90	9.10	10.70
Average ROE										
Book value	$14.95	$12.39	$12.90	$11.84	$10.68	$13.46	$12.64	$13.68	$13.26	$13.26
Average book value										
Average low market/book										
Low price		$29.00	$29.00	$28.10	$24.10	$22.30	$20.90	$19.00	$14.90	$17.40
High price		$40.40	$46.60	$47.00	$30.40	$35.90	$27.90	$25.40	$20.30	$21.30
Average high market/book										
Current ROE ratio										
Downside target price										
Average target price										
Upside target price										
Current price	**$39.13**									

Stock 4

	1993	1992	1991	1990	1989	1988	1987	1986	1985
Return on equity	10	NMF	NMF	4.60	11.10	15.00	9.80	5.70	6.70
Average ROE									
Book value	$41.00	$38.30	$40.07	$44.99	$44.11	$40.56	$35.15	$31.86	$31.19
Average book value									
Low price		$41.30	$37.60	$38.10	$52.90	$53.90	$39.90	$36.60	$29.00
Average low market/book									
High price		$62.10	$57.60	$68.50	$69.00	$68.50	$74.80	$55.40	$43.10
Average high market/book									
Current ROE ratio									
Downside target price									
Average target price									
Upside target price									
Current price	**$53.63**								

Stock 5

	1994	1993	1992	1991	1990	1989	1988	1987	1986	1985	1984
Return on equity	14	13	11.6	8.8	14.40	10.50	11.20	4.60	5.80	9.30	11.50
Average ROE											
Book value	$45.25	$42.97	$42.22	$42.51	$42.29	$39.38	$43.23	$46.13	$45.29	$45.47	$43.15
Average book value											
Low price		$67.50	$60.10	$63.50	$63.10	$45.40	$39.00	$32.00	$34.00	$29.30	$30.00
Average low market/book											
High price		$98.80	$75.40	$80.10	$81.60	$73.50	$52.00	$64.60	$48.10	$40.80	$40.30
Average high market/book											
Current ROE ratio											
Downside target price											
Average target price											
Upside target price											
Current price	**$87.13**										

Stock 6

	1993	1992	1991	1990	1989	1988	1987	1986	1985	1984	1983
Return on equity	18	18	16.4	23.60	23.10	22.10	21.30	17.40	14.60	9.30	6.70
Average ROE											
Book value	$10.35	$8.75	$7.43	$6.62	$5.62	$4.43	$3.50	$2.71	$2.29	$2.14	$2.54
Average book value											
Low price		$28.50	$23.40	$21.50	$16.20	$13.50	$10.30	$7.00	$3.70	$2.80	$3.00
Average low market/book											
High price		$45.30	$32.40	$34.10	$34.10	$17.10	$20.60	$13.70	$7.30	$4.30	$5.30
Average high market/book											
Current ROE ratio											
Downside target price											
Average target price											
Upside target price											
Current price	**$43.00**										

Stock 7

	1994	1993	1992	1991	1990	1989	1988	1987	1986	1985	1984
Return on equity	22	25	16.1	0.3	18.90	8.00	20.60	19.60	5.90	5.10	12.90
Average ROE											
Book value	$12.10	$10.15	$20.12	$18.79	$20.75	$20.48	$20.91	$18.55	$18.86	$19.37	$20.39
Average book value											
Low price		$40.40	$37.80	$37.60	$33.80	$40.00	$39.80	$42.00	$30.60	$27.50	$26.80
Avg. low market/book											
High price		$64.80	$50.80	$49.80	$43.90	$52.40	$53.30	$71.00	$46.70	$35.60	$34.70
Avg. high market/book											
Current ROE ratio											
Downside target price											
Average target price											
Upside target price											
Current price	$56.25										

Stock 8

	1993	1992	1991	1990	1989	1988	1987	1986	1985	1984	1983
Return on equity	15	14.2	16	15.20	15.40	16.10	14.40	15.60	18.60	19.20	16.90
Average ROE											
Book value	$27.48	$26.57	$28.12	$26.55	$24.20	$24.64	$24.38	$22.30	$19.90	$18.42	$17.40
Average book value											
Low price		$53.80	$49.60	$44.90	$41.50	$36.80	$33.30	$24.20	$22.10	$18.10	$14.30
Average low market/book											
High price		$65.50	$61.90	$55.10	$51.60	$47.80	$50.80	$37.10	$28.00	$22.80	$19.90
Average high market/book											
Current ROE ratio											
Downside target price											
Average target price											
Upside target price											
Current price	$61.13										

Stock 9

Stock 9	1992	1991	1990	1989	1988	1987	1986	1985	1984	1983	1982
Return on equity	9.5	5	14.10	13.60	14.70	13.70	13.90	20.50	24.80	23.60	22.10
Average ROE											
Book value	$75.80	$73.75	$74.96	$67.00	$66.96	$64.06	$56.67	$51.98	$43.23	$38.02	$33.13
Average book value											
Low price		$83.50	$94.50	$93.40	$104.50	$102.00	$119.30	$117.40	$99.00	$92.30	$55.60
Average low market/book											
High price		$139.80	$123.10	$130.90	$129.50	$175.90	$161.90	$158.80	$128.50	$134.30	$98.00
Average high market/book											
Current ROE ratio											
Downside target price											
Average target price											
Upside target price											
Current price	$89.00										

Stock 10

Stock 10	1992	1991	1990	1989	1988	1987	1986	1985	1984	1983	1982
Return on equity	7.5	7.6	12.50	16.80	15.50	9.10	6.70	3.00	6.10	5.80	4.60
Average ROE											
Book value	55.1	51.03	51.34	47.35	41.14	36.31	35.00	33.30	33.02	33.38	32.47
Average book value											
Low price		50.50	42.80	45.10	36.50	27.00	24.20	22.10	23.00	23.00	16.40
Average low market/book											
High price		78.30	59.80	58.80	49.40	57.80	40.10	28.90	29.90	30.00	25.80
Average high market/book											
Current ROE ratio											
Downside target price											
Average target price											
Upside target price											
Current price	$70.75										

Stock 11

	1994	1993	1992	1991	1990	1989	1988	1987	1986	1985	1984
Return on equity	16	17	16	17.8	19.20	20.50	18.90	18.80	19.10	19.30	19.40
Average ROE											
Book value	$19.15	$16.40	$14.59	$12.65	$11.09	$9.25	$9.09	$7.72	$6.45	$5.67	$4.94
Average book value											
Low price		$45.50	$38.50	$26.10	$25.00	$23.00	$20.40	$15.70	$16.20	$11.40	$9.10
Average low market/book											
High price		$59.10	$50.40	$39.90	$38.50	$34.90	$25.50	$30.60	$25.60	$18.20	$12.40
Average high market/book											
Current ROE ratio											
Downside target price											
Average target price											
Upside target price											
Current price	$57.00										

Stock 12

	1993	1992	1991	1990	1989	1988	1987	1986	1985	1984	1983
Return on equity	36.5	39	43.2	46.50	42.50	42.30	42.80	26.30	20.50	19.40	18.50
Average ROE											
Book value	$6.95	$5.50	$4.24	$3.30	$2.97	$2.40	$1.79	$2.09	$2.09	$1.96	$1.83
Average book value											
Low price		$40.60	$27.30	$22.30	$18.80	$16.00	$13.60	$7.50	$5.00	$4.30	$4.50
Average low market/book											
High price		$56.60	$55.70	$30.40	$26.90	$19.90	$24.80	$14.40	$7.70	$5.40	$5.80
Average high market/book											
Current ROE ratio											
Downside target price											
Average target price											
Upside target price											
Current price	$43.38										

Stock 13

	1995	1994	1993	1992	1991	1990	1989	1988	1987	1986	1985
Return on equity	21	20.5	18.4	8.7	14.30	14.60	20.30	20.60	8.60	17.90	15.10
Average ROE											
Book value	$15.30	$13.75	$16.81	$14.58	$14.43	$13.21	$12.90	$11.39	$10.11	$12.60	$11.41
Average book value											
Low price		$25.30	$22.40	$20.00	$18.00	$17.50	$26.40	$22.90	$20.80	$25.30	$17.90
Average low market/book											
High price		$33.10	$36.60	$25.40	$30.40	$35.30	$39.40	$30.40	$40.60	$35.10	$27.50
Average high market/book											
Current ROE ratio											
Downside target price											
Average target price											
Upside target price											
Current price	**$29.50**										

Stock 14

	1995	1994	1993	1992	1991	1990	1989	1988	1987	1986	1985
Return on equity	28.5	30	30.8	20.1	3.20	19.40	21.20	19.80	13.90	13.00	9.90
Average ROE											
Book value	$12.75	$10.65	$10.24	$14.12	$12.39	$12.90	$11.84	$10.68	$13.46	$12.64	$13.68
Average book value											
Low price		$49.50	$50.30	$36.60	$29.00	$29.00	$28.10	$24.10	$22.30	$20.90	$19.00
Average low market/book											
High price		$57.10	$65.00	$53.10	$40.40	$46.60	$47.00	$30.40	$35.90	$27.90	$25.40
Average high market/book											
Current ROE ratio											
Downside target price											
Average target price											
Upside target price											
Current price	**$50.25**										

Stock 15

	1992	1991	1990	1989	1988	1987	1986	1985	1984	1983	1982
Return on equity	10	10.4	14.10	15.70	13.60	11.90	11.50	9.70	11.60	9.30	8.50
Average ROE											
Book value	$25.50	$24.54	$24.16	$22.71	$21.36	$19.55	$18.25	$17.21	$16.69	$15.68	$14.96
Average book value											
Low price		$32.80	$31.40	$28.70	$25.30	$25.00	$19.80	$15.90	$14.10	$11.70	$10.00
Average low market/book											
High price		$50.00	$42.40	$42.20	$31.00	$43.70	$30.80	$23.10	$17.60	$18.30	$14.80
Average high market/book											
Current ROE ratio											
Downside target price											
Average target price											
Upside target price											
Current price									$46.63		

Stock 16

	1994	1993	1992	1991	1990	1989	1988	1987	1986	1985	1984
Return on equity	13	15	14.2	16	15.20	15.40	16.10	14.40	15.60	18.60	19.20
Average ROE											
Book value	$28.30	$27.48	$26.57	$28.12	$26.55	$24.20	$24.64	$24.38	$22.30	$19.90	$18.42
Average book value											
Low price		$57.80	$53.80	$49.60	$44.90	$41.50	$36.80	$33.30	$24.20	$22.10	$18.10
Average low market/book											
High price		$69.00	$65.50	$61.90	$55.10	$51.60	$47.80	$50.80	$37.10	$28.00	$22.80
Average high market/book											
Current ROE ratio											
Downside target price											
Average target price											
Upside target price											
Current price									$63.13		

Stock 17	1995	1994	1993	1992	1991	1990	1989	1988	1987	1986	1985
Return on equity	8.5	6	5	6.5	7.6	12.50	16.80	15.50	9.10	6.70	3.00
Average ROE											
Book value	$55.20	$52.10	$50.25	$50.46	$51.03	$51.34	$47.35	$41.14	$36.31	$35.00	$33.30
Average book value											
Low price		$60.60	$56.60	$58.50	$50.50	$42.80	$45.10	$36.50	$27.00	$24.20	$22.10
Average low market/book											
High price		$80.40	$72.00	$78.50	$78.30	$59.80	$58.80	$49.40	$57.80	$40.10	$28.90
Average high market/book											
Current ROE ratio											
Downside target price											
Average target price											
Upside target price											
Current price	**$75.38**										

Stock 18	1995	1994	1993	1992	1991	1990	1989	1988	1987	1986	1985
Return on equity	25.5	26	26.8	48.90	43.20	46.50	42.50	42.30	42.80	26.30	20.50
Average ROE											
Book value	$10.65	$9.30	$7.99	$4.37	$4.24	$3.30	$2.97	$2.40	$1.79	$2.09	$2.09
Average book value											
Low price		$28.10	$28.60	$40.60	$27.30	$22.30	$18.80	$16.00	$13.60	$7.50	$5.00
Average low market/book											
High price		$38.00	$44.10	$56.60	$55.70	$30.40	$26.90	$19.90	$24.80	$14.40	$7.70
Average high market/book											
Current ROE ratio											
Downside target price											
Average target price											
Upside target price											
Current price	**$38.13**										

Stock 19

	1992	1991	1990	1989	1988	1987	1986	1985	1984	1983	1982
Return on equity	16	18.4	14.90	0.00	17.30	1.70	17.00	16.10	13.90	13.90	16.30
Average ROE											
Book value	$32.65	$29.41	$25.29	$21.78	$30.52	$26.57	$27.42	$23.70	$20.85	$18.85	$17.11
Average book value											
Low price		$40.50	$29.60	$34.00	$30.80	$27.00	$29.50	$19.40	$14.10	$15.60	$11.40
Average low market/book											
High price		$70.50	$47.30	$48.10	$40.30	$53.60	$48.00	$33.00	$20.20	$21.60	$18.00
Average high market/book											
Current ROE ratio											
Downside target price											
Average target price											
Upside target price											
Current price										$68.63	

Stock 20

	1995	1994	1993	1992	1991	1990	1989	1988	1987	1986	1985
Return on equity	36	36.5	30.7	39.3	33.6	29.60	29.20	26.90	27.30	26.10	25.70
Average ROE											
Book value	$16.70	$15.00	$13.26	$13.43	$13.59	$12.90	$10.31	$8.31	$7.21	$5.94	$4.96
Average book value											
Low price		$47.30	$45.00	$70.10	$48.30	$36.00	$25.00	$20.10	$18.20	$11.00	$9.00
Average low market/book											
High price		$64.50	$77.60	$86.60	$81.80	$51.80	$45.80	$25.50	$31.10	$19.50	$11.90
Average high market/book											
Current ROE ratio											
Downside target price											
Average target price											
Upside target price											
Current price										$55.63	

Stock 21

	1993	1992	1991	1990	1989	1988	1987	1986	1985	1984	1983
Return on equity	20.5	20.6	22.9	19.60	19.40	16.10	13.10	11.90	12.00	16.90	18.50
Average ROE											
Book value	$12.00	$10.44	$8.49	$9.41	$8.05	$9.35	$8.49	$8.47	$7.87	$7.61	$6.94
Average book value											
Low price		$45.10	$38.00	$30.90	$21.10	$17.70	$15.00	$15.90	$12.60	$11.40	$12.60
Average low market/book											
High price		$55.80	$47.70	$45.60	$35.20	$22.00	$25.90	$20.60	$17.90	$15.00	$15.80
Average high market/book											
Current ROE ratio											
Downside target price											
Average target price											
Upside target price											
Current price	$53.63										

Stock 22

	1994	1993	1992	1991	1990	1989	1988	1987	1986	1985	1984
Return on equity	12	12.9	0	9	7.00	10.60	10.30	12.10	10.40	11.10	13.30
Average ROE											
Book value	$31.05	$28.80	$26.64	$40.29	$37.38	$39.77	$37.75	$35.89	$33.98	$31.79	$29.48
Average book value											
Low price		$42.00	$37.00	$24.40	$22.00	$36.50	$32.30	$26.00	$35.90	$30.90	$29.50
Average low market/book											
High price		$60.10	$48.00	$43.50	$41.90	$48.10	$46.30	$59.50	$50.40	$41.10	$40.40
Average high market/book											
Current ROE ratio											
Downside target price											
Average target price											
Upside target price											
Current price	$57.00										

Stock 23	1992	1991	1990	1989	1988	1987	1986	1985	1984	1983	1982
Return on equity	9.5	NMF	13.20	26.10	37.80	22.90	12.90	1.90	7.40	4.30	6.00
Average ROE											
Book value	$18.40	$17.55	$15.96	$16.83	$13.34	$9.43	$7.87	$19.82	$23.30	$23.32	$24.51
Average book value											
Low price		$15.40	$14.10	$22.80	$17.00	$15.50	$18.80	$12.00	$10.90	$17.00	$13.40
Average low market/book											
High price		$22.60	$24.90	$33.30	$28.40	$32.50	$33.20	$24.30	$21.80	$24.60	$20.30
Average high market/book											
Current ROE ratio											
Downside target price											
Average target price											
Upside target price											
Current price	**$20.25**										

Stock 24	1992	1991	1990	1989	1988	1987	1986	1985	1984	1983	1982
Return on equity	13	8	13.80	14.80	13.70	13.80	9.50	14.60	14.40	13.50	12.30
Average ROE											
Book value	$28.60	$26.20	$37.68	$33.69	$36.88	$32.90	$29.14	$31.58	$30.04	$27.21	$25.56
Average book value											
Low price		$42.10	$40.10	$39.90	$33.00	$30.00	$39.30	$34.50	$28.50	$26.90	$15.60
Average low market/book											
High price		$54.50	$62.50	$57.40	$42.60	$60.50	$56.30	$46.50	$41.60	$38.40	$29.40
Average high market/book											
Current ROE ratio											
Downside target price											
Average target price											
Upside target price											
Current price	**$54.25**										

Stock 25	1992	1991	1990	1989	1988	1987	1986	1985	1984	1983	1982
Return on equity	18.5	16.5	25.70	21.00	21.70	20.70	22.30	18.70	14.30	13.20	14.10
Average ROE											
Book value	$10.85	$9.50	$13.43	$15.10	$13.18	$12.46	$10.56	$10.52	$10.70	$9.74	$9.08
Average book value											
Low price		$13.80	$24.30	$25.60	$23.80	$20.00	$21.00	$12.70	$9.90	$9.30	$5.50
Average low market/book											
High price		$31.00	$39.40	$38.10	$28.70	$37.50	$31.30	$23.40	$14.20	$14.10	$10.10
Average high market/book											
Current ROE ratio											
Downside target price											
Average target price											
Upside target price											
Current price	**$18.00**										

Stock 26	1995	1994	1993	1992	1991	1990	1989	1988	1987	1986	1985
Return on equity	9	9	0	13.6	9.6	13.50	15.80	15.60	14.60	14.40	14.50
Average ROE											
Book value	$11.20	$10.30	$10.22	$15.64	$15.54	$18.00	$16.04	$14.34	$13.27	$11.25	$9.40
Average book value											
Low price		$12.90	$20.50	$26.00	$23.50	$22.90	$24.20	$17.10	$14.80	$14.50	$9.20
Average low market/book											
High price		$26.30	$32.80	$35.00	$36.40	$36.60	$36.10	$30.40	$29.80	$24.50	$15.60
Average high market/book											
Current ROE ratio											
Downside target price											
Average target price											
Upside target price											
Current price	**$15.00**										

Stock 27

	1993	1992	1991	1990	1989	1988	1987	1986	1985	1984	1983
Return on equity	38.5	37	33.6	29.60	29.20	26.90	27.30	26.10	25.70	25.30	22.40
Average ROE											
Book value	$16.80	$14.95	$13.59	$12.90	$10.31	$8.31	$7.21	$5.94	$4.96	$4.21	$4.03
Average book value											
Low price		$70.10	$48.30	$36.00	$25.00	$20.10	$18.20	$11.00	$9.00	$7.80	$6.80
Average low market/book											
High price		$86.60	$81.80	$51.80	$45.80	$25.50	$31.10	$19.50	$11.90	$10.40	$9.00
Average high market/book											
Current ROE ratio											
Downside target price											
Average target price											
Upside target price											
Current price	**$77.13**										

Stock 28

	1989	1988	1987	1986	1985	1984	1983	1982	1981	1980	1979
Return on equity	18.5	19.00	18.80	19.10	19.30	19.40	19.50	19.7	19.3	19.4	19.8
Average ROE											
Book value	$21.50	$18.20	$15.44	$12.90	$11.35	$9.88	$8.77	$7.56	$6.73	$5.61	$5.68
Average book value											
Low price		$40.80	$31.40	$32.50	$22.70	$18.10	$16.30	$11.50	$9.50	$7.10	$7.70
Average low market/book											
High price		$51.00	$61.10	$51.20	$36.20	$24.90	$22.10	$19.50	$14.40	$10.30	$10.30
Average high market/book											
Current ROE ratio											
Downside target price											
Average target price											
Upside target price											
Current price	**$46.75**										

Stock 29

	1989	1988	1987	1986	1985	1984	1983	1982	1981	1980	1979
Return on equity	28	30	27.3	26.1	25.7	25.3	22.4	21.3	20	20.2	20.6
Average ROE											
Book value	$39.80	$33.30	$28.83	$23.77	$19.84	$16.86	$16.14	$14.55	$13.18	$11.43	$9.92
Average book value											
Low price		$80.50	$72.60	$43.90	$36.00	$31.10	$27.00	$22.10	$21.00	$14.60	$15.60
Average low market/book											
High price		$101.50	$124.50	$78.00	$47.60	$41.60	$36.20	$33.90	$27.60	$24.30	$19.30
Average high market/book											
Current ROE ratio											
Downside target price											
Average target price											
Upside target price											
Current price	**$100.88**										

Stock 30

	1990	1989	1988	1987	1986	1985	1984	1983	1982	1981	1980
Return on equity	13.50	14	14.20	12.30	15.00	6.90	14.40	13.10	6.60	14.00	15.00
Average ROE											
Book value	$25.50	$23.90	$20.87	$21.04	$33.17	$32.82	$29.78	$37.45	$36.87	$33.13	$28.43
Average book value											
Low price		$31.80	$26.00	$36.80	$33.80	$28.30	$21.40	$19.20	$26.00	$26.00	$19.00
Average low market/book											
High price		$40.40	$49.30	$54.50	$48.10	$37.50	$38.80	$30.30	$39.90	$41.20	$33.00
Average high market/book											
Current ROE ratio											
Downside target price											
Average target price											
Upside target price											
Current price	**$35.38**										

Answers to Benchmark Investing's Self-Test

AlliedSignal (ALD)	1	1991	1990	1989	1988	1987	1986	1985	1984	1983	1982	1981
Return on equity		13.50	13.70	14.80	14.20	12.30	15.00	6.90	14.40	13.10	6.60	14.00
Average ROE	12.50											
Book value		$26.05	$25.10	$23.53	$22.09	$20.87	$21.04	$33.17	$32.82	$29.78	$37.45	$36.87
Average book value	$28.27											
Low price			$24.90	$31.80	$28.00	$26.00	$36.80	$33.80	$28.30	$21.40	$19.20	$26.00
Average low market/book	0.98											
High price			$37.90	$40.40	$36.90	$49.30	$54.50	$48.10	$37.50	$38.80	$30.30	$39.90
Average high market/book	1.46											
Current ROE ratio	1.08											
Downside target price	$27.49											
Average target price	$34.32											
Upside target price	$41.16			68.44% in 1991								
Current price	**$26.00**											

American Express	2	1992	1991	1990	1989	1988	1987	1986	1985	1984	1983	1982
Return on equity	12	14.50	14.60	20.30	20.60	8.60	17.90	15.10	13.20	13.10	12.70	19.00
Average ROE	15.65											
Book value		$16.65	$13.95	$13.21	$12.90	$11.39	$10.11	$12.60	$11.41	$10.10	$9.47	$7.96
Average book value	$11.31											
Low price			$18.00	$17.50	$26.40	$22.90	$20.80	$25.30	$17.90	$12.50	$14.00	$8.80
Average low market/book	1.63											
High price			$30.40	$35.30	$39.40	$30.40	$40.60	$35.10	$27.50	$19.50	$24.80	$17.70
Average high market/book	2.66											
Current ROE ratio	0.77											
Downside target price	$20.78											
Average target price	$27.36			26.24% in 1992								
Upside target price	$33.94											
Current price	**$20.50**											

AT&T (T)

	3	1992	1991	1990	1989	1988	1987	1986	1985	1984	1983
Return on equity		20	3.20	19.40	21.20	19.80	13.90	13.00	9.90	9.10	10.70
Average ROE	13.36										
Book value		$14.95	$12.39	$12.90	$11.84	$10.68	$13.46	$12.64	$13.68	$13.26	$13.26
Average book value	$12.68										
Low price			$29.00	$29.00	$28.10	$24.10	$22.30	$20.90	$19.00	$14.90	$17.40
Average low market/book	1.79										
High price			$40.40	$46.60	$47.00	$30.40	$35.90	$27.90	$25.40	$20.30	$21.30
Average high market/book	2.59										
Current ROE ratio	1.50		33.71% in 1992								
Downside target price	$40.16										
Average target price	$49.04										
Upside target price	$57.92										
Current price	**$39.13**										

Caterpillar (CAT)

	4	1993	1992	1991	1990	1989	1988	1987	1986	1985
Return on equity		10	NMF	NMF	4.60	11.10	15.00	9.80	5.70	6.70
Average ROE	7.86									
Book value		$41.00	$38.30	$40.07	$44.99	$44.11	$40.56	$35.15	$31.86	$31.19
Average book value	$38.28									
Low price			$41.30	$37.60	$38.10	$52.90	$53.90	$39.90	$36.60	$29.00
Average low market/book	1.08									
High price			$62.10	$57.60	$68.50	$69.00	$68.50	$74.80	$55.40	$43.10
Average high market/book	1.63									
Current ROE ratio	1.27		67.07% in 1993							
Downside target price	$56.09									
Average target price	$70.55									
Upside target price	$85.00									
Current price	**$53.63**									

Chevron (CHV)

Chevron (CHV)	5	1994	1993	1992	1991	1990	1989	1988	1987	1986	1985	1984
Return on equity		14	13	11.6	8.8	14.40	10.50	11.20	4.60	5.80	9.30	11.50
Average ROE	10.07											
Book value		$45.25	$42.97	$42.22	$42.51	$42.29	$39.38	$43.23	$46.13	$45.29	$45.47	$43.15
Average book value	$43.26											
Low price			$67.50	$60.10	$63.50	$63.10	$45.40	$39.00	$32.00	$34.00	$29.30	$30.00
Average low market/book	1.07											
High price			$98.80	$75.40	$80.10	$81.60	$73.50	$52.00	$64.60	$48.10	$40.80	$40.30
Average high market/book	1.51											
Current ROE ratio	1.39		6.69% in 1994									
Downside target price	$67.46											
Average target price	$81.36											
Upside target price	$95.27											
Current price	**$87.13**											

Disney (DIS)

Disney (DIS)	6	1993	1992	1991	1990	1989	1988	1987	1986	1985	1984	1983
Return on equity		18	18	16.4	23.60	23.10	22.10	21.30	17.40	14.60	9.30	6.70
Average ROE	17.25											
Book value		$10.35	$8.75	$7.43	$6.62	$5.62	$4.43	$3.50	$2.71	$2.29	$2.14	$2.54
Average book value	$4.60											
Low price			$28.50	$23.40	$21.50	$16.20	$13.50	$10.30	$7.00	$3.70	$2.80	$3.00
Average low market/book	2.82											
High price			$45.30	$32.40	$34.10	$34.10	$17.10	$20.60	$13.70	$7.30	$4.30	$5.30
Average high market/book	4.65											
Current ROE ratio	1.04		lost 0.30% in 1993									
Downside target price	$30.48											
Average target price	$40.37											
Upside target price	$50.26											
Current price	**$43.00**											

253

Eastman Kodak (EK)

Eastman Kodak (EK)	7	1994	1993	1992	1991	1990	1989	1988	1987	1986	1985	1984
Return on equity		22	25	16.1	0.3	18.90	8.00	20.60	19.60	5.90	5.10	12.90
Average ROE	13.24											
Book value		$12.10	$10.15	$20.12	$18.79	$20.75	$20.48	$20.91	$18.55	$18.86	$19.37	$20.39
Average book value	$18.84											
Low price			$40.40	$37.80	$37.60	$33.80	$40.00	$39.80	$42.00	$30.60	$27.50	$26.80
Avg. low market/book	1.89											
High price			$64.80	$50.80	$49.80	$43.90	$52.40	$53.30	$71.00	$46.70	$35.60	$34.70
Avg. high market/book	2.67											
Current ROE ratio	1.66											
Downside target price	$38.03			lost 12.09% in 1994								
Average target price	$45.86											
Upside target price	$53.69											
Current price	**$56.25**											

Exxon (XON)

Exxon (XON)	8	1993	1992	1991	1990	1989	1988	1987	1986	1985	1984	1983
Return on equity		15	14.2	16	15.20	15.40	16.10	14.40	15.60	18.60	19.20	16.90
Average ROE	16.16											
Book value		$27.48	$26.57	$28.12	$26.55	$24.20	$24.64	$24.38	$22.30	$19.90	$18.42	$17.40
Average book value	$23.25											
Low price			$53.80	$49.60	$44.90	$41.50	$36.80	$33.30	$24.20	$22.10	$18.10	$14.30
Average low market/book	1.46											
High price			$65.50	$61.90	$55.10	$51.60	$47.80	$50.80	$37.10	$28.00	$22.80	$19.90
Average high market/book	1.89											
Current ROE ratio	0.93		7.98% in 1993									
Downside target price	$37.15											
Average target price	$42.74											
Upside target price	$48.33											
Current price	**$61.13**											

IBM (IBM)

IBM (IBM)	9	1992	1991	1990	1989	1988	1987	1986	1985	1984	1983	1982
Return on equity												
Average ROE	16.60	9.5	5	14.10	13.60	14.70	13.70	13.90	20.50	24.80	23.60	22.10
Book value		$75.80	$73.75	$74.96	$67.00	$66.96	$64.06	$56.67	$51.98	$43.23	$38.02	$33.13
Average book value	$56.98											
Low price			$83.50	$94.50	$93.40	$104.50	$102.00	$119.30	$117.40	$99.00	$92.30	$55.60
Average low market/book	1.69											
High price			$139.80	$123.10	$130.90	$129.50	$175.90	$161.90	$158.80	$128.50	$134.30	$98.00
Average high market/book	2.42											
Current ROE ratio	0.57											
Downside target price	$73.21		lost 37.96% in 1992									
Average target price	$89.16											
Upside target price	$105.12											
Current price	**$89.00**											

International Paper (IP)

International Paper (IP)	10	1992	1991	1990	1989	1988	1987	1986	1985	1984	1983	1982
Return on equity												
Average ROE	8.77	7.5	7.6	12.50	16.80	15.50	9.10	6.70	3.00	6.10	5.80	4.60
Book value		$55.10	$51.03	$51.34	$47.35	$41.14	$36.31	$35.00	$33.30	$33.02	$33.38	$32.47
Average book value	$39.43											
Low price			$50.50	$42.80	$45.10	$36.50	$27.00	$24.20	$22.10	$23.00	$23.00	$16.40
Average low market/book	0.79											
High price			$78.30	$59.80	$58.80	$49.40	$57.80	$40.10	$28.90	$29.90	$30.00	$25.80
Average high market/book	1.16											
Current ROE ratio	0.86											
Downside target price	$37.11		lost 3.45% in 1992									
Average target price	$45.97											
Upside target price	$54.82											
Current price	**$70.75**											

McDonald's (MCD)

	11	1994	1993	1992	1991	1990	1989	1988	1987	1986	1985	1984
Return on equity	18.60											
Average ROE		16	17	16	17.8	19.20	20.50	18.90	18.80	19.10	19.30	19.40
Book value	$9.79											
Average book value		$19.15	$16.40	$14.59	$12.65	$11.09	$9.25	$9.09	$7.72	$6.45	$5.67	$4.94
Low price			$45.50	$38.50	$26.10	$25.00	$23.00	$20.40	$15.70	$16.20	$11.40	$9.10
Average low market/book	2.36											
High price			$59.10	$50.40	$39.90	$38.50	$34.90	$25.50	$30.60	$25.60	$18.20	$12.40
Average high market/book	3.42											
Current ROE ratio	0.86											
Downside target price	$38.87		3.45% in 1994									
Average target price	$47.64											
Upside target price	$56.41											
Current price	**$57.00**											

Merck (MRK)

	12	1993	1992	1991	1990	1989	1988	1987	1986	1985	1984	1983
Return on equity	34.10											
Average ROE		36.5	39	43.2	46.50	42.50	42.30	42.80	26.30	20.50	19.40	18.50
Book value	$2.82											
Average book value		$6.95	$5.50	$4.24	$3.30	$2.97	$2.40	$1.79	$2.09	$2.09	$1.96	$1.83
Low price			$40.60	$27.30	$22.30	$18.80	$16.00	$13.60	$7.50	$5.00	$4.30	$4.50
Average low market/book	5.68											
High price			$56.60	$55.70	$30.40	$26.90	$19.90	$24.80	$14.40	$7.70	$5.40	$5.80
Average high market/book	8.79											
Current ROE ratio	1.07											
Downside target price	$42.23		lost 18.37% in 1993									
Average target price	$53.81											
Upside target price	$65.39											
Current price	**$43.38**											

American Express	13	1995	1994	1993	1992	1991	1990	1989	1988	1987	1986	1985
Return on equity		21	20.5	18.4	8.7	14.30	14.60	20.30	20.60	8.60	17.90	15.10
Average ROE	15.90											
Book value		$15.30	$13.75	$16.81	$14.58	$14.43	$13.21	$12.90	$11.39	$10.11	$12.60	$11.41
Average book value	$13.12											
Low price			$25.30	$22.40	$20.00	$18.00	$17.50	$26.40	$22.90	$20.80	$25.30	$17.90
Average low market/book	1.65											
High price			$33.10	$36.60	$25.40	$30.40	$35.30	$39.40	$30.40	$40.60	$35.10	$27.50
Average high market/book	2.54											
Current ROE ratio	1.32											
Downside target price	$33.35				43.32% in 1995							
Average target price	$42.38											
Upside target price	$51.42											
Current price	**$29.50**											

AT&T (T)	14	1995	1994	1993	1992	1991	1990	1989	1988	1987	1986	1985
Return on equity		28.5	30	30.8	20.1	3.20	19.40	21.20	19.80	13.90	13.00	9.90
Average ROE	18.13											
Book value		$12.75	$10.65	$10.24	$14.12	$12.39	$12.90	$11.84	$10.68	$13.46	$12.64	$13.68
Average book value	$12.30											
Low price			$49.50	$50.30	$36.60	$29.00	$29.00	$28.10	$24.10	$22.30	$20.90	$19.00
Average low market/book	2.51											
High price			$57.10	$65.00	$53.10	$40.40	$46.60	$47.00	$30.40	$35.90	$27.90	$25.40
Average high market/book	3.48											
Current ROE ratio	1.57											
Downside target price	$50.30				31.48% in 1995							
Average target price	$60.07											
Upside target price	$69.85											
Current price	**$50.25**											

DuPont (DD)	15	1992	1991	1990	1989	1988	1987	1986	1985	1984	1983	1982
Return on equity		10	10.4	14.10	15.70	13.60	11.90	11.50	9.70	11.60	9.30	8.50
Average ROE	11.63											
Book value		$25.50	$24.54	$24.16	$22.71	$21.36	$19.55	$18.25	$17.21	$16.69	$15.68	$14.96
Average book value	$19.51											
Low price			$32.80	$31.40	$28.70	$25.30	$25.00	$19.80	$15.90	$14.10	$11.70	$10.00
Average low market/book	1.10											
High price			$50.00	$42.40	$42.20	$31.00	$43.70	$30.80	$23.10	$17.60	$18.30	$14.80
Average high market/book	1.61											
Current ROE ratio	0.86											
Downside target price	$24.13											
Average target price	$29.70											
Upside target price	$35.28											
Current price	**$46.63**											

4.80% in 1992

Exxon (XON)	16	1994	1993	1992	1991	1990	1989	1988	1987	1986	1985	1984
Return on equity		13	15	14.2	16	15.20	15.40	16.10	14.40	15.60	18.60	19.20
Average ROE	15.97											
Book value		$28.30	$27.48	$26.57	$28.12	$26.55	$24.20	$24.64	$24.38	$22.30	$19.90	$18.42
Average book value	$24.26											
Low price			$57.80	$53.80	$49.60	$44.90	$41.50	$36.80	$33.30	$24.20	$22.10	$18.10
Average low market/book	1.58											
High price			$69.00	$65.50	$61.90	$55.10	$51.60	$47.80	$50.80	$37.10	$28.00	$22.80
Average high market/book	2.02											
Current ROE ratio	0.81											
Downside target price	$36.29											
Average target price	$41.39											
Upside target price	$46.50											
Current price	**$63.13**											

0.84% in 1994

International Paper (IP)

	17	1995	1994	1993	1992	1991	1990	1989	1988	1987	1986	1985
Return on equity		8.5	6	5	6.5	7.6	12.50	16.80	15.50	9.10	6.70	3.00
Average ROE	8.87											
Book value		$55.20	$52.10	$50.25	$50.46	$51.03	$51.34	$47.35	$41.14	$36.31	$35.00	$33.30
Average book value	$44.83											
Low price			$60.60	$56.60	$58.50	$50.50	$42.80	$45.10	$36.50	$27.00	$24.20	$22.10
Average low market/book	0.95											
High price			$80.40	$72.00	$78.50	$78.30	$59.80	$58.80	$49.40	$57.80	$40.10	$28.90
Average high market/book	1.35				2.95% in 1995							
Current ROE ratio	0.96											
Downside target price	$50.02											
Average target price	$60.65											
Upside target price	$71.27											
Current price	**$75.38**											

Merck (MRK)

	18	1995	1994	1993	1992	1991	1990	1989	1988	1987	1986	1985
Return on equity		25.5	26	26.8	48.90	43.2	46.50	42.50	42.30	42.80	26.30	20.50
Average ROE	36.58											
Book value		$10.65	$9.30	$7.99	$4.37	$4.24	$3.30	$2.97	$2.40	$1.79	$2.09	$2.09
Average book value	$4.05											
Low price			$28.10	$28.60	$40.60	$27.30	$22.30	$18.80	$16.00	$13.60	$7.50	$5.00
Average low market/book	5.13											
High price			$38.00	$44.10	$56.60	$55.70	$30.40	$26.90	$19.90	$24.80	$14.40	$7.70
Average high market/book	7.86				75.37% in 1995							
Current ROE ratio	0.70											
Downside target price	$38.05											
Average target price	$48.19											
Upside target price	$58.33											
Current price	**$38.13**											

J. P. Morgan (JPM)

J. P. Morgan (JPM)	19	1992	1991	1990	1989	1988	1987	1986	1985	1984	1983	1982
Return on equity		16	18.4	14.90	0.00	17.30	1.70	17.00	16.10	13.90	13.90	16.30
Average ROE	12.95											
Book value		$32.65	$29.41	$25.29	$21.78	$30.52	$26.57	$27.42	$23.70	$20.85	$18.85	$17.11
Average book value	$24.15											
Low price			$40.50	$29.60	$34.00	$30.80	$27.00	$29.50	$19.40	$14.10	$15.60	$11.40
Average low market/book	1.04											
High price			$70.50	$47.30	$48.10	$40.30	$53.60	$48.00	$33.00	$20.20	$21.60	$18.00
Average high market/book	1.66				lost 1.02% in 1992							
Current ROE ratio	1.24											
Downside target price	$42.08											
Average target price	$54.50											
Upside target price	$66.92											
Current price	**$68.63**											

Philip Morris (MO)

Philip Morris (MO)	20	1995	1994	1993	1992	1991	1990	1989	1988	1987	1986	1985
Return on equity		36	36.5	30.7	39.3	33.6	29.60	29.20	26.90	27.30	26.10	25.70
Average ROE	30.49											
Book value		$16.70	$15.00	$13.26	$13.43	$13.59	$12.90	$10.31	$8.31	$7.21	$5.94	$4.96
Average book value	$10.49											
Low price			$47.30	$45.00	$70.10	$48.30	$36.00	$25.00	$20.10	$18.20	$11.00	$9.00
Average low market/book	3.15											
High price			$64.50	$77.60	$86.60	$81.80	$51.80	$45.80	$25.50	$31.10	$19.50	$11.90
Average high market/book	4.73			63.00% in 1995								
Current ROE ratio	1.18											
Downside target price	$62.02											
Average target price	$77.63											
Upside target price	$93.24											
Current price	**$55.63**											

Procter & Gamble (PG)	21	1993	1992	1991	1990	1989	1988	1987	1986	1985	1984	1983
Return on equity		20.5	20.6	22.9	19.60	19.40	16.10	13.10	11.90	12.00	16.90	18.50
Average ROE	17.10											
Book value		$12.00	$10.44	$8.49	$9.41	$8.05	$9.35	$8.49	$8.47	$7.87	$7.61	$6.94
Average book value	$8.51											
Low price			$45.10	$38.00	$30.90	$21.10	$17.70	$15.00	$15.90	$12.60	$11.40	$12.60
Average low market/book	2.59											
High price			$55.80	$47.70	$45.60	$35.20	$22.00	$25.90	$20.60	$17.90	$15.00	$15.80
Average high market/book	3.54											
Current ROE ratio	1.20	5.91% in 1993										
Downside target price	$37.23											
Average target price	$44.09											
Upside target price	$50.96											
Current price	**$53.63**											

Sears (S)	22	1994	1993	1992	1991	1990	1989	1988	1987	1986	1985	1984
Return on equity		12	12.9	0	9	7.00	10.60	10.30	12.10	10.40	11.10	13.30
Average ROE	9.67											
Book value		$31.05	$28.80	$26.64	$40.29	$37.38	$39.77	$37.75	$35.89	$33.98	$31.79	$29.48
Average book value	$34.18											
Low price			$42.00	$37.00	$24.40	$22.00	$36.50	$32.30	$26.00	$35.90	$30.90	$29.50
Average low market/book	0.93											
High price			$60.10	$48.00	$43.50	$41.90	$48.10	$46.30	$59.50	$50.40	$41.10	$40.40
Average high market/book	1.40											
Current ROE ratio	1.24	lost 16.49% in 1994										
Downside target price	$35.68											
Average target price	$44.86											
Upside target price	$54.04											
Current price	**$57.00**											

Union Carbide (UK)

	23	1992	1991	1990	1989	1988	1987	1986	1985	1984	1983	1982
Return on equity	13.25											
Average ROE		9.5	NMF	13.20	26.10	37.80	22.90	12.90	1.90	7.40	4.30	6.00
Book value		$18.40	$17.55	$15.96	$16.83	$13.34	$9.43	$7.87	$19.82	$23.30	$23.32	$24.51
Average book value	$17.19											
Low price			$15.40	$14.10	$22.80	$17.00	$15.50	$18.80	$12.00	$10.90	$17.00	$13.40
Average low market/book	0.91											
High price			$22.60	$24.90	$33.30	$28.40	$32.50	$33.20	$24.30	$21.80	$24.60	$20.30
Average high market/book	1.55											
Current ROE ratio	0.72											
Downside target price	$12.04			lost 13.53% in 1992								
Average target price	$16.22											
Upside target price	$20.40											
Current price	**20.25**											

United Technologies (UTX)

	24	1992	1991	1990	1989	1988	1987	1986	1985	1984	1983	1982
Return on equity	12.84											
Average ROE		13	8	13.80	14.80	13.70	13.80	9.50	14.60	14.40	13.50	12.30
Book value		$28.60	$26.20	$37.68	$33.69	$36.88	$32.90	$29.14	$31.58	$30.04	$27.21	$25.56
Average book value	$31.09											
Low price			$42.10	$40.10	$39.90	$33.00	$30.00	$39.30	$34.50	$28.50	$26.90	$15.60
Average low market/book	1.06											
High price			$54.50	$62.50	$57.40	$42.60	$60.50	$56.30	$46.50	$41.60	$38.40	$29.40
Average high market/book	1.58											
Current ROE ratio	1.01											
Downside target price	$30.73			lost 7.96% in 1992								
Average target price	$38.17											
Upside target price	$45.61											
Current price	**$54.25**											

Westinghouse (WX)

Westinghouse (WX)	25	1992	1991	1990	1989	1988	1987	1986	1985	1984	1983	1982
Return on equity	18.82											
Average ROE		18.5	16.5	25.70	21.00	21.70	20.70	22.30	18.70	14.30	13.20	14.10
Book value	$11.43											
Average book value		$10.85	$9.50	$13.43	$15.10	$13.18	$12.46	$10.56	$10.52	$10.70	$9.74	$9.08
Low price			$13.80	$24.30	$25.60	$23.80	$20.00	$21.00	$12.70	$9.90	$9.30	$5.50
Average low market/book	1.45											
High price			$31.00	$39.40	$38.10	$28.70	$37.50	$31.30	$23.40	$14.20	$14.10	$10.10
Average high market/book	2.34			lost 21.67% in 1992								
Current ROE ratio	0.98											
Downside target price	$15.48											
Average target price	$20.24											
Upside target price	$25.00											
Current price	**$18.00**											

Woolworth (Z)

Woolworth (Z)	26	1995	1994	1993	1992	1991	1990	1989	1988	1987	1986	1985
Return on equity	12.06											
Average ROE		9	9	0	13.6	9.6	13.50	15.80	15.60	14.60	14.40	14.50
Book value	$13.40											
Average book value		$11.20	$10.30	$10.22	$15.64	$15.54	$18.00	$16.04	$14.34	$13.27	$11.25	$9.40
Low price			$12.90	$20.50	$26.00	$23.50	$22.90	$24.20	$17.10	$14.80	$14.50	$9.20
Average low market/book	1.39											
High price			$26.30	$32.80	$35.00	$36.40	$36.60	$36.10	$30.40	$29.80	$24.50	$15.60
Average high market/book	2.26		lost 12.33% in 1995									
Current ROE ratio	0.75											
Downside target price	$11.58											
Average target price	$15.25											
Upside target price	$18.93											
Current price	**$15.00**											

Philip Morris (MO)

Philip Morris (MO)	27	1993	1992	1991	1990	1989	1988	1987	1986	1985	1984	1983
Return on equity		38.5	37	33.6	29.60	29.20	26.90	27.30	26.10	25.70	25.30	22.40
Average ROE	28.31											
Book value		$16.80	$14.95	$13.59	$12.90	$10.31	$8.31	$7.21	$5.94	$4.96	$4.21	$4.03
Average book value	$8.64											
Low price			$70.10	$48.30	$36.00	$25.00	$20.10	$18.20	$11.00	$9.00	$7.80	$6.80
Average low market/book	2.92											
High price			$86.60	$81.80	$51.80	$45.80	$25.50	$31.10	$19.50	$11.90	$10.40	$9.00
Average high market/book	4.32		lost 24.50% in 1993									
Current ROE ratio	1.36											
Downside target price	$66.71											
Average target price	$82.72											
Upside target price	$98.73											
Current price	**$77.13**											

McDonald's (MCD)

McDonald's (MCD)	28	1989	1988	1987	1986	1985	1984	1983	1982	1981	1980	1979
Return on equity		18.5	19.00	18.80	19.10	19.30	19.40	19.50	19.7	19.3	19.4	19.8
Average ROE	19.33											
Book value		$21.50	$18.20	$15.44	$12.90	$11.35	$9.88	$8.77	$7.56	$6.73	$5.61	$5.68
Average book value	$10.21											
Low price			$40.80	$31.40	$32.50	$22.70	$18.10	$16.30	$11.50	$9.50	$7.10	$7.70
Average low market/book	$1.93											
High price			$51.00	$61.10	$51.20	$36.20	$24.90	$22.10	$19.50	$14.40	$10.30	$10.30
Average high market/book	$2.95		49.8% in 1989									
Current ROE ratio	0.96											
Downside target price	$39.82											
Average target price	$50.23											
Upside target price	$60.65											
Current price	**$46.75**											

Philip Morris (MO)

Philip Morris (MO)	29	1989	1988	1987	1986	1985	1984	1983	1982	1981	1980	1979
Return on equity		28	30	27.3	26.1	25.7	25.3	22.4	21.3	20	20.2	20.6
Average ROE	23.89											
Book value		$39.80	$33.30	$28.83	$23.77	$19.84	$16.86	$16.14	$14.55	$13.18	$11.43	$9.92
Average book value	$18.78											
Low price			$80.50	$72.60	$43.90	$36.00	$31.10	$27.00	$22.10	$21.00	$14.60	$15.60
Average low market/book	$1.94											
High price			$101.50	$124.50	$78.00	$47.60	$41.60	$36.20	$33.90	$27.60	$24.30	$19.30
Average high market/book	$2.85											
Current ROE ratio	1.17											
Downside target price	$90.50			74.6% in 1989								
Average target price	$111.63											
Upside target price	$132.75											
Current price	**$100.88**											

Allied Signal (ALD)

Allied Signal (ALD)	30	1990	1989	1988	1987	1986	1985	1984	1983	1982	1981	1980
Return on equity		13.50	14	14.20	12.30	15.00	6.90	14.40	13.10	6.60	14.00	15.00
Average ROE	12.55											
Book value		$25.50	$23.90	$20.87	$21.04	$33.17	$32.82	$29.78	$37.45	$36.87	$33.13	$28.43
Average book value	$29.75											
Low price			$31.80	$26.00	$36.80	$33.80	$28.30	$21.40	$19.20	$26.00	$26.00	$19.00
Average low market/book	0.90											
High price			$40.40	$49.30	$54.50	$48.10	$37.50	$38.80	$30.30	$39.90	$41.20	$33.00
Average high market/book	1.39											
Current ROE ratio	1.08			lost 18.6% in 1990								
Downside target price	$24.74											
Average target price	$31.41											
Upside target price	$38.08											
Current price	**$35.38**											

The Dow Jones Industrial Stocks

1970–1971

Allied Corp.
Alcoa
Manville
AT&T
Bethlehem Steel
International Nickel
International Harvester
Standard Oil (California)
Owens-Illinois
U.S. Steel
DuPont
Eastman Kodak
Standard Oil (New Jersey)
General Electric
General Motors
Goodyear Tire
Chrysler
International Paper
American Can
American Tobacco
Swift
Anaconda
General Foods
Procter & Gamble
Sears
Texaco
Union Carbide
United Aircraft
Westinghouse
Woolworth

1972

Allied Corp.
Alcoa
Manville
AT&T
Bethlehem Steel
International Nickel
International Harvester
Standard Oil (California)
Owens-Illinois
U.S. Steel
DuPont
Eastman Kodak
Exxon (name changed from
    Standard Oil–New Jersey)
General Electric
General Motors
Goodyear Tire
Chrysler
International Paper
American Can
American Tobacco
Swift
Anaconda
General Foods
Procter & Gamble
Sears
Texaco
Union Carbide
United Aircraft
Westinghouse
Woolworth

1973–1974

Allied Corp.
Alcoa
Manville
AT&T
Bethlehem Steel
International Nickel
International Harvester
Standard Oil (California)
Owens-Illinois
U.S. Steel
DuPont
Eastman Kodak
Exxon
General Electric
General Motors
Goodyear Tire
Chrysler
International Paper
American Can
American Tobacco
Esmark (name changed from
    Swift, 1973)
Anaconda
General Foods
Procter & Gamble
Sears
Texaco
Union Carbide
United Aircraft
Westinghouse
Woolworth

1975

Allied Corp.
Alcoa
Manville
AT&T
Bethlehem Steel
International Nickel
International Harvester
Standard Oil (California)
Owens-Illinois
U.S. Steel
DuPont
Eastman Kodak
Exxon
General Electric
General Motors
Goodyear Tire
Chrysler
International Paper
American Can
American Tobacco
Esmark
Anaconda
General Foods
Procter & Gamble
Sears
Texaco
Union Carbide
United Technologies (name
    changed from United
    Aircraft)
Westinghouse
Woolworth

1976–1978

Allied Corp.
Alcoa
Manville
AT&T
Bethlehem Steel
Inco (named changed from
     International Nickel, 1976)
International Harvester
Standard Oil (California)
Owens-Illinois
U.S. Steel
DuPont
Eastman Kodak
Exxon
General Electric
General Motors
Goodyear Tire
Chrysler
International Paper
American Can
American Tobacco
Esmark
MMM (replaced Anaconda,
     August 9, 1976)
General Foods
Procter & Gamble
Sears
Texaco
Union Carbide
United Technologies
Westinghouse
Woolworth

1979–1981

Allied Corp.
Alcoa
Manville
AT&T
Bethlehem Steel
International Nickel
International Harvester
Standard Oil (California)
Owens-Illinois
U.S. Steel
DuPont
Eastman Kodak
Exxon
General Electric
General Motors
Goodyear Tire
IBM (replaced Chrysler,
     June 29, 1979)
International Paper
American Can
American Tobacco
Merck (replaced Esmark,
     June 29, 1979)
MMM
General Foods
Procter & Gamble
Sears
Texaco
Union Carbide
United Technologies
Westinghouse
Woolworth

1982–1983

Allied Corp.
Alcoa
American Express (replaced
    Manville, August 30, 1982)
AT&T
Bethlehem Steel
International Nickel
International Harvester
Standard Oil (California)
Owens-Illinois
U.S. Steel
DuPont
Eastman Kodak
Exxon
General Electric
General Motors
Goodyear Tire
IBM
International Paper
American Can
American Tobacco
Merck
MMM
General Foods
Procter & Gamble
Sears
Texaco
Union Carbide
United Technologies
Westinghouse
Woolworth

1984

Allied Corp.
Alcoa
American Express
AT&T
Bethlehem Steel
International Nickel
International Harvester
Chevron (name changed from
    Standard Oil–California)
Owens-Illinois
U.S. Steel
DuPont
Eastman Kodak
Exxon
General Electric
General Motors
Goodyear Tire
IBM
International Paper
American Can
American Tobacco
Merck
MMM
General Foods
Procter & Gamble
Sears
Texaco
Union Carbide
United Technologies
Westinghouse
Woolworth

1985

Allied-Signal (name changed
    from Allied Corp.)
Alcoa
American Express
AT&T
Bethlehem Steel
International Nickel
International Harvester
Chevron
Owens-Illinois
U.S. Steel
DuPont
Eastman Kodak
Exxon
General Electric
General Motors
Goodyear Tire
IBM
International Paper
American Can
McDonald's (replaced
    American Tobacco,
    October 30, 1985)
Merck
MMM
Philip Morris (replaced
    General Foods,
    October 30, 1985)
Procter & Gamble
Sears
Texaco
Union Carbide
United Technologies
Westinghouse
Woolworth

1986

Allied-Signal
Alcoa
American Express
AT&T
Bethlehem Steel
International Nickel
Navistar (name changed from
    International Harvester)
Chevron
Owens-Illinois
USX (name changed from U.S.
    Steel)
DuPont
Eastman Kodak
Exxon
General Electric
General Motors
Goodyear Tire
IBM
International Paper
American Can
McDonald's
Merck
MMM
Philip Morris
Procter & Gamble
Sears
Texaco
Union Carbide
United Technologies
Westinghouse
Woolworth

1987–1990

Allied-Signal
Alcoa
American Express
AT&T
Bethlehem Steel
Boeing (replaced Inco, March
    12, 1987)
Navistar
Chevron
Coca-Cola (replaced
    Owens-Illinois, March 12,
    1987)
USX
DuPont
Eastman Kodak
Exxon
General Electric
General Motors
Goodyear Tire
IBM
International Paper
Primerica (name changed
    from American Can,
    April 29, 1987)
McDonald's
Merck
MMM
Philip Morris
Procter & Gamble
Sears
Texaco
Union Carbide
United Technologies
Westinghouse
Woolworth

1991–1992

Allied-Signal
Alcoa
American Express
AT&T
Bethlehem Steel
Boeing
Caterpillar (replaced Navistar,
    May 6, 1991)
Chevron
Coca-Cola
Disney (replaced USX,
    May 6, 1991)
DuPont
Eastman Kodak
Exxon
General Electric
General Motors
Goodyear Tire
IBM
International Paper
J.P. Morgan (replaced
    Primerica, May 6, 1991)
McDonald's
Merck
MMM
Philip Morris
Procter & Gamble
Sears
Texaco
Union Carbide
United Technologies
Westinghouse
Woolworth

1993–1996

AlliedSignal (name changed
    from Allied-Signal, April
    26, 1993)
Alcoa
American Express AT&T
Bethlehem Steel
Boeing
Caterpillar
Chevron
Coca-Cola
Disney
DuPont
Eastman Kodak
Exxon
General Electric
General Motors
Goodyear Tire
IBM
International Paper
J. P. Morgan
McDonald's
Merck
MMM
Philip Morris
Procter & Gamble
Sears
Texaco
Union Carbide
United Technologies
Westinghouse
Woolworth

1997

AlliedSignal
Alcoa
American Express
AT&T
Johnson & Johnson (replaced
    Bethlehem Steel, March 17)
Boeing
Caterpillar
Chevron
Coca-Cola
Disney
DuPont
Eastman Kodak
Exxon
General Electric
General Motors
Goodyear Tire
IBM
International Paper
J. P. Morgan
McDonald's
Merck
MMM
Philip Morris
Procter & Gamble
Sears
Hewlett-Packard (replaced
    Texaco, March 17)
Union Carbide
United Technologies
Travelers (replaced
    Westinghouse, March 17)
Wal-Mart (replaced
    Woolworth, March 17)

TOTAL RETURNS IN PERCENTAGES

Year	ALD	AA	AXP	T	BS	BA
1973	73.41%	40.61%	-31.24%	0.33%	17.96%	-48.96%
1974	-38.97%	-36.94%	-39.72%	-4.67%	-17.65%	33.00%
1975	22.26%	33.77%	44.27%	21.62%	43.22%	61.19%
1976	24.63%	51.84%	12.83%	32.09%	28.90%	88.57%
1977	15.86%	-16.18%	-8.74%	1.73%	-43.96%	29.54%
1978	-32.01%	6.49%	-14.58%	7.60%	-2.37%	287.69%
1979	80.07%	20.37%	8.62%	-5.74%	15.29%	9.32%
1980	13.83%	14.49%	41.29%	1.44%	32.43%	-10.08%
1981	-14.51%	-7.96%	14.60%	33.79%	-5.78%	-45.85%
1982	-19.84%	27.41%	50.59%	10.26%	-11.61%	56.76%
1983	79.61%	48.63%	5.42%	13.43%	51.17%	33.27%
1984	-2.39%	-14.87%	19.25%	15.80%	-36.49%	32.62%
1985	40.72%	7.30%	44.32%	34.36%	-9.00%	41.15%
1986	-3.48%	-8.90%	9.41%	4.80%	-60.00%	0.14%
1987	-25.11%	41.55%	-56.95%	12.80%	168.00%	-30.37%
1988	21.42%	22.57%	19.72%	10.93%	38.81%	68.05%
1989	12.86%	38.79%	34.21%	62.43%	-20.09%	49.79%
1990	-17.42%	-19.17%	-38.00%	-30.89%	-17.55%	17.17%
1991	68.44%	14.80%	3.93%	34.25%	-2.37%	7.43%
1992	40.15%	13.75%	26.24%	33.71%	14.29%	-13.86%
1993	32.50%	-0.91%	28.14%	5.53%	27.37%	10.27%
1994	-12.28%	27.17%	-1.39%	-1.77%	-11.68%	10.40%
1995	42.00%	24.16%	43.32%	31.48%	-22.89%	68.89%
1996	42.95%	23.07%	38.71%	-6.30%	-36.02%	37.27%
Total	444.70%	351.84%	254.25%	319.01%	139.98%	793.40%
Average	18.53%	14.66%	10.59%	13.29%	5.83%	33.06%
Cumulative	1905.52%	1472.57%	290.83%	1312.88%	-33.83	11486.48%

Year	CAT	CHV	KO	DIS	DD	EK
1973	3.01%	-3.77%	-13.60%	-60.03%	-7.18%	-20.74%
1974	-26.15%	-8.44%	-56.44%	-54.41%	-38.53%	-44.15%
1975	47.62%	26.50%	59.49%	133.89%	41.47%	72.08%
1976	27.87%	46.95%	-0.74%	-5.02%	11.19%	-17.01%
1977	-2.66%	0.57%	-1.82%	-15.01%	-6.65%	-38.12%
1978	10.49%	27.19%	22.46%	1.11%	10.70%	19.03%
1979	-4.51%	26.45%	-16.92%	13.03%	2.65%	-13.15%
1980	11.72%	82.88%	3.00%	15.81%	10.84%	51.29%
1981	-0.17%	-9.38%	11.13%	3.90%	-4.76%	7.00%

Year	CAT	CHV	KO	DIS	DD	EK
1982	−23.38%	−19.77%	56.89%	23.35%	2.75%	25.85%
1983	21.50%	15.70%	8.08%	−14.90%	51.64%	−7.35%
1984	−31.75%	−2.82%	21.75%	16.06%	0.77%	−0.91%
1985	37.10%	29.68%	40.28%	89.90%	43.18%	10.99%
1986	−3.27%	25.31%	37.72%	54.47%	28.25%	40.71%
1987	55.76%	−7.38%	3.96%	38.13%	7.95%	−24.93%
1988	3.83%	21.89%	20.20%	11.61%	5.25%	−4.13%
1989	−7.15%	54.21%	76.16%	71.04%	44.29%	−4.42%
1990	−17.37%	11.66%	22.46%	−8.32%	−6.46%	6.08%
1991	−4.40%	−0.52%	74.65%	13.47%	31.46%	20.71%
1992	22.90%	3.12%	5.76%	50.89%	4.80%	−11.92%
1993	67.07%	30.40%	8.19%	−0.30%	6.11%	43.83%
1994	24.90%	6.69%	17.14%	8.58%	20.10%	−12.09%
1995	8.74%	21.68%	45.88%	28.75%	28.11%	43.66%
1996	30.64%	28.06%	43.43%	19.17%	37.89%	22.16%
Total	253.34%	406.86%	489.11%	435.17%	325.82%	164.47%
Average	10.56%	16.95%	20.38%	18.13%	13.58%	6.85%
Cumulative	507.02%	2682.33%	3487.44%	1062.38%	1278.12%	103.36%

Year	XON	GE	GM	GT	IBM	IP
1973	12.42%	−11.57%	36.67%	−48.54%	−21.88%	28.38%
1974	−25.99%	−44.48%	25.96%	−8.82%	−29.66%	−27.87%
1975	45.13%	43.00%	95.20%	77.48%	37.36%	67.13%
1976	26.93%	24.15%	45.82%	14.25%	28.04%	22.73%
1977	−4.66%	−6.74%	−11.24%	−22.32%	1.57%	−33.58%
1978	8.98%	−0.69%	−4.95%	1.01%	13.35%	−12.00%
1979	20.19%	31.20%	2.88%	−12.09%	−9.13%	7.40%
1980	56.05%	26.76%	−4.10%	34.37%	10.78%	20.00%
1981	−15.06%	1.23%	−9.11%	27.25%	−11.14%	−1.13%
1982	4.80%	71.15%	68.25%	91.58%	75.28%	29.78%
1983	36.05%	27.39%	23.73%	−9.21%	30.61%	26.93%
1984	29.39%	0.00%	11.76%	−9.47%	4.28%	−4.62%
1985	30.19%	32.26%	0.80%	27.35%	29.87%	−1.35%
1986	33.74%	21.40%	0.89%	39.12%	−20.00%	52.76%
1987	−40.21%	−45.69%	0.57%	47.10%	−0.08%	−40.49%
1988	21.05%	4.59%	44.20%	−11.96%	9.33%	12.79%
1989	18.86%	47.93%	8.38%	−11.39%	−18.88%	25.41%
1990	8.30%	−8.13%	−11.54%	−52.47%	25.20%	−2.55%
1991	22.82%	36.88%	−11.34%	185.49%	−16.96%	35.38%
1992	5.06%	14.69%	16.52%	28.86%	−37.96%	−3.45%

Year	XON	GE	GM	GT	IBM	IP
1993	7.98%	25.61%	72.65%	35.51%	15.28%	4.20%
1994	0.84%	−0.02%	−21.77%	−24.85%	31.86%	13.74%
1995	38.49%	44.39%	28.13%	37.76%	25.69%	2.95%
1996	24.64%	39.97%	8.45%	15.43%	67.21%	9.56%
Total	365.99%	357.38%	416.81%	450.44%	240.02%	232.10%
Average	15.25%	14.89%	17.37%	18.77%	10.00%	9.67%
Cumulative	1741.35%	1163.63%	2264.51%	909.22%	350.78%	380.09%

Year	JPM	MCD	MRK	MMM	MO	PG
1973	34.25%	−25.25%	−8.05%	−7.67%	−1.75%	−16.09%
1974	−22.68%	−48.46%	−16.09%	−39.25%	−14.95%	−9.46%
1975	6.86%	98.72%	6.41%	23.27%	12.42%	11.53%
1976	8.50%	−8.39%	0.37%	4.66%	18.62%	7.51%
1977	−20.00%	−3.13%	−16.33%	−11.35%	2.53%	−5.71%
1978	10.64%	−9.60%	24.87%	34.29%	17.04%	6.64%
1979	7.48%	−5.12%	9.68%	−16.59%	5.53%	−12.97%
1980	17.68%	14.26%	19.94%	22.99%	24.36%	−2.66%
1981	10.16%	36.18%	3.50%	−2.54%	17.16%	22.21%
1982	31.91%	40.39%	1.85%	43.49%	27.84%	52.22%
1983	5.33%	18.45%	10.13%	14.40%	24.25%	0.01%
1984	22.45%	11.47%	7.33%	−0.58%	16.94%	4.44%
1985	68.98%	58.40%	49.13%	18.60%	14.38%	26.93%
1986	32.49%	14.50%	82.93%	33.96%	68.27%	13.27%
1987	8.82%	−26.51%	29.94%	−41.61%	22.96%	15.58%
1988	0.34%	10.64%	11.73%	−0.40%	23.82%	5.18%
1989	30.92%	45.69%	37.04%	32.63%	68.55%	65.29%
1990	3.57%	−15.23%	18.72%	11.36%	27.87%	25.87%
1991	59.10%	31.69%	87.98%	14.72%	58.59%	10.62%
1992	−1.02%	29.34%	−20.25%	9.01%	−1.11%	16.55%
1993	9.17%	17.78%	−18.37%	11.37%	−24.50%	5.91%
1994	−15.08%	3.45%	14.22%	1.40%	8.50%	13.82%
1995	48.32%	55.18%	75.37%	27.88%	63.00%	36.29%
1996	25.78%	1.20%	23.59%	28.08%	30.08%	31.72%
Total	383.97%	345.65%	435.64%	212.12%	510.40%	324.70%
Average	16.00%	14.40%	18.15%	8.84%	21.27%	13.53%
Cumulative	2179.71	897.67%	2654.90%	343.72%	6470.04%	1429.72%

Year	S	TX	UK	UTX	WX	Z	DJIA	Benchmark
1973	−29.30%	−17.05%	−27.61%	−43.71%	−38.71%	−37.36%	−13.12%	−3.22%
1974	−37.50%	−21.79%	27.66%	45.64%	−56.73%	−42.42%	−23.14%	−5.13%
1975	37.50%	21.56%	53.53%	48.28%	43.50%	147.33%	44.40%	73.28%
1976	9.40%	27.27%	5.30%	72.73%	39.10%	22.50%	22.72%	35.01%
1977	−15.60%	2.70%	−29.23%	−3.47%	8.56%	−22.04%	−12.71%	−3.16%
1978	−24.90%	−6.72%	−10.29%	13.94%	−2.87%	10.07%	2.69%	6.24%
1979	−2.30%	29.82%	32.09%	16.27%	26.95%	36.90%	10.52%	17.43%
1980	−7.20%	74.72%	27.00%	46.98%	54.16%	5.67%	21.41%	35.44%
1981	14.60%	−25.42%	8.81%	−27.62%	−7.85%	−20.00%	−3.40%	7.84%
1982	95.20%	3.41%	9.32%	41.38%	59.51%	53.75%	25.79%	65.20%
1983	28.20%	24.90%	25.09%	32.56%	45.47%	42.71%	25.65%	35.67%
1984	−9.70%	3.48%	−36.03%	3.81%	−1.02%	10.46%	1.08%	16.16%
1985	28.30%	−3.30%	102.08%	24.55%	74.74%	67.51%	32.78%	50.33%
1986	6.20%	29.58%	48.85%	8.34%	28.31%	32.53%	26.92%	68.27%
1987	−10.10%	5.92%	3.33%	−23.32%	−7.82%	−7.39%	6.02%	47.09%
1988	27.10%	43.29%	13.33%	25.98%	9.66%	54.52%	15.95%	23.05%
1989	−1.10%	37.11%	−5.38%	35.81%	44.99%	27.44%	31.71%	21.03%
1990	−27.96%	7.63%	−25.27%	−8.43%	−19.32%	−1.71%	−0.57%	15.63%
1991	57.13%	6.53%	29.73%	17.06%	−31.93%	−8.86%	23.93%	25.69%
1992	25.40%	2.78%	−13.53%	−7.96%	−21.67%	23.55%	7.34%	14.92%
1993	29.01%	13.72%	39.09%	32.56%	8.59%	−16.12%	16.72%	38.04%
1994	−16.49%	−2.58%	34.63%	4.48%	−11.89%	−37.48%	4.95%	11.36%
1995	53.59%	36.44%	30.19%	54.15%	35.35%	−12.33%	36.48%	37.81%
1996	20.31%	29.15%	11.01%	44.29%	22.59%	69.23%	28.57%	45.14%
Total	249.79%	323.15%	353.70%	454.30%	301.67%	398.46%	332.69%	673.34%
Average	10.41%	13.46%	14.74%	18.93%	12.57%	16.60%	13.86%	28.06%
Cumulative	330.42%	1204.08%	1045.23%	2890.18%	418.85%	816.99%	1604.02%	26,933.41%

GREATEST BULL RUNS

Starting Date	Ending Date	Dow Start	Dow Finish	Percentage Change	Duration in Days
6/13/49	12/13/61	161.60	734.90	354.76	4566
8/24/21	9/3/29	63.90	381.17	496.51	2932
10/11/90	12/31/97	2365.10	7908.25	234.37	2638
8/12/82	8/25/87	776.92	2722.42	250.41	1839
4/28/42	5/29/46	92.92	212.50	128.69	1492
6/26/62	2/9/66	535.76	995.14	85.74	1324
2/28/78	4/27/81	742.12	1024.05	37.99	1154
10/19/87	7/16/90	1738.41	2999.75	72.56	1001
5/26/70	1/11/73	631.15	1051.69	66.63	961
7/26/34	3/10/37	85.51	194.40	127.34	958

WORST DAILY POINT LOSSES

The Dow Jones Industrial Average suffered its worst point drop ever on Monday, October 27, 1997, falling more than 554 points. Below are the 10 biggest daily point drops in the Dow.

Date	Point Drop	Percentage Drop
October 27, 1997	554.26	7.2
October 19, 1987	508.00	22.6
August 15, 1997	247.37	3.1
January 9, 1998	222.20	2.8
June 23, 1997	192.95	2.5
October 13, 1989	190.58	6.9
March 8, 1996	171.24	3.0
July 15, 1996	161.05	2.9
March 13, 1997	160.48	2.3
March 31, 1997	157.11	2.3

WORST DAILY PERCENTAGE LOSSES

The Dow Jones Industrial Average suffered its worst percent loss ever on Monday, October 19, 1987. Below are the 10 biggest percentage losses in the Dow.

Date	Point Drop	Percentage Drop
October 19, 1987	508.00	22.61
October 28, 1929	38.33	12.82
October 29, 1929	30.57	11.73
November 6, 1929	25.55	11.73
December 18, 1899	5.57	8.72
August 12, 1932	5.79	8.40
March 14, 1907	6.89	8.04
October 26, 1987	153.83	8.04
July 21, 1933	7.55	7.84
October 18, 1937	10.57	7.75

INDEX

Bold indicates display matter; *n* indicates a footnote.

Abelson, Reed, 12
Added value and Sharpe ratios, 204
Advisors, professional, 211–213
(*See also* Professional managers)
Aetna Life & Casualty, 209
Against the Gods (Bernstein), 210*n*1
AIM Value Fund, 13
Airbus, 103
Alcan, 89
Alcoa (AA), 43, 55, 87–90, **88**
Allen, Robert E., 99
Allied Chemical & Dye Corporation, 84
Allied Corp., 83, 138
AlliedSignal (ALD), 77–78, **82,** 82–87, 180–181, **251, 265**
Allstate Insurance, 133, 135
Aluminum Company of America, 87
Aluminum Ltd, 89
American Express (AXP), 2, 30, 36, 43, 50, **91,** 91–95, **251, 257**
American Express Bank, 92–93
American Express Financial Advisors (AEFA), 92
American Heritage Growth Fund, 218
American Telephone & Telegraph, 97
Analysts (*see* Professional managers)
Angelis, Michael De, 2
Appreciation, unrealized, 218
Armstrong, C. Michael, 97, 99
Arrow Electronics, 81
Artisan Small Cap Fund, 212–213
Asset allocation and risk, 205
Asset base and ROE, 67
Asset mix and retirement savings, 10, 18, **20**
Associated Press, 219
AT&T, 118
AT&T Corp (T), 30, 36, 95–99, **96, 252, 257**
Auerbach, Jon G., 12

Balcor Real Estate, 93
Ball, Robert, 17
Bargain companies, 7–8, 65–67, 73, 86

Bargain companies (*Cont.*)
(*See also* Stock selection)
Baron, Ron, 205
Baron Asset Fund, 205
Barrett company, 84
Barron's, 11, 36, 43, 86, 195, 220, 224, 231
Baruch, Bernard, 176
BBN Planet, 98
Beating the market, system for, 81
(*See also* Benchmark investing)
Beating the Street (Lynch), 176–177, 230
Behavior, investment, 6, 63, 209, 226
Behavioral finance, 182, 215
Bell, Alexander Graham, 96
Benchmark investing:
advantages and disadvantages of, 25–26
analysis (1991–1996), 30, 36, 43, 50, 55, 57
basic strategy, 7–8, 9
cumulative total return (1991–1996), 25
and diversification, 200
Dow monitors (1973–1996), 138, **140–163**
as forecasting tool, 183–185, **189**
formula for, 68–70, 78–79
future potential of company, 182–183
holding periods, 177–179
and LEAPS, 185, 187–189
performance (1973–1996), **61–62, 139**
philosophy behind, 64–68
result comparisons (1991–1996), **61**
results (1973-1997), 30, **31**
risk-adjusted returns vs. Dow, **204**
self-test, 233–235, 236–250
skeptical approach to, 15–16
target prices and adjustments, 65–66
tenets of, 71–74
true value revealed, 183
as valuation tool, 26
winning picks, **138**
[*See also* Dow Jones Industrial Average (DJIA); mentors for

investors; Stock purchases; Stock selection]
Benson & Hedges, 130
Berger 100 Fund, 218
Berkshire-Hathaway, 199, 200
Bernstein, Peter L., 195, 210
Best, Daniel, 105
Best Tractor, 105
Bethlehem Steel, 190, 192
Bible, Geoffrey, 130, 131
Big Blue [*see* International Business Machines (IBM)]
Biggs, Barton, 224
Black Monday, 27–28
Boeing, Bill, 102
Boeing Airplane Company, 102
The Boeing Company (BA), 30, 70, 100–103, **101**
Bonds, **19, 20,** 20–21
Book value, 67, 68, 69, 78–79
Bosch, Robert, 85
Bossidy, Lawrence A., 85, 86
Boston Company, 93
Breed Technologies, 85
Brennan, Edward, 135
Bre-X, 11
Brown & Williamson Tobacco Company, 130
Bryne, Andrew, 88
Buffetology (Buffett, M.), 199
Buffett, Mary, 199*n*4
Buffett, Warren:
vs. benchmark investing, 7–8
benchmark used, 76–78
and diversification, 199, 205
on goal setting, 216
and Graham, Benjamin, 1–2, 226, 229
as long-term investor, 24
market timing, 210–211
purchase considerations, 5, 27, 70, 94
and Ruane, Bill, 226
vs. stock market, 200
wealth progression, **3**
(*See also* Mentors for investors)
Business Week, 213*n*2, 220
Buy-and-hold strategy, 218, 225
Buyback program, 76, 124, 131
Buying stocks (*see* Stock purchases)
Buy-sell recommendations (1990-1995), **220**
C. J. Root Glass Company, 109

279